The Gītā and Tulasī-Rāmāyaṇa:
Their Common Call for the Good of All

OTHER BOOKS BY THE SAME AUTHOR

1. The Social Role of the Gītā: How and Why
2. The Social Message of the Gītā Symbolized as Lokasaṁgraha
3. Tulasī-Rāmāyaṇa: Jagmangal-Parayana
   (तुलसी रामायण... जगमंगल-परायण)
4. Mānas Evam Gītā: Lokmangal-Gunjita
   (मानस एवं गीता... लोकमंगल-गुञ्जिता)
5. Lokasaṁgrahasandesh
   (लोकसंग्रह सन्देश)

The Gītā and Tulasī-Rāmāyaṇa:
Their Common Call for the Good of All

SATYA P. AGARWAL
Ph.D. (UC, Berkeley)
Center for South Asia Studies
University of California
Berkeley, California,
U.S.A.

Publishers:
URMILA AGARWAL
11293, Ridermark Row, Columbia,
Maryland 21044 U.S.A.

First Edition: 2000

ISBN: 81-208-1752-4

Distributors:
URMILA AGARWAL
C-157 Anand Vihar
Delhi 110 092

MOTILAL BANARSIDASS
41 U.A. Bungalow Road, Jawahar Nagar
Delhi 110 007 (India)

PRINTED IN INDIA
BY JAINENDRA PRAKASH JAIN AT SHRI JAINENDRA PRESS,
A-45 NARAINA, PHASE I, NEW DELHI 110 028

To

Dr. Natwerlal S. Jānī
Gītā-scholar and Social Worker

prerakā mam śikṣakāḥ
pitāmātāgurujanāḥ
bhaginī bhrātaro bhāryā
śṛeṣṭho jānīnatavaraḥ

Contents

	Preface	ix
	Acknowledgements	xiii
1.	Underlying Spirit of Vedas and Other Sources—Concern for the Good of All	1
2.	Ten Points of the Message of Gītā and Mānas	23
3.	Call to Follow Dharma that Unites—Avibhaktam Vibhakteṣu	31
4.	Call to Participate in God's Work—Mat-Karma or Rāma-Kāj	50
5.	Call to Follow the Spiritually Perfect—Yogārūḍha or Sant	66
6.	Call to Adapt to Changing Needs—Desh-Kāla-Pātra	92
7.	Call for the Good of All—Sarvabhūtahitaṃ or Sakal-Mangal	105
8.	Call for the Good of the World—Lokaśaṃgraha or Jag-Mangal	118
9.	Call to Avoid Self-Centred Attitudes—Nirmamo Nirahaṃkāraḥ	131
10.	Call for Even-Minded Vision—Samadriṣṭi	140
11.	Call not to Succumb to Evil—Āsurī Sampat or Kaliyug	154
12.	Call to Promote Virtues—Daivī Sampat or Rāma-rājya	165
13.	How to Re-invigorate the Call for the Good of All	178

Appendices

I. Six Descriptions of the Spiritually Perfect in the Gītā 197

II. Initial Declaration of the Mānas About Jag-Mangal and Sarva-Hit 207

III. Kaliyuga—Tulasī's Description of a Society under the Grip of Unrighteousness 219

IV. Rāma-rājya—Tulasī's Description of an Ideal Society Based on Jag-Mangal 229

Notes 237

Index 243

Preface

The year 2000 has already received, and is still receiving, special attention all over the world from leaders of thought and action, who are doing at least two things. First, they are taking stock of the progress that they have made so far in their respective fields. Secondly, they are making elaborate plans to face the challenges of the twenty-first century. The socio-spiritual field is a part of this wide network. There is undoubtedly an element of competition and commercialization associated with such activities. However, even those who do not hanker after personal gains (and do not want to adopt a commercial approach) need to protect the social cause for which they stand, particularly if the cause is spiritually worthwhile and the effort called for is free from violence and dishonesty. I, as an admirer of the Bhagwad-Gītā (or Gītā for short) and Tulasī-Rāmāyaṇa (or Mānas for short), strongly feel that the promoters of the universal message of these two great books need to be alert in making their views known now, so as not to let a great cause suffer from lack of appropriate and timely action.

I must specify as to what particular aspects of the Gītā and the Mānas need, in my opinion, to be promoted during the present year. The necessary specification can be summarized in three steps. First, that the Gītā's message is to encourage all the citizens to put an end to discrimination, injustice and conflicts, through (non-governmental) programmes based on social harmony, justice and social service. Secondly, that the Mānas too, contains practically the same message as the Gītā, if we focus attention on the right verses (of the Mānas) and interpret them properly. Thirdly, that both these books are in favour of adjusting religious practices to changing social needs, and therefore the 'dharma' that they envisage for the conflict-ridden society of today needs to emphasize a broad ideal like 'avibhaktaṃ vibhakteṣu', i.e. to bring about unity in the midst of diversity.

From the above, I hope that no one gets the impression that I stand alone in spelling out the universal message of the Gītā and the Mānas.Great leaders like Swami Vivekananda, Mahatma Gandhi,

Sadhu Vaswani, and Vinoba Bhave—to name only a few—have played a leading role in this regard. For the Gītā in particular, such ideas formed the basis of the pioneering work done by Lokmanya Tilak and Śrī Aurobindo. Scholars like Dr. Radhakrishnan, D.S. Sarma, Pandit Ram Kinkar Upadhyay and Shivananda—again to name only a few—have explained the message of one or both of these books to large audiences world-wide.

Although the universal message of the Gītā and the Mānas has the strong backing of academicians as well as activists, there still exist some who interpret these two books from a different perspective. The Indian tradition has always recognized the right of scholars to put forward an interpretation that is 'svasya ca priyatātmanaḥ', i.e. the one that satisfies their Ātman. But Manusmṛti (where these words occur) has explained this further by saying that it refers to that action (or opinion) which does not make one feel ashamed. The Mahābhārata has gone a step further by advising not to do anything which either would make the doer feel ashamed or 'yadanyeṣāṃ hitaṃ na syād', i.e. which is not beneficial to others.

I feel that the Bṛhadaranyaka Upaniṣad's famous story entitled 'Da Da Da' (narrated below) also envisages the possibility as well as the desirability of interpreting the same word (or syllable 'da' in the story) in different ways (viz. damaḥ, dānaṃ, dayā in the story), if the underlying approach is to arrive at 'hitaṃ', i.e. the good of oneself as well as of others—

"Three kinds of Prajapati's sons—gods, men, and demons—lived with their father as students. After finishing their studies, the gods said to Prajapati, 'Please teach us.' He told them the syllable 'Da' and asked, 'Have you understood?' The gods said, 'We have. You say to us : discipline yourselves.' Prajapati said, 'Yes, you have understood.'

"Then men said to him, 'Please teach us.' Prajapati told them the same syllable 'Da' and asked, 'Have you understood?' Men said, 'We have. You say to us : be charitable.' Prajapati said, 'Yes, you have understood.'

"Then demons said to Prajapati, 'Please teach us.' He told them the same syllable 'Da' and asked, 'Have you understood?' Demons said, 'We have. You say to us : have compassion.' Prajapati said, 'Yes, you have understood.' "

The preceding analysis gives me confidence that the message of 'sarva-hitaṃ' (good of all) represents a common minimum core acceptable to all categories of interpreters of the Gītā and the Mānas. This should cause no surprise because 'hitaṃ' (or its equivalent) was stated repeatedly to be the purpose of what Lord Krishna told Arjuna in the Gītā, and also of the 'kathā' that Tulasīdāsa wrote in his Mānas, as illustrated by the following quotations (two from each of them)—

> *vakṣyāmi hitakāṃyayā* (X.1)
> (I shall speak with the desire to do 'hitaṃ')
>
> *vakṣyāmi te hitaṃ* (XVIII.64)
> (I shall speak what is 'hitaṃ' for you).
>
> *kahiun kathā sansār-hit* (Araṇyakāṇḍa)
> (Whatever I said was for 'hitaṃ' of the world)
>
> *Rām-kathā jag-mangal-karnī* (Balakāṇḍa)
> (Rām-kathā will bring about jag-mangal (good of the world)).

Although I am linking my present publication to the special attention that is being given world-wide to the year 2000, I should not fail to point out another linkage, viz. that between this publication and the five earlier ones of mine, all of which were devoted to the universal message of either the Gītā or the Mānas or both. A brief description of each of them will clarify this linkage. The first publication entitled *"The Social Role of the Gītā : How and Why"*, which was brought out in 1993, was a detailed (two-part) study on the social relevance of the Gītā. Part one provided an in-depth analysis of how new interpretations of the Gītā played a significant role in the social history of India during the nineteenth and twentieth centuries. Part Two explained how the social applications of the Gītā were linked with its most important teaching for the modern age, viz. lokasaṃgraha, the good of the society. Prof. B.A. van Nooten, writing the Preface, characterized my book as the 'most meritorious work from one of Berkeley's distingunished alumni'. The then Governor of the State of Maryland (USA), William Donald Schaefer, recognized this as 'dedication and service to your fellowmen' and honoured me with "Governor's Citation".

The second publication came out in 1995 and it was entitled *"The Social Message of The Gītā Symbolized as Lokasaṃgraha"*. It consisted of two hundred self-composed Sanskrit verses and a detailed English commentary thereon. Prof. Madhav Deshpande, writing the Preface, characterized this book as "unique". The then President of India, Dr. Shankar Dayal Sharma, expressed his admiration for this study at the book-release function held at Rashtrapati Bhawan, New Delhi, in July 1995.

The Third publication came out in 1997 and it was in Hindi, carrying the title *"Tulasi-Ramayana : Jagmangal-Parāyana"*. Parallel to the lokasaṃgraha-message of the Gītā (explained in the earlier books), the subject-matter of this study was "jag-mangal" (i.e. good of the world) as formulated by Tulasīdāsa in the Mānas. This book won the Kunti Goyal International Award, and the then President of India, Dr. Shankar Dayal Sharma, again honoured me at the book-release function held at Rashtrapati Bhawan, New Delhi, in January 1997.

The fourth publication came out in 1998, and this too was in Hindi, carrying the title *"Mānas Evam Gītā : Lokmangal-Gunjitā"*. Here the lokasaṃgraha message of the Gītā and the jagmangal-message of the Mānas were brought together and explained within a common framework. The fifth publication came out in 1999, and it conveyed the social message of the Gītā in Sanskrit verses, carrying the title *"Lokasaṃgraha-Sandeśaḥ"* The International Conference on Tulasīdāsa and His Works, held at Florida International University, Miami, Florida, USA, in November 1999, honoured me for both these publications by giving me the International Tulasī Award.

The present publication, being number six in the series, is a continuation of what I have been writing since 1993. There are three notable features of this study. First, I have shown that the lokasaṃgraha-message of the Gītā has been presented in that scripture from ten different but inter-connected angles, so that it can appeal to various types of listeners. Secondly, I have shown that the jagmangal-message of the Mānas can also be explained from the same ten angles as are applicable to the Gītā. Thirdly, I have shown that serious concern for the good of all has been an integral part of the Indian tradition right from the Vedas, and the comprehensive ten-point call of the Gītā represented the high point of this tradition—and that the Mānas (written in the simple language of the villagers) helped spread the same call among common people. It is my earnest hope that these ideas will help shape (to howsoever small an extent) the socio-spiritual outlook of (at least some) citizens of the world and strengthen their resolve to face the challenges of the twenty-first century in a spirit of mutual cooperation based on social harmony, justice and social service.

SATYA P. AGARWAL

Acknowledgements

The ideas presented in this book (or rather in the entire series of books in which the present book is number six) have been formulated, slowly but steadily, as a result of nearly sixty years of close association with scholars and activists, and to all of them I want to express my indebtedness and gratitude.

To begin with, I respectfully recall the great contribution of my parents. My mother, Shrimati Sita Devi, was not only an admirer of Rāmacharitmānas herself, but she also lovingly transferred that admiration to the hearts of her children (including me). My father, Shri Ram Swarup, tried to explain to me in simple Hindi, as early as in 1942, some of the new ideas contained in Tilak's *Gita-Rahasya*.

Shri Hanuman Prasad Poddar, editor of Gita Press, Gorakhpur, who was a close friend of my father, introduced me to various scholarly writings on the Gītā and the Mānas. Similar guidance was given to me by my elder brothers, cousin brother, and teachers of Hindi and Sanskrit.

Although my study of the various scriptures went on, during my stay at Berkeley from 1948 onward, practical examples of karmayoga on a modest scale, under Indian conditions, were provided by my father-in-law, Shri Dwarka Prasad Mital (who was a freedom-fighter with Mahatma Gandhi), and my uncle-in-law, Shri Dilip Singh Mital (who worked with Vinoba Bhave).

After my retirement from the United Nations, the Indian community in Cairo, Egypt, led by Dr. R.S.S. Sarma and Dr. M. Sivamurthy, who organized so many socio-religious activities, enabled me, during 1988-89, to share my views on the Gītā and the Mānas, on a weekly basis, with members of an active Study Group.

During July-August 1990, I and my wife Urmila had an excellent opportunity to hold discussions on 'lokasaṃgraha' with Gītā-scholars in Canada, of whom special mention should be made of Prof. K. Sivaraman, Prof. Arvind Sharma, Prof. J.G. Arapura,

Prof. V. Subramaniam, and Prof. K. Mishra (then visiting from Banaras Hindu University). In June 1991, we had the privilege of talking about 'lokasaṃgraha' with Swami Chinmayananda. In January 1992, we can never forget how Swami Ranganathananda, under medical advice to take rest, asked us to come and see him, to consult about 'lokasaṃgraha'. Dr. V. Madhusudan Reddy and Dr. Karan Singh provided an insight into Śrī Aurobindo's interpretation of 'lokasaṃgraha'. Shri Shivananda reviewed for us what he had written on the Gītā and the Mānas.

From February 1992, the renewal of my old ties with the University of California, Berkeley, enabled me to start giving a concrete shape to my ideas on 'lokasaṃgraha'. Prof. Robert P. Goldman, Chairman, and Dr. Steven M. Poulos, Vice-Chairman, Center for South Asia Studies, kindly obtained for me a new University-linked identity, namely, as an honorary Research Associate. At the technical level, Dr. Barend A. van Nooten and Dr. Linda Hess of the Berkeley campus, and Swami Aparananda of the Berkeley-based Ramakrishna Mission, provided several sessions of useful discussion on 'lokasaṃgraha'. My first book in the present series entitled *"The Social Role of the Gita : How and Why"* came out in August 1993.

In November 1994, the Governor of the State of Maryland, William Donald Schaefer, encouraged me by conferring upon me the Governor's Citation, and by recognizing my writings as an act of social service. Prof. M.V. Mathur presented me this Citation on behalf of the Governor, and added his own words of appreciation and encouragement.

On July 10, 1995, the President of India, Dr. Shankar Dayal Sharma, honoured me at the Rashtrapati Bhawan, New Delhi, for my second book entitled *"The Social Message of the Gita : Symbolized as Lokasaṃgraha"*. Shri T.N. Chaturvedi, M.P. also expressed admiration for my contribution.

In October 1996, Prof. Satish C. Goyal announced that my third book entitled *"Tulasī-Rāmāyaṇa : Jagmangal Parāyaṇa"* has won the Kunti Goyal International Award. The book-release ceremony was performed on January 31, 1997 at the Rashtrapati Bhawan, New Delhi, and the President of India, Dr. Shankar Dayal Sharma spoke words of praise. On August 10, 1997, the Mānas Sangam, Kanpur (under the leadership of Shri Badri Narayan Tiwari) conferred on me a special Hindi Literary Award (marking 500 years of Tulasī's birth).

My fourth book, published in 1998, was entitled *"Mānas Evam Gītā:*

Lokmangal-Gunjitā", and this was followed, in 1999, by the fifth book entitled *"Lokasaṃgraha-Sandeśaḥ."* Honouring these two books, Dr. Bhu Dev Sharma, Dr. Ram Prakash Agarwal and Shri Satya D. Gupta, acting on behalf of the International Conference on Tulasīdāsa and his Works (held at Florida International University), conferred upon me the International Tulasī Award in November 1999.

During 1999-2000, when the present book was being drafted, special words of encouragement and admiration were spoken by Dr. Natwerlal S. Jani, who was himself a great scholar and social worker, but who is no more with us now. As a mark of my gratefulness to Dr. Jani, I have dedicated this book to him. Other scholars and/or activists who gave valuable support include Dr. B.P. Shah, Prof. Ram Das Lamb, Acharya Sohanlal Ramrang, Shri Lallan Prasad Vyas, Dr. M.K. Gautam, Dr. Piyush Agrawal, Dr. Jagdish Rustagi, Shri Ravi Maharaj, Shri Satya Narayan Maharaj, Shri Baldeo O. Girwarr, Shri Rajendra Arun, Prof. Radhey Shyam Dwivedi, Shri P.C. Gupta, Prof. Usha Gupta, Prof. Rajnikant M. Pancholi, Shri Parvesh Swani, and Pandit Padmaraj Joshi.

Within my own family or svajanam, in the language of the Gītā, my wife Urmila's role as an active research partner has already been referred in the above paragraphs. Over and above that, she provided not only constant companionship and encouragement but also very valuable feedback, based on her contacts with temple groups and cultural associations. Technical and moral support came from all the members of the family, viz. Nishkam, Kokila, Seema, David Harding, Isha, Kiran, Priya and Maya. Close relatives who rendered valuable help, include Shri Harish Kashyap, Shrimati Nirmala Gupta, Renu Mital, Dr. K.M. Mital, Shri M.M. Agarwal, Shri Arya Bhushan, Dr. K.V. Mital, and Abhay Bhushan. To all of them as well as to many others who rendered help but whose names are not specifically mentioned (in order to keep this list short), I express my sincere thankfulness.

15 April, 2000 SATYA P. AGARWAL

CHAPTER ONE

Underlying Spirit of Vedas and Other Sources—Concern for the Good of All

1.1. The focus of attention in this book is the social message of the Gītā and Tulasī-Rāmāyaṇa. However, there is no intention to imply anything like a monopoly of ideas or exclusiveness of outlook. In other words, no claim is made that the social message suddenly appeared in these two books, from nowhere. What we want to say is that, although serious concern for the good of all did exist in the Indian tradition right from the Vedas, and such concern has been maintained through many writings for thousands of years, a comprehensive ten-point call emanating from a single source took a visible shape in the Gītā and was later re-enunciated in simpler language in Tulasī-Rāmāyaṇa. The last statement about the similarity between the Gītā and Tulasī-Rāmāyaṇa may surprise those who look mainly at the outer form and style of story narration, because these two books refer to events of two different yugas or periods of time and are written in two different styles. What is similar is the inner content that gives the social message, as will be explained in this book.

1.2. Our aim in the present chapter is to quote and briefly explain selected extracts from the Vedas, Upaniṣads, Mahābhārata, Vālmīki-Rāmāyaṇa, and other important writings that express concern for the good of all. We want to make it clear that these selections are only illustrative. Furthermore, the various quotations given in this chapter are not necessarily in a chronological order.

Five Quotations from the Vedas

1.3. Before presenting selected Vedic utterances aimed at achieving the good of all, we feel it is necessary to refer to a basic question that is raised by some critics of the Vedic approach relating to social organization. This question can be formulated in the following form. Since the varṇa-system of dividing the society into four classes—brāhmin, kṣatriya, vaiśya, śūdra—was started in Vedic times, why not blame the Vedic leaders for the anti-social features of the caste system which is a degenerated form of the varṇa system? It is beyond the scope of the present book to attempt a detailed answer to this question. We have no hesitation in criticizing the anti-social characteristics of the caste system, the most repugnant element of which was 'untouchability'. However, we feel that the blame for this need not be assigned entirely to the Vedic people because the social degeneration occurred over a long period of time, and so the leaders of later ages too must receive a part of the blame.

1.4. The first of the five, selected Vedic utterances that proclaim the concern for the good of all is the famous gāyatrī mantra—

> *aum bhūrbhuvaḥ svaḥ tatsaviturvareṇyaṃ bhargo devasya*
> *dhīmahi dhiyo yo naḥ pracodayāt.*

Simple Meaning—God alone is everywhere and everything—He is this world, the higher worlds and the heaven. We pray to Him and meditate on Him in the form of the effulgence of the sun. May He inspire us and guide us so that our intellect may remain steady on the right path.

Why do we identify the gāyatrī mantra as the most well-known Vedic proclamation of the desire for the good of all? One obvious reason is that the words 'dhīmahi' and 'naḥ' refer to plural numbers which show that this prayer is for collective welfare and not for the good of any individual. Another speciality of the gāyatrī mantra is that through it we pray to God for the right intellect, not for material gain. In other words, the gāyatrī mantra prays for the good of all which can be achieved by the right intellect of all.

1.5. The second quotation that expresses the Vedic concern for the good of all is in the form of a warning addressed to those who neglect other living beings and prepare food merely for their own consumption—

> *Moghamannaṃ vindate aprachetāḥ satyam bravīmi vadha it*
> *sa tasya nāryamaṇaṃ puṣyati no sakhāyaṃ kevalāgho*
> *bhavati kevalādī.*

Simple Meaning—This stupid man eats in vain, I am telling the truth that such eating will lead to his destruction because he is not promoting the cause of God in the form of fire by not feeding his fellow-beings. One who prepares food merely for one's own consumption is a sinner.

How this mantra expresses the concern for the good of all is explained by Shivananda in his commentary on the Gītā. We give below the gist in English of what Shivananda wrote in Hindi—

"This mantra seeks to promote the well-being and happiness of all by ensuring adequate food for all. This reminds us of the following śloka or verse which summarizes in simple words what Indian culture stands for—

sarve bhavantu sukhinaḥ sarve santu nirāmayāḥ
sarve bhadrāṇi paśyantu mā kaścid duḥkhbhāg bhavet.

Simple Meaning—May all be happy, may all be free from diseases, may all look to the good of others, may none suffer from sorrow."[1]

1.6. The third quotation that seeks to promote the good of all, forms part of every mantra that is uttered at the time of performing a Vedic yajña—the common English word for yajña being 'sacrifice'. Each such mantra ends with the words 'idaṃ na mama' meaning 'this is not mine'. The performer of the yajña offers sesame, ghee, etc. to God through the medium of the sacrificial fire and declares that he is giving up his sense of ownership and attachment to the various objects. Rather than quote the full mantras chanted during a yajña, we want to highlight the social significance of the words 'idaṃ na mama'. These words sought to make people unselfish, free from the sense of 'I' and 'mine'. It is obvious that the Vedic concern for the good of all is conveyed by the words 'idaṃ na mama' which occur repeatedly in the Vedic texts.

1.7. The fourth quotation that provides the philosophical basis of social harmony is the following mantra of Rigveda which is the oldest of the four Vedas—

ekaṃ sad viprā bahudhā vadanti.

Simple Meaning—God is One although learned people call Him by many names.

When people grasp the message of this mantra, they realize the foolishness in creating divisions in the society on the basis of different names used to call God. Liberal thinking cultivated by this mantra can obviously make a significant contribution to the good of all.

1.8. The fifth quotation that expresses the Vedic concern for the good of all is the last mantra of Rigveda—this being the last mantra, the closing three words are uttered twice—

samānī va ākūtiḥ samānā hridayāni vaḥ
samānamastu vo manaḥ yathā vaḥ susahāsati
yathā vaḥ susahāsati.

Simple Meaning—May you all think along similar lines, may you all have similar emotions, may you all have similar views. Such a sense of unity will make your society strong, will make your society strong.

This mantra not only speaks of the Vedic concern for the good of all but also shows the way of achieving it, namely, through a sense of unity which is created by a similarity of freely expressed views, not imposed by force.

Five Quotations from the Upaniṣads too

1.9. We ended the five quotations from the Vedas by recalling the last mantra of the Rigveda. Now, while selecting the five quotations from the Upaniṣads, we begin with the Śāntipāṭha or peace invocation which is uttered in the beginning of Kaṭhopaniṣad as well as several other Upaniṣads—

aum saha nāvavatu saha nau bhunaktu saha vīryaṃkaravāvahai
tejasvi nāvadhītamastu mā vidviṣāvahai
aum śāntiḥ śāntiḥ śāntiḥ

Simple Meaning—Om! May Brahman protect us, develop us and nourish us. May we be full of energy. May our studies illumine us. May we never hate each other. Om! Peace! Peace! Peace!

1.10. The above invocation emphasizes, among other things, freedom from hatred—and this was viewed by the Upaniṣads as an important element for achieving the good of all. A similar emphasis has been given in the Īśa Upaniṣad from which we present the following verse, as the second quotation from the Upaniṣads—

yastu sarvāṇi bhūtāni ātmanyevānupaśyati
sarvabhūteṣu chātmānaṃ tato na vijugupsate.

Simple Meaning—The person who realizes all beings as not distinct from his own self, and his own self as the Self of all beings, does not, by virtue of that perception, hate any one.

1.11. The third quotation referring to all-round development of individuals, families and the whole society, is from Kaṭhopaniṣad. For a clear understanding of this, it is necessary to grasp the essence of the dialogue that takes place between Yama—the God of death and dharma—and Naciketā—a young boy—. Yama classifies life's goals into two categories, viz. preyas and śreyas. Preyas means that which is pleasant, immediately attractive. Śreyas means good, that which conduces to true welfare, which is ultimately beneficial.

In terms of the four puruṣārthas or goals of life or values, preyas can be equated with artha and kāma, i.e. material and psychological values. Similarly, śreyas can be equated with dharma and mokṣa, i.e. moral and spiritual values. If both preyas and śreyas are achieved, as will be shown to happen in the case of Naciketā, that will signify all-round progress as well as spiritual enlightenment.

Yama asks Naciketā to specify three boons which he will grant, and the way Naciketā formulates his choices and preferences helps us derive the message of the Upaniṣad. For the first boon, Naciketā says—

śāntasaṅkalpaḥ sumanā...prathamaṃ varaṃ vriṇe.

Simple Meaning—My father was angry with me, so I choose as the first boon that he may be cheerful and free from anxiety and anger.

For the second boon, Naciketā says—

...agniṃ...prabrūhi...etad dvitīyena vriṇe vareṇa.

Simple Meaning—Secondly, teach me agni, that is, all sacrificial practices which will give me material opulence and psychological satisfaction, i.e. preyas.

For the third and final boon, Naciketā says—

...etad vidyām...varāṇāmeṣa varastritīyaḥ.

Simple Meaning—Finally, teach me about Ātman which never dies, so that I may achieve śreyas.

Yama had no objection to the granting of the first two boons, but he tried to dissuade Naciketā from the third boon—offering in its place more of preyas. However, Naciketā insisted on achieving śreyas too, and Yama finally granted the third boon also. This becomes clear from the last verse of Kaṭhopaniṣad—

...nāciketo'tha labdhvā vidyāmetām yogavidhiṃ ca kritsnaṃ.

Simple Meaning—In the end, Naciketā received everything, i.e. father's grace, yogavidhi, i.e. preyas, and vidyā, i.e. śreyas.

This quotation from Kaṭhopaniṣad, if properly interpreted, shows the way in which the good of all can be achieved.

1.12. The fourth quotation is from Chāndogya Upaniṣad. King Ashvapati describes the happy state of affairs in his kingdom which shows that attempts to achieve the good of all were made in that society—

na me steno janapade na kadaryo na madyapaḥ
nānāhitāgnirnāvidvān na svairī svairiṇī kutaḥ.

Simple Meaning—In my kingdom there is no thief, no miser, no drunkard, no non-performer of yajña, no uneducated, no adulterer, so how can there be any adulteress?

1.13. The fifth quotation relates to the importance given in the Upaniṣads to ahiṃsā, i.e. non-violence. By way of illustration, we refer to two Upaniṣads, so the full quotation is made up of two components.

The first component occurs in Ārunikopaniṣad which suggests that special effort should be made to cultivate four virtues of which non-violence is one—

brahmacaryam, ahimsām ca, aparigrahaṃ ca, satyaṃ ca, yatnena
he rakṣato he rakṣato he rakṣata iti.

Simple Meaning—Try your best to cultivate and maintain four virtues, viz. brahmcarya (self-control and discipline), non-violence, non-possessiveness, and truth.

The second component occurs in Chāndogya Upaniṣad which views worldly life itself as a yajña—

puruṣo vāva yajñaḥ...atha yat tapo dānaṃ ārjavaṃ ahiṃsā satyavacanaṃ iti
tā asya dakṣiṇāḥ.

Simple Meaning—The entire human life is a yajña...Tapas (discipline), dānam (sharing), uprightness, non-violence, truthfulness—these are indicators of the completeness of the yajña, like the dakṣiṇā or gift given to the priest.

Besides the above-mentioned five quotations, we may recall that another Upaniṣadic text entitled "da, da, da" has also been referred to in the Preface to this book.

Three Problems that Challenged the Approach of the Vedas and the Upaniṣads

1.14. The Vedas and the Upaniṣads did try to protect the interests of all the members of the society, and they achieved a good deal of success too. However, we need to examine why their success was not complete. Three main problems confronted them—with some force during the Vedic and Upaniṣadic times themselves, and even more forcefully in the times that followed. In the following paragraphs, we shall have a close look into these problems, and that will also help clarify the role that the Gītā played in the period that followed the Vedas and the Upaniṣads.

1.15. The first problem was that of access. The knowledge of the Vedas and the Upaniṣads remained confined to a small section of the society. Orthodox opinion even raised the issue of entitlement—such opinion unhesitatingly proclaimed that lower sections of the society were not entitled to study the Vedas and the Upaniṣads. How then was the deep knowledge contained in the Vedas and the Upaniṣads supposed to reach the society as a whole? The Vedas did not establish any organization for this purpose—and the history of the world's religions lends support to the Vedic approach, because such organizations tend to become centers of rigidity and orthodoxy with the passage of time. Vedic thinkers had hoped that scholars and social workers, acting in their individual capacity, would spread the message of the Vedas and the Upaniṣads to the common people. Such hopes were fulfilled to a great extent, but significant gaps did remain because of lack of universal education. The result was that disadvantaged sections of the society were denied direct access to Vedic as well as Upaniṣadic knowledge, either on grounds of entitlement or because of lack of education. Such people depended heavily on priests whose exploitative tendencies became prominent over long periods of time.

1.16. The second problem was that religious and spiritual practices, that were prominent during the Vedic and the Upaniṣadic times, started facing criticism at the hands of social reformers who questioned the relevance of those practices under changed circumstances. For example, people admiring non-violence began protesting against those yajñas in which animals were sacrificed. Furthermore, intellectuals expressed dissatisfaction with the rituals in general, saying that such external practices diverted people's attention away from internal concepts that really counted. They pointed out that the most important concept of the yajña, symbolized by the words 'idam na mama', was pushed to the background because these words were often uttered like a parrot without realizing that the underlying idea was to make people unselfish. In fact, the Upaniṣads themselves gave priority to jñāna or knowledge in preference to the Vedic karma-kāṇḍa or rituals. However, with the further passage of time, the Upaniṣads themselves faced criticism on the ground that they were often interpreted as encouraging abstract discussion aimed at self-realization but divorced from practical problems of the society. The sannyāsa-oriented, i.e. renunciatory approach of many of the Upaniṣads appeared to encourage escapism, and so did not find favour with social reformers. They pointed out that common people were getting the wrong message. For example, although the real purpose of the law of karma, as envisaged in the Upaniṣads, was to keep people away from bad deeds, common people misinterpreted it and ignored poor sufferers on the plea that such suffering was due to their past karma.

1.17. The third problem was related to social stratification which gradually degenerated into social disunity to such an extent that even in the face of external invasions, different parts of the society could not present a united front, resulting in the subjugation of the Indian people. Social disunity at critical times represented an inability to adjust socio-religious ideas to changing circumstances. The question as to why this occurred needs to be examined in the light of the history of different religions. In general, it can be argued that those religions which have a founder are more likely to get tied to rigid approaches because leaders other than the founder may not carry adequate weight in their attempt to get rid of rigidities. Hinduism has an in-built advantage because it is not tied to any founder. However, to keep such an open, democratic religion up-to-date, creative and continuously meaningful, it is necessary that each member of the society stay alert and fulfill his or her obligation to hold the society together. When the caste divisions proved to be an obstacle in matters of socio-religious unity, necessary adjustment therein was obviously needed. But religious leaders in medieval India seem to have worsened the situation instead of narrowing the social divisions. In other words, the high expectations that the Vedas and the Upaniṣads had assumed for the future generations of Hindus, were not adequately fulfilled during medieval times.

Gītā's Role in Providing the Necessary Corrective

1.18. A close look into the problems that challenged the approach of the Vedas and the Upaniṣads helps clarify the role that the Gītā played. The question as to how the good of the society can be given the highest priority was raised and answered by the Gītā. The style of presentation was, however, indirect because it made use of a dialogue. To get to the core of the Gītā's message was thus not so simple as one might wish. But it did bring together in a single book, relevant ideas of the Vedas and the Upaniṣads and added thereto the concept of selfless service as well as devotion to God. By doing all this within the span of seven hundred verses, the Gītā made it relatively easy to bring out the message of the good of all. An in-depth analysis of the Gītā from the viewpoint of the good of all—this is the subject matter of a large part of this book, and the rest of the book adopts the same attitude towards Tulasī-Rāmāyaṇa. At this point, it may be enough to say that ten aspects of this analysis will be presented in the forthcoming chapters of the book—just as complete knowledge of anything calls for a look at it from ten angles.

1.19. K.M. Panikkar has adopted an historical approach to the evolution of social philosophy in ancient India, and made a comparative assessment of the respective contributions of the Vedas, the Upaniṣads, and the Gītā, from the viewpoint of Lokasaṃgraha or the good of the world. The conclusion arrived at by Panikkar is in line with what we have written above. Here are his words—

> "The social theory behind the Lokasaṃgraha doctrine of the Gītā is most important. The conception of a world order which it is the duty of the individual to uphold by dedicating his activity towards that end, runs all through the teaching of the Gītā. The earlier Vedic religion had no such conception. Nor did the later thinkers who built up the comprehensive structure of Upaniṣadic thought devote any attention to social development. For the first time the Gītā gives a social content to religion and emphasizes the welfare of the world as the purpose of all action."[2]

1.20. Swami Raṅganāthānanda's analysis and conclusions about the respective roles of the Upaniṣads and the Gītā, in regard to the evolution of practical spirituality in ancient India, are similar to those of Panikkar stated above (although Panikkar's analysis had covered the Vedas too). Speaking on the message of the Upaniṣads, Swami Raṅganāthānanda said—

"Religion in India, as also elsewhere, has experienced a recurring opposition, often irreconcilable, between the path of the mystic and that of the man of action, between the claims of the beyond and the claims of this world. Upaniṣadic verses pointedly seek to resolve this opposition in the light of the synoptic and total vision of reality achieved in Vedānta. But what the Upaniṣads do is only to offer hints and suggestions. It was left to the Bhagavad-Gītā of a later age to capture the energy and charm of this vision in a comprehensive statement of practical spirituality."[3]

Illustrations from the Mahābhārata

1.21. Although the Gītā contains in a nutshell (with some explanation) all the important elements of dharma oriented to the good of all, it is useful to look for further elaboration of some of these elements in the Mahābhārata also, because the Gītā is structurally a part of the Mahābhārata. By utilizing nearly one hundred thousand verses, Vyāsa, the author of the Mahābhārata was able to explain fully, among other things, the social dimensions of dharma. For example, the Gītā has referred briefly to King Janaka as an exemplary karmayogin devoted to the good of all. While explaining this section of the Gītā, Lokamanya Tilak has presented details from the Mahābhārata that illustrate the ideas and actions of Janaka. Chapter eight of the present book, in which the Lokasaṃgraha ideas will be discussed, will be the right place to show linkages between the Gītā and the rest of the Mahābhārata, in regard to the role of Janaka.

1.22. But there is much else in the Mahābhārata which need not wait till chapter eight of this book. For example, there are stories about persons who made sacrifices for the sake of the world, and of whom there is no specific mention in the Gītā. Rishi Dadhīci is one of them. The Mahābhārata begins that story with a description of the atrocities committed by a demon named Vrittrāsur. Feeling helpless against the might of this demon, the gods made a deep search as to what special weapon could overpower him. They discovered that only a weapon made from the bones of Rishi Dadhīci can kill Vrittrāsur. So all the gods assembled and went to the Rishi, praying for help—

arhasi lokahitārthaṃ kartum svaśarīratyāgaṃ.

Simple Meaning—O Rishi, for the sake of the world, can you please give up your body?

The Mahābhārata says that Rishi Dadhīci gladly acceded to the request of the gods and voluntarily gave up his life—thus becoming instrumental in saving the world from the horrors caused by Vrittrāsur.

1.23. Acharya Vinoba has selected from the Mahābhārata three other stories that illustrate specific elements of the message of universal welfare contained in a nutshell in the Gītā. As already mentioned in paragraph 1.15 of this book, certain sections of the society, according to orthodox opinion, were not entitled to the knowledge and practices of the Vedas and the Upaniṣads. The Gītā eliminated all barriers in the path of spirituality, and the Mahābhārata wrote interesting stories to confirm this in the minds of common listeners. For example, the Gītā proclaimed in verse IX.32—

> *striyo vaiśyās tathā śūdrās te'pi yānti parāṃ gatiṃ.*

> ***Simple Meaning***—Lord Krishna said that the state of perfect bliss is attainable by all, for example, women, vaiśyas, śūdras—all can achieve perfection.

1.24. The three stories from the Mahābhārata, which Acharya Vinoba selected, relate to these three categories of persons, showing that they even taught important persons who came to them for instruction. Here are the three stories narrated by Acharya Vinoba, but translated by one of his disciples—

> "You may go on discussing whether women have the right to study the Vedas, but here, in the Mahābhārata, we see before our eyes Sulabhā teaching divine wisdom to king Janak. ...The story of the vaish-merchant-Tulādhār is similar. The brahmin Jājali goes to him in search of wisdom... The third story is of Vyādh, the hunter. An arrogant brahmin ascetic was asked by his guru to approach the hunter and learn wisdom from him."[4]

Vālmīki Rāmāyaṇa—Portrayal of Ideal Characters

1.25. While the longest epic, the Mahābhārata promotes the concept of Lokasaṃgraha through innumerable stories, the other epic, the Vālmīki Rāyāmaṇa achieves the same objective by describing exemplary characters like Rāma, Sītā, and others. The Rāmāyaṇa has become popular in many countries outside India too, and many versions of the story have appeared in a large number of languages.

1.26. Rishi Vālmīki is regarded as 'Ādi-Kavi' or the first poet. He has himself described the special circumstances under which the metrical composition or 'śloka' came out of tongue as a divine inspiration. The creator Brahmā linked the origin of 'śloka' to 'śoka' or grief which Vālmīki felt because of compassion towards a bird that was killed by a hunter. The uniquely meaningful beginning of the Vālmīki-Rāmāyaṇa, which sets the tone for the entire epic, has been beautifully told by C. Rajagopalachari in the following words—

"One morning, Saint Nārada came on a visit to Vālmīki's āśrama or hermitage. Vālmīki asked the sage, 'Please tell me who among the heroes of this world is the highest in virtue and wisdom'. Nārada replied, 'Rāma is the hero that you ask for.'...

"The next day, Vālmīki's mind was still full of Rāma's story. As he was walking along the river-bank, he saw on a nearby tree two loving Krauncha-birds singing in their joy of life and love. Suddenly, the male bird fell down, hit by a hunter's arrow. The female bird, seeing her lover rolling on the ground, lamented in piteous fashion. Observing this, Vālmīki burst into a curse—O hunter, as you have killed one of these love-intoxicated birds, you will wander homeless all your long years...

"Vālmīki was wondering why he lost himself in anger...To him in meditation, Brahmā said—Be not afraid. These things happened to start you on the story of Rāma. From 'śoka' (sorrow) sprang the 'śloka' (verse) and in this metre and rhythm the story should be told...With my blessings, you shall sing Rāma's story, for the benefit of the world."[5]

1.27. The belief that Rāma was an Avatāra or incarnation of Viṣṇu was not so widespread in Vālmīki's time as it became later on. So Vālmīki depicted Rāma as an ideal man and Sītā as an ideal woman. From his very childhood, Rāma was a source of happiness for all. As he grew up, he set standards of right behavior—as a son, as a brother, as a student. On the occasion of Sītā's 'svayam-vara' i.e. husband-choosing function, Rāma gave a tangible proof that he was unbeatable in valour too, but he remained calm and free from egotism. Sītā too behaved as an ideal daughter of Janaka. Later on when Kaikeyī made a tricky move which resulted in Rāma, Sītā and Lakṣmaṇa going into exile for fourteen years, Rāma behaved like an ideal karmayogin, treating the pleasant and the unpleasant alike and bearing no ill-will even towards Kaikeyī.

1.28. Modern critics of Vālmīki-Rāmāyaṇa often pick up a few instances like the killing of Bāli, disfiguring of Shurpanakhā, fire-ordeal of Sītā, and finally the banishment of Sītā, to question the claim that

Rāma and Sītā were ideal characters. In the opinion of this author, the fact that standards change with the lapse of time needs to be recognized. Later writer of Rāmāyaṇa, for example, Tulasīdāsa omitted the banishment of Sītā because it appeared to him to be inappropriate. He placed a greater emphasis on the message of good of all, and he gave it through Rāma-rājya or the ideal rule of Rāma and Sītā.

1.29. Continuing with the Vālmīki-Rāmāyaṇa, it is significant that, although Rāma and Sītā were great in the palaces of Ayodhyā and Mithila, they became even greater when they walked through thick forests and established one-ness with the forest dwellers. The development in Rāma's character reached a high point when, on seeing the skeletons of saints killed by rakṣasas or demons, he proclaimed his determination to put an end to the misery of the people by overpowering the demons—

kṣatriyairdhāryate chāpo nārtaśabdo bhavediti.

Simple Meaning—Rāma said, kṣatriyas use their strength only to ensure that oppression and misery of innocent people come to an end.

1.30. Vālmīki attached much importance to Rāma's establishing friendly ties with Sugrīva, the king of monkeys. Swami Vivekananda interpreted this as the coming together of the people from the north and the south. Modern interpreters see in this a message of inter-racial unity. Similarly, the victory of unarmed monkeys over the heavily armed demons represented the victory of good over evil.

1.31. Ignoring the critical opinion of some of the modern writers, Swami Vivekananda found Vālmīki's portrayal of Sītā as a glorious ideal for women. Sītā gave up the palace of Ayodhyā and insisted on walking through forests and dangerous places to go hand-in-hand with her husband Rāma. Wherever she went, she treated the elderly women and the wives of the Rishis with the same respect as she had shown for her mother-in-law Kauśalyā. Even as a prisoner of Rāvaṇa in Laṇkā, Sītā maintained her faithfulness to the marriage-vows. Vālmīki showed how evil forces could not subdue sublime virtues of Sītā.

1.32. Besides Rāma and Sītā, Vālmīki depicted several other exemplary characters. Bharat's devotion to his elder brother Rāma, and his refusal to be a part of the royal conspiracy even though his mother Kaikeyī wanted that, gave to the society the message of self-sacrifice for a right cause. Rāma's mother Kauśalyā gave precedence to family unity at the cost of personal happiness. Jaṭāyu gladly sacrificed his life in an attempt to rescue Sītā from the wicked Rāvaṇa. Hanumān showed how a true karmayogin could penetrate the heavily guarded fortress of Laṅkā and give to Sītā the much-needed message of hope sent by Rāma.

1.33. The story of Vibhīṣaṇa, the younger brother of Rāvaṇa, is significant in two ways. First, the words used by Rāma for accepting Vibhīṣaṇa's surrender and for putting an end to all his fears, provide an indication that Rāma was an incarnation of Viṣṇu. Secondly, Vibhīṣaṇa showed the way in which a person, in spite of close associations with demons, could give up the path of evil and join the forces of the good. According to Mahatma Gandhi, Vibhiṣaṇa adopted the path of non-cooperation with evil and so could be called a Satyāgrahī in modern terminology. The assurance given by Rāma, to anyone following Vibhīṣaṇa's example, is expressed in the following verse—

sakrideva prapannāya tavāsmīti yo yācate
abhayaṃ sarvabhūtebhyo dadāmyetad vrataṃ mama.

Simple Meaning—Rāma says, let every one listen to my promise—if someone tells Me even once "I am yours" and comes to me for shelter and protection, I bestow on him complete fearlessness.

Highest Priority to Non-Violence by Buddhism and Jainism

1.34. Although the primary attention of this book is on Vedic and related sources, a brief mention needs to be made of the important contribution of Buddhism and Jainism too. The reform movement to make yajñas free from animal-sacrifice was strongly supported by Buddhist and Jain thinkers. We have already given, in paragraph 1.13, Upaniṣadic quotations that glorify non-violence. Subsequently, the Mahābhārata declared non-violence as the highest dharma—"ahiṃsā paramo dharmaḥ". The Buddhists and the Jains insisted that glorification of non-violence must go hand-in-hand with visible signs of adherence thereto in day-to-day life, for example, the practice of vegetarian food.

Emperor Aśoka's Messages of Social Harmony and Tolerance

1.35. Emperor Aśoka has a special place in world history because of his efforts to promote non-violence, peace and equal respect to all religions. During the early part of his rule, he attacked and conquerred Kaliṅga province, but the sight of killings and horrors of war brought about a change of heart. Personally he became a Buddhist but to the society as a whole he gave the message of equal respect for all religions. He made special efforts to put an end to animal-sacrifice.

Hindu Influences on Mahāyāna Buddhism

1.36. Buddhism spread from India to other parts of Asia, and historians have identified two branches or variants of this religion. The older variant is known as Theravāda or Hīnayāna; it became popular in Sri Lanka, Burma, Thailand and other countries of South-east Asia. The latter variant is known as Mahāyāna which became popular in Tibet, China, Japan etc. From the viewpoint of the philosophy that gives prominence to the good of all, rather than to individual salvation or Nirvāṇa, the Mahāyāna variant has attracted greater attention. The reason is that a practitioner of Mahāyāna, on attaining perfection, is not keen on achieving Nirvāṇa because he or she would rather stay on in the world to help suffering humanity. This Mahāyāna ideal is known as Bodhisattva and scholars of comparative religion find it to be similar to the Pūrṇa-yogin of the Gītā. In the opinion of Lokmanya Tilak, the social service-oriented ideas of Mahāyāna Buddhism, which were not so prominent in the older variant i.e. Hīnayāna, are indicative of the influence of the Gītā. Dr. Radhakrishnan also says—

> "The two chief works of Mahāyāna Buddhism—The Awakening of Faith in the Mahāyāna, and the Lotus of the True Law—are deeply indebted to the teaching of the Gītā."[6]

We need not go into further details.

Glorification of Non-Violence by Patañjali

1.37. The Yogaśāstra of Maharshi Patañjali has given an indication of the type of miraculous improvement in social relationship that can be achieved through non-violence—

> *ahiṃsāpratiṣṭhāyāṃ tatsannidhau vairatyāgaḥ.*

> ***Simple Meaning***—When the practice of non-violence becomes perfect, i.e. in the presence of a non-violent saint, even violent beings give up their enmity.

This assurance of Patañjali has exercised a healthy influence on Satyāgrahī's who are guided by the faith that the heart of the oppressors would undergo a change because of non-violent resistance to unjust practices. Critics of Mahatma Gandhi often used to point out that there were no visible signs of any change of heart on the part of the British rulers. In reply, Gandhi would refer to Patañjali's assurance and would conclude that the practice of non-violence by the Satyāgrahī's had not achieved perfection. In other words, the need was, said Gandhi, to carry non-violence to perfection rather than give it up.

Manusmṛti's Support to Non-Violence and to Five Yajñas

1.38. In continuation of the above, we want to say that Patañjali has listed non-violence as one of the virtues that together constitute 'yama' or self-discipline. Manusmṛti too has sung praises of non-violence. Besides this, Manusmṛti has spoken of the importance of five Maha-yajñas. The idea underlying these yajñas is that every householder should consider as a debt, the help received from others, and that the yajñas present an attempt to discharge this debt. These yajñas are different from the ones which are performed with the help of ghee, wood and other commodities. The five Mahā-yajñas prescribed for householders by Manusmṛti are—

(i) Brahma-yajña or a study of the Vedas
(ii) Deva-yajña or prayer to deities
(iii) Pitri-yajña or offerings dedicated to ancestors
(iv) Manuṣya-yajña or hospitality to human beings
(v) Bhūta-yajña or offering of food to other creatures.

The concern shown by Manusmṛti for 'loka-vivriddhi' i.e. growth or prosperity of the people, will be referred to in chapter eight.

Desire to do Good to all Glorified in Bhāgavat-Purāṇa

1.39. The main purpose of the Purānas was to spread religious ideas among common people through the medium of stories. Many of these stories that advocate fasting for achieving heaven or material rewards, do not obviously reach the highest standard of the Gītā which speaks of niṣkām-karma i.e. performance of duty without hankering after selfish gains. Critics of the Purāṇas also blame them for spreading superstition and orthodoxy among illiterate people. Rather than look into the negative side of the Purāṇas, we propose to pick up verses that glorify the desire to do good to all. For example, the following verse from Bhāgavat-Mahāpurāṇa deserves mention—

ahiṃsā satyamasteyaṃ akāmakrodhalobhanā
bhūtapriyahitehā ca dharmo 'yaṃ sārvavārṇikaḥ.

Simple Meaning—For people of all the varṇas, seven elements of dharma are important, viz., non-violence, truth, absence of avarice, unselfishness, freedom from anger, freedom from greed, and desire to do good to all.

Another relevant quotation from the same Purāṇa gives the assurance that devotion to God puts an end to caste distinctions—

bhaktiḥ punāti manniṣṭhā śvapākānapi sambhavān.

Simple Meaning—Bhagavān says—genuine devotion to Me (i.e. God) makes every one pure, even those who are called Cāṇḍals because they eat dog's meat.

Ideal of Helping Others Praised by Kālidāsa and Bhartrihari

1.40. Sanskrit literature is full of verses providing the ideal of helping others. For our present purposes, two quotations should suffice. The first one is from Kālidāsa's Abhijñāna-shākuntalam where the good of the world has been given priority over individual happiness—

svasukhanirabhilāṣaḥ khidyase lokahite.

Simple Meaning—That person is admirable who is willing to put into background the desire for personal happiness, in order to promote the good of the world.

1.41. The second quotation is from the Nītiśataka of Bhartrihari. He has classified human beings into four categories on the basis of whether they give priority to selfish interest or to the good of others. To the highest category belong the saints who promote the interests of others by giving up their own. The full text of Bhartrihari's verse is—

ete satpuruṣāḥ parārthaghatakāḥ svārthān parityajya ye
sāmānyāstu parārthamudyamabhritah svārthāvirodhena ye
te'mi mānuṣarākṣasāḥ parahitam svārthāya nighnanti ye
ye nighnanti nirarthakaṃ parahitaṃ te ke na jānīmahe.

Simple Meaning—Those who take care of the good of others, even at the cost of their own, I call them 'good'. Those who are engaged in tasks that benefit others, but do not put their own interests at risk, I call them 'ordinary'. Those who work contrary to the good of others, in order to promote their own, I call them 'demons' that look like human beings. Those who destroy what might do good to others, and do this without any valid reason (i.e. even though their own interests might be hurt at the same time), I do not know what to call them (because they are worse than demons).

Importance of Helping Others as Expressed in Modern Indian Languages

1.42. When modern languages took the place of Sanskrit, popular literature inspiring devotion to God arose all over India, the basis of which was Rāmāyaṇa, Mahābhārata, Bhāgavat-Purāṇa, etc. The new versions of Rāmāyaṇa introduced certain changes in what Vālmīki had written, mainly because Rāma was now accepted as an Avatāra of Vishṇu, and not merely as an ideal man. Kamban's Tamil-Rāmāyaṇa, Krittivasa's Bangla-Rāmāyaṇa, and Tulasīdāsa's Hindi-Rāmāyaṇa—all these became great favourites in their respective regions. A parallel development took place, focussing attention on Krishna as another Avatāra of Vishṇu. Among Hindi poets who composed songs of devotion addressed to Krishna, the most popular were Sūrdās and Mirābāī. Many saints-poets utilized the teachings of Rāmāyaṇa, Gītā and other scriptures and composed devotional and inspiring songs to spread the religious and spiritual message among common people. For our present purposes, brief quotations from the songs composed by three saints should suffice, viz. Narsi Mehta, Kabir and Tukaram.

1.43. A song of Saint Narsi Mehta of Gujarat was a favourite of Mahatma Gandhi. This song (in Gujarati language) glorifies those who help others, and we quote a part of it—

Vaishnavajan to tene kahiye je pir parāi jāne re
par duhkhe upkār kare toye man abhimān na āne re.

Simple Meaning—A true bhakta or devotee of Vishṇu is one who feels pain when others are in pain, who tries to remove the sufferings of others, and who does this without any feeling of egotism.

1.44. Saint Kabir of Uttar Pradesh did not attach much importance to any particular form of the Infinite. He conveyed the message of the good of all in very simple and effective Hindi—

Kabirā kharā bazār men sab ki mānge khair
na kāhu se dostī na kāhu se vair

Simple Meaning—Kabir says, standing in the market place, I pray for the welfare of all, making no distinction between friends and enemies.

1.45. Saint Tukaram of Maharashtra, through songs composed in Marathi language, instructed common people to view all beings as various forms of God. Such a view obviously promotes the good of all. Acharya Vinoba has rendered Saint Tukaram's Marathi songs into simple Hindi, like the following—

nar nārī bachche sab hī nārāyaṇ
aisā merā man banāo prabhu.

Simple Meaning—O God, give me such understanding that I consider everyone as God, be they men, women or children.

1.46. Shivanand is of the opinion that the message of the good of all, as conveyed by Indian saints, carried weight because many of them belonged to poor sections of the society and had themselves experienced sufferings and hardships in their own lives. The gist of Shivanand's ideas, expressed in Hindi, can be conveyed in the following words—

> "Large numbers of bhaktas and saints of India, who achieved fame and popularity, were born in what are commonly called lower castes, for example, Namdev (tailor), Kabir (weaver), Dadu (cotton processor), Raidas (leather-worker), Sena (barber), Nabhadas (harijan), Sadana (butcher), Narhari (goldsmith), Savanta (gardener), Tukaram (harijan), Chokhamela and Gulabrao Maharaj (untouchables). Several of the saints were Muslims or Christians who belonged to poorer sections of the society. In fact, according to Nārad-bhakti-sūtras, all distinctions of caste, education, appearance, family, property, occupation, etc. disappear because of genuine devotion to God."[7]

Tulasī-Rāmāyaṇa's Priority to the Good of All

1.47. Among the Hindi language books that give priority to the good of all, Tulasī-Rāmāyaṇa i.e. Rāmcharitmānas or Mānas (for short), has a unique place. The one word or idea that is prominent in the Mānas from the beginning to the end is "mangal" which means "good". Of course, Tulasīdāsa or Tulasī (for short) has used several synonyms of 'mangal' too. In order to clarify that he has in mind the good of all, Tulasī has used jag-mangal or sakal-mangal which mean, respectively, good of the world, and good of all. This entire book of ours is devoted to a thorough discussion of the good of all as depicted in the Mānas, along with the Gītā. Therefore, is will not be appropriate to write in detail at this point about the priority given by the Mānas to the good of all.

1.48. In paragraph 1.19 above, we quoted K.M. Panikkar who summarized the special contribution of the Gītā in comparison to the Vedas and the Upaniṣads. A similar comparison between Tulasī on the one hand, and Mirābāi and Sūrdās, on the other, has been presented by Shripal Singh Kshem. We give below in English, a glimpse of what Kshem has written in beautiful and literary Hindi—

> "Mirābāi gave the message of surrendering to God—and this represented the complete merger of Mira's individual self into Lord Krishna's Universal Self, ignoring worldly criticism and mundane considerations. Similarly, Sūrdās was whole heartedly devoted to the

singing of adoration for the 'lilā' or 'sport' of Lord Krishna as a child of Vrindavan. He sang about how the Lord played with his dearest devotees rather than about what the Lord did to tackle the overall social and wordly problems.

"In the writings of Goswami Tulasīdāsa, on the other hand, the main purpose of God's incarnation is the good of the world based on harmonization and cooperation. Tulasī directed his spiritual pursuits to the attainment of the good of all and he made this the aim of his poetry, too. His entire philosophy was directed to achieve the good of all."[8]

How Gītā and Mānas are Special and Similar too

1.49. The preceding paragraphs make it clear that we are fully justified in viewing the Gītā and the Mānas as two pillars that hold the banner of the good of all. We now want to draw attention to historical events that helped discover similarities between these two books. The biggest event that saw the simultaneous utilization of both these books was the freedom struggle of India. Mahatma Gandhi based his technique of non-violent Satyagraha on the principles of the Gītā. Subsequently, when asked to describe the social ideal of independent India, he put before the people the picture of Rām-rājya as narrated in the Mānas. Since details relating to these topics will be presented in chapters twelve and thirteen of this book, it is not necessary to write more about them at this point. However, since references to the good of all in selected books have been included in the present chapter, it seems appropriate to refer here to five more books that took the lead in discovering similarities between the Gītā and the Mānas.

1.50. The first book was Acharya Vinoba's *Sthitaprajña-darshan* which was published in 1946 and which specifically gave some quotations from the Mānas to illustrate the ideas of the Gītā.[9] Thereafter, in 1962 came the second book—a small booklet written by Sadhu T.L. Vaswani which was entitled 'Śrī Rāma' and which was printed at Loksangraha Press, Poona. In the concluding chapter, Vaswani wrote—

> "Tulasī's Rāmāyaṇa is a treasure-house for bhaktas of Śrī Rāma. From that classic of bhakti (devotion), are selected the "sayings" which are given below...Śrī Rāma's "sayings" given here remind me of Śrī Krishna's "sayings" in the Gītā. Rich are they in the beauty of wisdom as are the orient pearls in the Indian Ocean."[10]

1.51. Along with the "sayings" presented by Sādhu Vāswāni, the name of the press where this book was printed calls for our attention because the word 'Loksangraha' is from the Gītā and it stands for the good of the world, like the word 'Jagmangal' of the Mānas. More on these two words in chapter eight.

1.52. The author of the third book is Balkoba Bhave, the younger brother of Acharya Vinoba. In his *Gītā-Tattva-Bodh*, he quoted many verses of the Mānas that went hand-in-hand with specific verses of the Gītā. The second edition of this book was published in 1981.[11] The fourth book entitled *Gītā-Rasāmrit* of Shivanand adopted the same style as that of the third one. The second edition of Shivanand's book was published in 1986.[12]

1.53. The author of the fifth book, published in 1987, is Pandit Ramkinkar Upādhyāy. The book consists of two parts and is entitled *A Comparative Study of Mānas and Gitā,* The author has devoted special attention to the dialogue between Rāma and Vibhīshan that takes place in Laṅkā-kāṇḍa of the Mānas. We shall cover this topic in chapter twelve. An English language rendering of the conclusion of the book (written in Hindi) is given below—

> "Just as the warrior, the charioter and the chariot... all three are needed for victory on the battlefield, similarly Jñāna, bhakti and karma—all three are needed for success in life. Only when we have jñānayoga in the mind, karmayoga in the body, and bhaktiyoga in the heart, can we overpower the evil."[13]

The Object of This Book

1.54. The broad objective of this book is to explain how the Gītā and the Mānas give the message of the good of all, and also to show that there are strong similarities between these two great books in this regard. The process of fulfilment of this objective consists of providing answers to the following five questions—

Question One—Why have we selected the Gītā and the Mānas, out of so many religious books that have been written and that together constitute the Vedic tradition? (We want to add that this question has already been answered in the present chapter.)

Question Two—What are the key words or phrases that help in explaining the message of the good of all, as formulated in the Gītā, and what type of interpretation is needed for this purpose?

Question Three—How did the Mānas, while accepting the broad approach of the Gītā, modify the Gītā's terminology? In other words, what new words or phrases did the Mānas use and what type of interpretation is needed to establish similarities between the two books?

Question Four—How did the people respond to the message of the Gītā and the Mānas? More specifically, when and to what extent, did the Pandits and others oppose or accept the message, and how did the society lose or gain thereby?

Question Five—What preliminary suggestion can we give to further promote the message of the Gītā and the Mānas so that individuals as well as the society and the country—and ultimately the whole world—may benefit, socially, culturally, morally, economically, and politically?

Scope of the Remaining Chapters

1.55. As already mentioned, question one has been answered in the present chapter. Questions two and three are strongly linked to each other because of similarities between the Gītā and the Mānas. Therefore, answers to these two questions will be given simultaneously. Furthermore, since there are ten key words or phrases to be explained (reference chapter two), adequate answers to questions two and three will require ten more chapters (after chapter two)—and will be completed in chapter twelve. Finally, questions four and five will be answered, one after the other, in chapter thirteen.

Selected verses of the Gītā and the Mānas will be presented i.e. the original text with accompanying English language meaning—in four Appendices.

Chapter Two

Ten Points of the Message of Gītā and Mānas

2.1. As already stated in paragraph 1.54, the process of fulfilment of the objective of this book consists of providing answers to five questions. Of these, question one has already been answered in chapter one. The present chapter begins consideration of questions two and three simultaneously, because of similarities between the Gītā and the Mānas. Detailed answers to these two questions will be given in the course of eleven chapters—one for identifying ten key words or phrases, and ten more for explaining them at the rate of one per chapter. Thus the task that we start in this chapter will be completed in chapter twelve. That will leave questions four and five to be answered in chapter thirteen.

Identification of Key Words or Phrases in the Gītā

2.2. For purposes of identifying the key words or phrases, of the Gītā as well as the Mānas, we begin the search for them from the ancient source, i.e. the Gītā, and then see how the Mānas has simplified some of those words or phrases. This procedure does not put the Mānas to any disadvantage because we shall find many instances where the Gītā expresses ideas in only one or two verses but the Mānas explains them in detail.

2.3. We believe that the message of Gītā is universal and that Arjuna is only an instrument through whom the message has been delivered. The foundation of the call for the good of all is the faith that, in reality, God is looking after the whole universe, and therefore, human beings too can best worship God by putting in their best in the work that God does. According to the Gītā, God is the basis of the unity of mankind, which in turn is the essence of dharma, because God is 'śāśvatadharmagoptā (XI.18) i.e. the protector of dharma that is free from man-made narrowmindedness. A follower of such broad-based dharma views the whole world as one family—this being a translation of the ancient Indian ideal 'vasudhaiva kuṭumbakaṃ'. To see unity in the midst of diversity is referred to in the Gītā as 'avibhaktam vibhakteṣu' (XVIII.20). We identify this as the first key phrase.

2.4. In the process of identifying the concept of unifying dharma, our attention was drawn to the basis thereof, viz. God's work as the sustainer of the world. Another expression for God's work is 'suhṛdaṃ sarvabhūtānām' (V.29), i.e. the friend who does good to all without expecting any return. And connected therewith is the call of Lord Krishna to participate in God's work, i.e. 'mat-karma' (XI.55). We identify this as the second key expression, conveying the message of the good of all.

2.5. In broad-based dharma, although the primary example-setter is God, the Gītā has listed several others also whose conduct can inspire mankind to work for the good of all. Such a list includes the sun, Manu, Ikṣvāku and Janaka—but these should be viewed only as illustrative because the Gītā has used the expression 'Janaka and others' (IV.1 and III.20). In another context (IV.15), the Gītā has stated that all those who have worked hard for the welfare of mankind have shown the way for others to follow. An appropriate expression for such commendable conduct is 'yogārūḍha-vritti', i.e. the spontaneous social work of those who have achieved spiritual perfection through any of the yogas like karma, bhakti or jñāna. The word 'yogārūḍha' occurs twice in the Gītā (VI.3, 4). We identify this as the third key expression. To complete the description of such persons, the Gītā talks about them under six different categories, in chapters II, V, VI, XII, XIV and XVIII. The expression 'sant' also occurs once in the Gītā (III.13). All these references tell us about yogārūḍha-vritti.

Adjustments to Changing Needs

2.6. Although the way shown by God or perfect persons is mentioned as example-setting, the Gītā has clarified that it is neither necessary nor advisable to stick to their path blindly, i.e. without changes or adjustments. The favourite expression of the Gītā to convey this message is 'deśe kāle ca pātre ca' (XVII.20) which means that dharma has to be relevant to the particular place, time and social needs. We identify this as the fourth key expression.

2.7. Since example-setting persons are usually of a high status, a doubt could arise in the minds of ordinary people whether acts of social service are supposed to be undertaken only by a selected few. The Gītā removes this doubt in two ways. First, it says that whatever a person does, it should be in accordance with one's 'pauruṣaṃ' or capacity because otherwise the act becomes tamasika or harmful (XVIII.25). Secondly, the Gītā says that acts of social service do not become great by virtue of quantitative measures, because what counts is the motivation or genuine desire to help—in fact, even a small amount of work done in accordance with dharma achieves a lot (II.40).

2.8. A consideration of pauruṣaṃ or capacity provides an indication of a limited role that an individual can play. A similar indication is given by using the prefix 'sva'—meaning one's own—to karma or dharma. In other words, Gītā-expressions like svakarma or svadharma indirectly convey the idea that individuals have limited capacities. In spite of such limitation, the Gītā speaks of the ideal of 'sarvabhūtahitaṃ', i.e. the good of all beings. We identify this word (which occurs twice in the Gītā, V.25 and XII.4) as the fifth key expression. Only by understanding the process of harmonization between 'sva' and 'sarva', can we hope to grasp the Gītā's message of trying one's best to achieve the good of all.

Prominence of Lokasaṃgraha

2.9. Although 'sarvabhūtahitaṃ' is the most explicit word for the good of all beings, the Gītā also uses one more expression, viz. 'lokasaṃgraha' to convey the message of the good of the world. In this context, the Gītā classifies human desires into two categories, viz. desires for selfish gains and desires for the good of the world. Those who entertain desires only for selfish gains are condemned by the Gītā as 'kāmakāmī'. On the other hand, the expression 'niṣkama karmayogins' is used to glorify those who perform their duties (including social service) without entertaining the desire for selfish gains, i.e. their desires are for the good of the world. Verse III.25 establishes a strong link between niṣkāma karma and lokasaṃgraha—the former representing the technique of work, and the latter representing its purpose. Because of the conceptual importance of this link—and also other reasons—the word 'lokasaṃgraha' has occupied a prominent place, among all the expressions that are used in the Gītā for the message of the good of all. We identify this as the sixth key expression.

2.10. The Gītā says that svadharma, aimed at sarvabhūtahitaṃ, will bring about svahitaṃ also, because all members of the society are inter-related. This follows from verse III.11 which summarizes the social philosophy of the Gītā. In terms of practical behaviour, this philosophy calls for a big change in ordinary people's priorites as well as attitudes. This can be stated in two steps. First, considering 'me' as the doer, a higher priority needs to be given to the social good rather than to 'my' good— and this is what the Gītā calls 'nirmama' or giving up the sense of mine. Secondly, priority needs to be shifted from a self-centered approach to a non-egotistic approach—and this is what the Gītā calls 'nirahaṃkāra' or giving up egotism. Putting both of these ideas together, we get the expression 'nirmamo nirahaṃkārah' which occurs twice in the Gītā (II.71 and XII.13). We identify this as the seventh key expression.

2.11. The Gītā has raised the question, "Why should we have the desire to do good to all?" and reminded us that the most effective answer to this is provided by the Vedantic philosophy according to which the same 'Ātman' is in all the beings. However, since merely academic knowledge of the philosophy is not enough by itself, the Gītā wants that it should be put into practice too. A follower of such an approach can be characterized as practising even-minded social behaviour or equal vision or 'samadriṣṭi' in the language of the Gītā. We identify this as the eighth key expression.

2.12. Although the Gītā wants that its message of the good of all should spread far and wide, it warns us against harbouring an unrealistic hope that anti-social elements will disappear from the face of the earth. In the terminology of the Gītā, the society will remain a mixture of sattva-rajas-tamas, i.e. good, average, and bad components. Among tāmasika or bad components, the most harmful from the viewpoint of universal welfare are—violence, hatred, injustice, etc. Of the various expressions that the Gītā uses for anti-social elements, 'āsurī sampat' can be considered special because it suggests that forces of evil try to entrap people by their dangerous practice of forming a chain. We identify this as the ninth key expression. By warning us of the damage that such forces can cause, the Gītā has indirectly strengthened its call for the good of all.

2.13. We now come to the last of the key words or phrases, viz. 'daivī sampat' which is the opposite of what we described in the preceding paragraph. We identify this as the tenth key expression. Glorification of virtues is a favouritic topic of the Gītā. In fact, repeated descriptions of 'yogārūḍha-vritti', already referred to in paragraph 2.5, can also be included in this topic. The inclusion of 'daivī sampat' in the selected list of ten is considered necessary for purposes of indicating the way of overpowering 'āsurī sampat'. The most important virtues are obviously those that can remedy the ills listed in the preceding paragraph. The promotion of virtues like non-violence, compassion, sharing, etc. is an important way of supporting the message of the good of all.

Ten Key Expressions at a Glance

2.14. In the light of the above, the ten key words or phrases, that play an important role in conveying the Gītā's message of the good of all, are listed below, along with simple English rendering thereof—

(1) Dharma that unites—Avibhaktam vibhakteṣu;
(2) God's work—Matkarma;
(3) Service spontaneously rendered by saints—yogārūḍha vritti;
(4) Adapting religious practices to changing needs—desh-kāla-pātra;
(5) Doing good to all beings—sarvabhūtahitaṃ;
(6) Good of the world—lokasaṃgraha;
(7) Going beyond mineness and egotism—nirmamo nirahaṃkāraḥ;
(8) Even-minded vision—samadriṣṭi;
(9) Not to succumb to forces of evil—āsurī sampat; and
(10) Promote virtues—daivī sampat.

It should be clarified that no in-built order of importance is associated with the sequence of presentation of expressions in the above list. For example, the most prominent word "lokasaṃgraha" has been listed in the sixth place.

Terminological Modifications in the Mānas

2.15. The approach of the Mānas, for giving the message of the good of all, is practically the same as that of the Gītā. Therefore the same ten concepts, which underlie the list of the preceding paragraph, are valid for the Mānas too. However, since the language of the Mānas is simple Hindi, most of the Sanskrit words have been replaced by their Hindi equivalents. In two cases, viz. 'āsurī sampat' and 'daivī sampat', considerations other than linguistic assumed importance. Rather than explain this point here, we present below what Tulasī has done for each of the ten expressions, one by one.

2.16. (1) ***Avibhaktam vibhakteṣu.*** These words of the Gītā, drawing attention to the essential unity of all mankind, occur in the context of 'sāttvika jñāna'. The Mānas also has the same unifying vision, but the expression that we propose to choose is linked with 'bhakti'. We feel that the message of unity is the main thing, while the difference in the context (bhakti versus jñāna) is not so important in the present case. Accordingly, the counterpart of the first key expression that we identify is from Uttarakāṇḍa (i.e. canto VII)—

kehi san karahin virodh.

i.e. because of the unifying vision, with whom can a bhakta have any conflict?

More on these Mānas-words in chapter five.

(2) ***Mat-karma.*** In the Gītā, Lord Krishna uses the expression 'mat-karma' meaning 'my work'. To put it in the wider context, we have translated it as 'God's work'. The obvious equivalent of this in the Mānas is 'Rāmkāj', which means 'Rām's work', i.e. 'God's work'. This expression occurs repeatedly in the Mānas, but the way it has been used in Kishkindhākāṇḍa, Sundarakāṇḍa, and Laṅkākāṇḍa (i.e. cantos. IV, V, VI) has special significance, as we shall explain in chapter four.

(3) ***Yogārūḍha-vritti.*** We mentioned in paragraph 2.5 that the Gītā has used several expressions for spiritually perfect persons. We have picked up 'yogārūḍha' because it can be applied to such persons in general, irrespective of the yoga or yogas which took them to perfection. We also drew attention to the fact that the word 'sant' occurs once in the Gītā. The same word 'sant'—being also a Hindi word—is Tulasī's favourite. For 'vritti' Tulasī uses the expression 'lakshaṇa'. So the equivalent of the third item in our list is 'sant-lakshaṇa', which occurs all over the Mānas.

(4) ***Desh-kāla-pātra.*** This expression of the Gītā, suggesting adjustment to changing needs, has three components which mean, respectively, place, time, and worthiness or suitability of the person who receives help. The first two of these three terms occur quite frequently in the Mānas too. We have picked up the following expression from Ayodhyākāṇḍa—

desh kāla lakhi samaya samājū

which has four components—the first two being the same as in the Gītā (i.e. desh, kāla), the third component (samaya) means 'circumstances', and the fourth component (samāj) means 'society'. The word 'lakhi' means 'taking into account'. So the Mānas-expression says, "taking into account place, time, circumstances, and society". Therefore, the Mānas not only conveys what the Gītā does in the present context, but even goes a step further.

(5) ***Sarvabhūtahitaṃ.*** This expression of the Gītā has been translated by Tulasī in a variety of ways. For example, we have, in the Mānas, sarva-hit, sarvaśreyaskarī, sakal-hit, sakal-mangal, sab kahn hit, sakal-sukh, and so on. But by far the most frequently found expression is 'sakal mangal' which we have picked up as the counterpart of 'sarvabhūtahitaṃ'.

(6) ***Lokasaṃgraha.*** In this case too, the Mānas contains several expressions which are practically synonyms. For example, we have jagmangal, jagat-hit, sansār-hit, vishva-upkār, sakal-lok-hit, and so on. But 'jag-mangal' is our choice, because the purpose of writing Ram-kathā has been linked by Tulasī with 'jag-mangal'.

(7) ***Nirmamo nirahaṃkārah.*** The Mānas does not have a short and straightforward translation of this expression. Laṅkākāṇḍa has a rather long expression—

"maiṇ aru mor muḍhatā tyāgū"

which means "give up the arrogance of I and mine". Uttarakānḍa has a shorter expression—

"gat.....mamtā mad.... moh"

i.e. "give up mine-ness, arrogance, and ignorance."

Of these two, the former expression, although longer, is closer to 'nirmamo nirahaṃkārah', and therefore that is our choice. We shall give details in chapter nine.

(8) ***Samadrishṭi.*** This expression is based on verse V.18, of the Gītā which uses the word 'samadarshinah.' meaning 'they have samadrishṭi or equal vision'. The word 'samadarshī' occurs in the Mānas too, for example, in Kishkindhākāṇḍa. Therefore, we can say that the expression 'samadrishṭi' can be used in relation to the Gītā as well as the Mānas.

(9) ***Āsurī sampat.*** This expression in the Gītā refers to 'forces of evil'. Subsequent to the Gītā, a time-cycle was formulated in terms of four yugas—satya, tretā, dvāpar, and kali—the assumption being that virtue gave way to evil as time moved from satyayuga to kaliyuga. According to this classification, Tulasīdāsa wrote the Mānas in kaliyuga which was practically a synonym for evil. In fact, the Mānas contains

a section in Uttarakāṇḍa which describes the degeneration that had taken place in kaliyuga. We have picked up the word 'kaliyuga' as a counterpart of 'āsurī sampat'.

(10) *Daivī sampat.* This expression in the Gītā, representing the opposite of 'āsurī sampat', refers to 'virtues'. In terms of the four yugas, the counterpart of 'daivī sampat' should be 'satyayuga'. However, Tulasī says in the Uttarakāṇḍa of the Mānas that, when Lord Rāma became king, the condition of the society resembled 'satyayuga' (although Lord Rāma appeared as an incanation of Vishṇu in tretāyuga). Thus the description of 'Rāma-rājya' in Uttarakāṇḍa (being opposite to kaliyuga) refers to an ideal state based on virtues. So it is appropriate that we have picked up 'Rām-rājya' as a counterpart of 'daivī sampat'.

Choosing Expressions for Chapter-Titles

2.17. The ten key pairs of expressions that we have selected (in paragraphs 2.2 to 2.16) will be explained in chapters three to twelve. Since the discussion in these chapters will be based on the Gītā as well as the Mānas, it will be helpful to include, as far as feasible, expressions from both the books in the titles of these chapters. At the same time, English equivalents of these expressions are necessary for the convenience of readers. Since we do not want titles that are too long, we plan to adopt a selective approach in relation to the Mānas-expressions. The choices made under this approach are summarized below—

(a) Expression (viii)—samadriṣṭi—poses no problem because it is applicable to the Gītā as well as the Mānas.

(b) Six expressions of the Mānas, being short, can be included in chapter titles, along with the Gītā-expressions, and these are (ii), (iii), (v), (vi), (ix), (x).

(c) The remaining three expressions of the Mānas, being rather long, pose problems relating to their inclusion in the chapter-titles. So these are not included, and they are (i), (iv) and (vii).

CHAPTER - THREE

Call to Follow Dharma that Unites—Avibhaktam Vibhakteṣu

3.1. In the previous chapter, we initially identified ten key words or phrases through which the message of the good of all has been given in the Gītā. Then we pointed out that the same words or phrases or their Hindi equivalents or variants thereof could be used in relation to the Mānas too. In the present chapter, we explain the first of the ten key expressions, and follow the same procedure as before, that is, give quotations first from the Gītā, and then from the Mānas. The following nine chapters will similarly take up the remaining key words or phrases, explaining one of them in each chapter. All this forms a part of the process through which questions two and three, out of the five listed in paragraph 1.54, will be answered.

Dharma of Harmonization Through Broad-Mindedness

3.2. The basic concept of dharma is to hold people together, voluntarily and not by force. Therefore, 'dharma that unites'—which is a part of the title of this chapter—looks for common elements rather than those that divide. The Gītā's words—'avibhaktam vibhakteṣu'—which occur in verse XVIII.20, convey the same idea, because their literal meaning is "See unity in the midst of diversity". The Gītā also uses another expression 'śāsvatadharma' which literally means 'eternal dharma' but which implies that it is free from man-made narrow-mindedness. Another equivalent English expression for that could be 'broad-based dharma' which has certain advantages for modern readers.

3.3. The underlying approach of the Gītā towards dharma can be characterized as 'harmonization', which implies integration and not conflict. In his commentary on the Gītā, Dr. Radhakrishnan has explained the comprehensive nature of religious unity which the Gītā achieved--

"The different elements which, at the period of composition of the Gītā, were competing with each other within the Hindu system, are brought together and integrated into a comprehensive synthesis, free and large, subtle and profound. The teacher refines and reconciles the different currents of thought, the Vedic cult of sacrifice, the Upaniṣad teaching of the transcendent Brahman, the Bhāgavata theism and tender piety, the Sāṅkhya dualism and the yoga meditation. He draws all these living elements of Hindu life and thought into an organic unity. He adopts the method, not of denial but of penetration and shows how these different lines of thought converge towards the same end."[1]

3.4. Let us look as the underlying causes of disunity. Some of the issues causing religious conflicts are—by what name to call God, whose prayers does God accept, and so on. The Gītā declares that devotees of God may choose any name that appeals to them, and similarly that God accepts all prayers that come from the devotees' hearts. Verse IV.11 contains a summary of such declaration—

ye yathā māṃ prapadyante tāṃs tathai'va bhajāmyahaṃ
mama vartmā'nuvartante manuṣyāḥ pārtha sarvaśaḥ.

Simple Meaning— Lord Krishna says, as men approach me, so do I accept them; whatever path they follow, they come to me.

3.5. This is one of the verses which Swami Vivekananda used in his address to the Parliament of World's Religions in Chicago in 1893. The practical significance of this verse is explained by Dr. Radhakrishnan in a long commentary, a part of which is reproduced below—

"The same God is worshipped by all. The differences of conception and approach are determined by local colouring and social adaptation. All manifestations belong to the same supreme...God is the rewarder of all who diligently seek Him, whatever views of God they may hold. The spiritually immature are unwilling to recognize other gods than their own. Their attachment to their creed makes them blind to the larger unity of the Godhead. This is the result of egotism in the domain of religious ideas. The Gītā, on the other hand, affirms that though beliefs and practices may be many and varied, spiritual realization to which these are the means is one."[2]

3.6. In chapter VII, the Gītā says explicitly that worshippers of God can be of many kinds, that they are all admirable, but that the best worshippers are those who combine knowledge with devotion, i.e. they worship God for no material gain for themselves. We reproduce below verse VII.16 and the first half of verse VII.18—

chaturvidhā bhajante māṃ janāḥ sukritino'rjuna
ārto jijñāsurarthārthī jñānī ca bharatarṣabha
udārāḥ sarva evai'te jñānī tvātmai'va me matam.

Simple Meaning—The virtuous ones who worship Me are of four kinds—the man in distress, the seeker for knowledge, the seeker for wealth, and the man of wisdom...All these are admirable but the devotee who is a jñānin too is verily Myself.

3.7. An important word in verse VII.18 is 'udārāḥ' which has been translated as admirable. Apte's Sanskrit-Hindi dictionary has further explained the meaning of this word by quoting "udāracharitānām tu vasudhaiva kuṭumbakam" which means that 'udāra' people are those who view the whole world as one family.

3.8. The above-mentioned ideas of the Gītā have been broadly incorporated into the Mānas too, but the terminology has obviously been modified. For example, parallel to Gītā's 'avibhaktam vibhakteṣu', the Mānas says in Uttarakāṇḍa—'kehi san karahin virodh', i.e. because of the unifying vision, with whom can a bhakta have any conflict? Similarly, instead of Gītā's 'śāsvatadharma', the Mānas simply uses the word 'dharma' but has declared, again in Uttarakāṇḍa, that

parhit saris dharma nahi bhāī.

which means that there is no dharma as great as 'helping others'.

3.9. Parallel to the Gītā verse IV.11, we have the Mānas declaration made in Bālakāṇḍa (i.e. canto. I)—

jinh kī rahī bhāvanā jaisī
prabhu murati tinh dekhī taisī.

Simple Meaning—Each one saw in God's face, the form that appealed to him or her.

3.10. Following the example of the Gītā, Tulasīdāsa tried to harmonize the different religious beliefs that prevailed in his time. Two quotations from the Mānas would be sufficient to illustrate this. First, he says in Bālakāṇḍa, it is immaterial whether one believes that God is formless or that God has a form—

sagunahi agunahi nahin kachhu bhedā
gāvahin muni purān budh vedā.

Simple Meaning—There is no difference between 'saguṇa' (God with forms and attributes), and 'nirguṇa' (God without form and attributes). This is the opinion of sages, purāṇas, pandits and Vedas.

3.11. Secondly, Tulasī was very keen that worshippers of Rāma (i.e. Vishṇu), and worshippers of Śiva should not think that they are different from each other. There are many declarations in the Mānas to this effect. We present here only one of them, viz. Rāma's declaration in Laṅkākāṇḍa (i.e. canto. VI)—

shankarpriya mam drohī
shivdrohī mam dās
te nar karahin kalap bhari
ghor narak mahn vās.

Simple Meaning—Those people will be doomed who worship Me and oppose Shiva, and similarly those also will be doomed who worship Shiva and oppose Me.

3.12. Corresponding to Gītā verses referred to in paragraph 3.6, the same, four kinds of devotees are mentioned in the Mānas too, and the highest place is given to one who combines knowledge with devotion. Here is a short extract from Bālakāṇḍa—and we have omitted details about the four kinds of devotees—

rām bhagat jag chāri prakārā
sukriti chāriu anagh udārā...
jñānī prabhuhi visheshi piārā.

Simple Meaning—In the world, there are four kinds of devotees of Rāma. All of them perform good deeds, are sinless, and 'udār' too,...Of these four, the devotee who is also a jñāni is particularly dear to Rāma.

3.13. It is noteworthy that Tulasī uses the same word 'udār' which the Gītā uses in verse VII.18. We quoted another Sanskrit text in paragraph 3.7 and interpreted 'udār' as those people who view the whole world as one family. Parallel to that, we have the following explanation of 'udār' given by Tulasī in Uttarakāṇḍa—

sab udār sab parupkārī

which means that, in Rāmrājya, all the people were 'udār' and they helped each other.

Dharma of Virtues—Promoted by Avatāra Declaration

3.14. Shri Rāma of the Mānas and Shri Krishna of the Gītā—both are Avatāras or incarnations of Vishṇu i.e. God. The concept of Avatāra in Vedic dharma is based on the belief that God cares for the welfare of all the people, so much so that He is willing to intervene in times of crisis. Whenever unrighteousness and injustice take control over the affairs of the human society, then an Avatāra of God comes down on earth and helps those who are struggling to uphold dharma and social justice. Three important implications of this belief need to be clearly stated. First, that there are many Avatāras—not one—and therefore a belief in "only one" Avatāra or "the last" Avatāra is contrary to the Vedic doctrine. Secondly, the arrival of an Avatāra is not in a vacuum, that is, human effort is presumed to be constantly going on for the maintenance of dharma. Thirdly, the Avatāra doctrine is a built-in mechanism to bring the practice of dharma in tune with the changing needs of the society. Although the basic principle of dharma, like the welfare of all without any discrimination, remains intact, the details as to how this is to be achieved need to be readjusted from time to time, and this is taken care of by an Avatāra. Details relating to this particular aspect will be presented in chapter six.

3.15. Before looking into the Avatāra declarations of the Gītā and the Mānas, it is useful to see what types of evil deeds prevailed in the society prior to the intervention by the Avatāra. Taking the Gītā first, the following four topics are relevant to throw light on this issue—

(a) Evil-mindedness and misdeeds of the Kauravas
(b) Unrighteousness that necessitates God's intervention
(c) Demoniac characteristics
(d) Tāmasika or bad tendencies

3.16. A detailed discussion on items (b) to (d) will be presented in chapter eleven. Here it should suffice to draw attention to the main words that refer to the evil deeds of the Kauravas led by Duryodhana. They have been called wicked (duṣkṛtām), evil-minded (durbuddhi), greedy (lobhī), demoniac (āsurī), tāmasika (perverted), and felons (ātatāyinaḥ). Swami Chidbhavananda has listed some of the crimes, because of which, the felons, according to Hindu tradition, were punishable by death, no sin attaching to one who killed them—

"The Kauravas had secretly set fire to the residence where the Pāṇḍavas were expected to be sleeping; they had surreptitiously tried to poison their food and had attempted murder of the Pāṇḍavas who were legitimate heirs to the throne; deceitfully they had tried to deprive the Pāṇḍavas of their kingdom, wealth and wife."[3]

3.17. Next, let us look at the description of the evil deeds of the rākṣasas or the demons, as given in the Bālakāṇḍa of the Mānas—

barani na jāi anīti ghor nisāchar jo karahin
hinsā par ati prīti tinh ke pāpahi kavani miti...
giri sari sindhu bhār nahin mohī
jas mohi garua ek paradrohī.

Simple Meaning—Tulasī says, the unjust and evil deeds of the demons are indescribable. Since violence is their creed, there can be no limit to their sins...Mother Earth said that big mountains, oceans and rivers were less of a burden to her than a single person who is anti-social and who tries to harm others.

Three sins of the demons have been identified as particularly harmful to the society—

(i) pardroh i.e. harming others
(ii) violence
(iii) injustice

3.18. A knowledge of the evil deeds of the demons is helpful for obtaining a clear understanding of the purpose for which the Avatāra came to the earth. In fact, stating the purpose is part of the Avatāra declaration of both the books. For example, the Gītā's declaration contains three purposes, as the following two verses (IV.7-8) show—

yadā yadā hi dharmasya glānirbhavati bhārata
abhyutthānamadharmasya tadā'tmānaṃsrijāmyahaṃ
paritrāṇāya sādhūnāṃvināś'āya ca duṣkṛtāṃ
dharmasaṃsthāpanārthāya sambhavāmi yuge-yuge.

Simple Meaning—Lord Krishna declares, whenever there is a decline of righteousness and rise of unrighteousness, then I incarnate Myself. For the protection of the good, for the destruction of the wicked, and for the establishment of righteousness, I come into being from age to age.

3.19. Next, the Avatāra declaration of the Mānas which is broadly similar to that of the Gītā, but which is slightly more detailed, as the following extract from Bālakāṇḍa shows—

jab jab hoi dharam kai hānī
bādhahin asur adham abhimānī
karahin anīti jāi nahin barni
sīdahin vipra dhenu sur dharnī
tab tab prabhu dhari vividh sarirā
harahin kripānidhi sajjan pirā
asur māri thāpahin suranh rākhahin nij shruti setu
jag vistārahin visad jas rām janma kar hetu
soi jas gāi bhagat bhav tarahīn
kripāsindhu janhit tanu dharahīn.

Simple Meaning—Tulasī says, whenever dharma loses ground and arrogant monsters gain an upper hand, and they unjustly cause harm to learned people, cows, gods, and to the Mother Earth herself, then God appears, in forms that vary from yuga to yuga. God is compassionate and He will not let good people suffer for long. When God appeared as Rāma, He overpowered the demons and restored the rule of gods and of righteousness. Rāma made it known to all that He will never let dharma lose the battle. This assurance and this message gives strength to good people. In fact, Rāma takes Avatāra for the sake of good people.

3.20. An obvious component of the dharma, as re-established by the Avatāra, is to avoid the evil deeds of the demons. For example, in the case of Krishna, since the Kauravas had insulted Draupadī, a woman, an important teaching of the Gītā is to ensure respectful behaviour to all members of the society, irrespective of age, sex, etc. Acharya Vinoba has interpreted verses IX.11-13 of the Gītā for highlighting this message. Because of the importance of this point, we want to draw attention to it here, leaving the details to be presented in chapter ten which will discuss behavioural issues.

3.21. A brief reference may still be made here to a parallel text of the Mānas. Tulasī says in Sundarakāṇḍa (i.e. canto. V) that the demon Rāvaṇa, by insulting his younger brother Vibhīshaṇa, really dragged himself down the path of destruction—

sādhu avagyā turat bhavānī
kar kalyān akhil kai hānī.

Simple Meaning—If a good person is insulted by anyone, then the person who insults is sure to come to immense grief.

Dharma of Social Service—Presented from Four Angles

3.22. So far we have discussed two aspects of dharma, viz. harmonization, and promotion of virtues. The third aspect of dharma that the Gītā and the Mānas have emphasized is 'vishva-seva' or service of the world or social service. The seva-related message has been given in both the books from many angles, so that, one way or the other, it may reach all types of readers. Although repetitiveness was considered as a literary drawback in India, the authors of these books were prepared to be criticized on that account rather than miss out on any valid angle for conveying such an important message. We present below four ways in which the Gītā and the Mānas have given the message of social service.

(a) ***God is the Root of the World-Tree***

3.23. There are some who take the view that an individual or 'jīva' could worship God by establishing a direct relationship with Him and that the world or 'jagat' could be left out of this relationship, to take care of itself. Since such persons are indifferent to social welfare, they cannot claim to be followers of the Gītā. The message of the Gītā is—give up attachment to the world, but never give up action that is beneficial to the world. Lokmanya Tilak has warned that by leaving out the world, no individual can establish complete unity with God—

> "If a man seeks unity with the Deity, he must necessarily seek unity with the interests of the world also, and work for it. If he does not, then the unity is not perfect, because that is union between two elements out of the three (man and Deity), and the third (the world) is left out. I have thus solved the question for myself and I hold that serving the world, and thus serving His will, is the surest way of salvation, and this way can be followed by remaining in the world and not going away from it."[4]

3.24. The message that God is very much interested in the welfare of the world has been conveyed by the Gītā in many ways. In the present context, we want to draw attention to the concept that God is the root of the world-tree and is thus the source from which the whole world receives its sustenance. Verse XV.1 says—

ūrdhvamūlamadhaḥśākhaṃ ...

Simple Meaning—The world-tree has its root above and branches below.

Dr. Radhakrishnan says in his commentary on this verse that

"As the tree originates in God, it is said to have its roots 'above'; as it extends into the world, its branches are said to go 'downwards'. The world is a living organism united with the supreme."[5]

3.25. The same idea has been expressed in the Mānas too. The following extract from Uttarakāṇḍa attributes to God, the continuous flowering and appearance of new leaves on the world-tree—

pallavat phūlat naval nit sansār vitap namāmahe
avatār nar sansār bhār vibhanji dāruṇ dukh dahe
jay pranatpāl dayāl prabhu sanjukt'sakti namāmahe.

Simple Meaning—O God, You are visible to us as the world-tree, and it is because of You that we see continuously new leaves and flowers on it. Our salutations to You. When the demons became a burden to the world, You came as an Avatāra in the form of Man i.e. Rāma, and put an end to deep sorrows. You are the most compassionate, You protect those who seek Your help. We bow to You as well as Your Shakti i.e. Sita Victory to You.

3.26. How should we visualize the inter-relationship between God, jagat and jīva? An answer to this question in the form of a single verse has been attempted by Indian thinkers. For example, the following verse summarizes the Vedānta philosophy, including the Māyā dectrine, of Ādi Shankaracharya—

ślokārdhena pravakṣyāmi
yaduktam granthakoṭibhiḥ
brahma satyam jaganmithyā
jīvo brahmaiva nāparaḥ.

Simple Meaning—I will explain in half a verse what has been said in millions of books. Brahman is satya or real, jagat or the world is mithyā or unreal, and jīva or the individual is none other than Brahman himself.

3.27. Acharya Vinoba suggested that, for highlighting the message of social service, it is preferable not to view the world as 'mithyā', but rather as 'sphūrtī' or vibrant manifestation. His formulation is summarized in the following verse—

vedavedāntagītānāṃ vinunā sāra uddhritaḥ
brahma satyam jagat sphūrtir jīvanaṃ satyaśodhanaṃ.

Simple Meaning—Vinu i.e. Vinoba has extracted the essence of the Vedas, the Vedānta, and the Gītā—Brahman is satya or real, jagat is sphūrti or vibrant manifestation, and the goal of life is to carry on the search for Truth.

3.28. P.M. Thomas views Vinoba's verse as containing a new interpretation of the Gītā—

> "This is a new aspect of the Gītā which Bhave (i.e. Vinoba) has brought out...By ascribing a relative reality to the world as opposed to total unreality, Bhave is building a metaphysical basis for his ideology of serving the poor."[6]

3.29. Acharya Vinoba himself considers his own formulation as an attempt to further incorporate scientific ideas into Vedānta. Nargolkar quotes Vinoba—

> "I do not think I have made any great departure from the general teaching of the Vedānta philosophy. On the contrary, my statement brings about a happy reconciliation between Vedānta and the age of science."[7]

3.30. Our intention in paragraph 3.26-29 was to prepare the background for incorporating the tree-concept into the ideas of Shankaracharya and Vinoba. To achieve this, we note that the starting words in the second half of both the verses given above are 'brahma satyam'. We feel that by beginning instead with the words 'brahma mūlaṃ', the tree-concept becomes prominent, and on that basis, the Gītā's message of social service can be stated even more explicitly. To this end, we present below a third verse composed by Satya i.e. the author of this book. The first half of this verse is similar to that of Vinoba because the idea of the world-tree occurs in the Vedas and the Upaniṣads, and of course in the Gītā as we mentioned in paragraph 3.24. After this clarification, we write the Sanskrit text of the new verse—

> *vedavedāntagītānaṃ satyena sāra uddhritaḥ*
> *brahma mūlaṃ jagad vrikṣo jīva ubhayasevakaḥ.*

Simple Meaning—Satya has extracted the essence of the Vedas, the Vedānta and the Gītā—Brahman is the root, jagat or the world is the tree, and the role of jīva is to serve both of them.[8]

P. Sankaranarayanan is of opinion that

"New interpretations of the Gītā have led many Indians to appreciate the dictum that service of man is service of God, that 'mānava sevā' is 'Mādhava sevā'."[9]

(b) ***Capabilities are God-given***

3.31. From the tenth chapter of the Gītā, called "vibhūtiyoga", we can derive, among other things, two messages, viz. (i) that all capabilities are God-given, and (ii) that, as a follow-up of the first message, these capabilities should be so used that the entire world gets the benefit, and not merely the person who has the capability. It will be useful to present some of the verses of the tenth chapter that help us understand these ideas.

3.32. First, we have the famous declaration of Lord Krishna in verse X.41—

yad-yad vibhūtimatsattvaṃ śrīmadūrjitameva vā
tat-tadevā'vagaccha tvaṃ mama tejoṃśasambhavaṃ.

Simple Meaning—Whatsoever being there is, endowed with glory and grace and vigour, know that to have sprung from a fragment of God's splendour.

Dr. Radhakrishnan explains this as follows—

"While all things are supported by God, things of beauty and splendour reveal Him more than others. Every deed of heroism, every life of sacrifice, every work of genius, is a revelation of the Divine. The epic moments of a man's life are inexplicably beyond the finite mind of man."[10]

3.33. Secondly, the question is to what use God-given capabilities should be put. Lord Krishna uses the expression 'hitakāmyayā' in verse X.1 which means 'prompted by the desire to do good', So that is the specific purpose of all that He says. In fact, one of the 'vibhūtis' mentioned in verse X.35 is 'gāyatrī' and we have, in paragraph 1.4, chosen gāyatrī-mantra as the most well-known Vedic pronouncement of the desire for the good of all. Similarly, in verse X.31, there is a reference to Lord Rāma's skill as a warrior and we mentioned in paragraph 1.29 that such skill was used only to save innocent people from the clutches of the demons. The Gītā's advice relating to the proper use of capabilities occurs also in chapters other than the tenth. For example, the last verse of the Gītā, viz. XVIII.78, uses the words 'bhūti' and 'dhruvā nīti' simultaneously. Since 'bhūti' is a synonym of 'vibhūti' and 'dhruvā nīti' stands for perfect morality, Dr. Radhakrishnan finds in this verse, the fulfilment of "the double purpose of human life, viz. personal perfection and social efficiency".[11]

3.34. The idea that God-given capabilities should be used for the benefit of all, has been expressed repeatedly in Sanskrit literature. Inspiration is drawn from natural phenomena and objects. For example, clouds, rivers, trees—all give the same message, and one of the most popular verses containing it is the following—

svayaṃ na khādanti phalāni vrikṣāḥ
pivanti nāmbhaḥ svayameva nadyaḥ
dhārādharo varṣati nātmahetoḥ
paropakārāya satām vibhūtiḥ.

Simple Meaning—Trees do not eat their own fruits themselves, rivers do not drink their own water themselves, clouds do not use their own water for themselves. Similarly, good people use their capabilities for the good of others.

3.35. We now move to the Mānas which has fully accepted Gītā's ideas about the source as well as proper use of capabilities. First, we have the famous statement of Bharat in Ayodhyākāṇḍa (i.e. canto II) that corresponds to verse X.41 of the Gītā—

sampati sab raghupati kai āhī.

Simple Meaning—All property, all prosperity belongs to God, not to me.

Acharya Vinoba referred to these words of the Mānas when he appealed to people that they should share their land, wealth, etc. with the poor.

3.36. Another famous statement of the Mānas about the source of capabilities is made by Hanumān in Sundarakāṇḍa (i.e. canto V)—

nāghi sindhu hātakpur jārā
nisichar gan badhi vipin ujārā
so sab tav pratāp raghurāī
nath na kachhu mor prabhutāī.

Simple Meaning—O Rāma, you are asking me how I was able to cross the ocean, how I was able to set fire to the golden city of Laṅkā, how I was able to kill so many demons, and how I was able to destroy their orchards. To tell you the truth, all this strength came from You, none of this is mine.

3.37. Next, about the proper use of God-given capabilities, the most well-known statement by Tulasī occurs in the early part of Bālakāṇḍa (i.e. canto I)—

> *kīrati bhaniti bhūti bhali soī*
> *sursari sam sab kahn hit hoī.*

Simple Meaning—Only that glory, poetry and prosperity is good which, like the holy river Ganga, contributes to the good of all.

3.38. The same idea is repeated by Tulasī in the closing part of Uttarakāṇḍa (i.e. canto VII)—

> *so dhan dhanya pratham gati jākī*
> *dhanya punya rat mati soi pākī.*

Simple Meaning—Only that wealth is worth having which is used for dāna i.e. sharing. This is called the first way of spending money. (To complete the list of ways in which money can be spent, the second way is 'bhog' i.e. enjoyment, and the third way is 'nāsh' i.e. loss or destructive uses). Similarly, only that intellect is mature and worth having which orients us towards 'puṇya' i.e. good deeds done for the benefit of the society.

3.39. Regarding the use of capabilities, we have so far looked at what Tulasī suggested. The point that we have made is further strengthened when we consider what Tulasī did. It is well known that Tulasī had the God-given gift of writing poetry, and also that he used it for the good of all. Although he could write Sanskrit poetry too, he preferred to write in 'girā grāmya' i.e. common language of the village people because he wanted to bring sacred Rāmāyaṇa within their reach. Pandits of Banaras opposed him because of this because they felt that the sanctity of the scripture will be lost if it was written in any language other than 'dev-vāṇī, i.e. the language of the gods i.e. Sanskrit. Eventually, Tulasī's mission was fulfilled and the Mānas became *sakallokhitkārī*, i.e. it contributed to the good of all the people.

(c) ***Lesson of the Cosmic Vision***

3.40. Scriptures say that cosmic vision can be experienced only through God's grace. Therefore, only a few instances of this have been described. In the Gītā, the whole of the eleventh chapter is devoted to Arjuna's request, and Lord Krishna's agreeing thereto, combined with the delivery of an important message as to what Arjuna should get out of the rare experience of the cosmic vision. In the Mānas, there are two instances of this, viz. first, related to Rāma's mother, Kaushalyā, and the second, related to Kākbhushuṇḍī, the famous devotee of Lord Rāma. Kaushalyā's vision has been described only briefly in Bālakāṇḍa. However, the cosmic vision by Kākbhushuṇḍi has been described in detail in Uttarakāṇḍa. For purposes of the present section we shall refer to this vision only, as far as the Mānas is concerned.

3.41. To start with the Gītā, verse XI.13 tells us what Arjuna saw—and the words used are somewhat like the ones that we have used in the title of the present chapter, viz. avibhaktaṃ vibhakteṣu—

tatrai'kasthaṃ jagat kṛtsnaṃ pravibhaktamanekadhā
apaśyaddevadevasya śarīre pāndavastadā.

Simple Meaning—In the body of the God of gods, Arjuna beheld the whole universe, with its manifold divisions gathered together in One.

Dr. Radhakrishnan comments that

"The vision is a revelation of the potential divinity of all earthly life."[12]

A glimpse of how Arjuna felt and spoke can be had from verses XI.14 and 16, of which we give below the first verse in full and the second only partly—

tataḥ sa vismayāvisto hriṣṭaromā dhananjayaḥ
praṇamya śirasā devaṃ kṛtāñjalirabhāṣata.

Simple Meaning—Arjuna was struck with amazement, his hair stood on end. He bowed down his head to the Lord and spoke with hands folded in salutation.

nāntaṃ na madhyaṃ na punastavādiṃ
paśyāmi viśveśvara viśvarūpa.

Simple Meaning—Arjuna said, "I see not Thy end nor Thy middle nor Thy beginning, O Lord of the Universe, O Form Universal."

3.42. Acharya Vinoba has suggested—and it is indeed a useful suggestion—that after getting a glimpse of how Arjuna felt and spoke, we need to concentrate our attention on the closing words of chapter XI, viz.—

nirvairaḥ sarvabhūteṣu yaḥ sa māmeti pāṇḍava.

Simple Meaning—Lord Krishna says—One who is free from enmity to all creatures, comes to Me, O Arjuna!

Thus the description of the cosmic vision in the Gītā ends with the delivery of the message that contributes to the good of all.

3.43. In the Mānas too, Kākbhushuṇḍī's experience—i.e. what he saw and how he felt—is comparable to that of Arjuna. For example, Kākbhushuṇḍī expresses his inability—while speaking to Garuḍa—to recall and to describe what he saw in the cosmic vision—

jo nahin dekhā nahin sunā jo manahūṃ na samāi
so sab adbhut dekheūṇ baraṇi kavani vidhi jāi.

Simple Meaning—I am unable to describe what I saw. The cosmic vision showed me what I had never seen before, also what I had never heard of before, in fact what I had never even imagined before.

Kākbhushuṇḍī recalls that he was feeling perplexed and confused, but says he—

dekhi kripāl vikal mohi vihase tab raghubīr.

Simple Meaning—My confusion ended when I saw that Lord Rāma—who is full of compassion—was smiling.

3.44. As in the Gītā, the description of the cosmic vision in the Mānas too ends with the delivery of the message contributing to universal welfare. From the words spoken by Lord Rāma to Kākbhushuṇḍī in Uttarakāṇḍa, the following two extracts will suffice, for getting a glimpse of the message—

akhil vishva yah mor upāyā
sab par mohi barābari dāyā.

Simple Meaning—Lord Rāma said—The entire universe and all the beings have been created by Me, and I have equal compassion towards all of them.

purush napunsak nāri vā jīva charāchar koi
sarva bhāva bhaj kapaṭ taji mohi param priya soi
satya kahaun khag tohi śuchi sevak mam prānpriya.

Simple Meaning—O Kākbhushuṇḍī, I am telling you a profound truth. The dearest to me is 'śuchi sevak' i.e. one who serves all beings with a pure mind i.e. without any selfish motive. I make no distinction on grounds of sex or species. All I need is, that my bhakta should have no desire to cheat any one, and should serve others with 'sarva bhāva' i.e. wholeheartedly.

It may be mentioned that the words 'sarva bhāvena bhajati', which must have inspired Tulasīdāsa to write the above quoted Mānas expression, occur in verse XV.19 of the Gītā.

(d) ***God as the Inner Voice***

3.45. Both the Gītā and the Mānas have described situations when a sincere follower of dharma finds it hard to decide which path, among the various possible ones, should be chosen. Before telling how these two books tackle this problem, we want to say that the question of choosing the right path has been raised and answered by the Mahābhārata and Manusmṛti also. For example, in the Mahābhārata, replying to Yakṣa's question, Yudhishthira says—

> *tarko'pratiṣthaḥ shrutayo vibhinna*
> *naiko risiryasya vachaḥ pramāṇaṃ*
> *dharmasya tattvaṃnihitam guhāyāṃ*
> *mahājano yena gataḥ sa panthāḥ.*

Simple Meaning—Inferential logic alone cannot help in making a clear and good choice. In the Śrutis, i.e. the Vedas and the Upaniṣads too, various answers to the same question can be found. As for the Smrities, it is difficult to identify a single Rishi who can be considered more authoritative than others. So, in a way, it looks as if the essence of dharma is hidden in a cave. A practical solution to the problem is to follow the path shown by "mahājana".

The expression "mahājana" is usually translated as "a great man" or "a venerable person", although Arvind Sharma takes it to mean "a majority of people", or "the great mass of people".[13]

3.46. Next, we want to draw attention to the views of Manusmṛti—

> *vedaḥ smritiḥ sadāchāraḥ*
> *svasya cha priyamātmanaḥ*
> *etaccaturvidhaṃ prāhuḥ*
> *sākṣāddharmasya lakṣaṇaṃ.*

Simple Meaning—The Vedas, the Smrities, good behaviour, and the satisfaction of one's Ātman, are the four main characteristics of dharma.

3.47. The expression "satisfaction of one's Ātman", which occurs in the above verse of Manusmṛti, is of particular interest to us in the present section. Manusmriti itself has explained it in another context by saying that it refers to that action by doing which one does not feel ashamed.

The Mahābhārata has gone a step further by advising not to perform any action which either would make the doer feel ashamed or

yadanyeṣām hitaṃ na syād.

i.e. which is not beneficial to others.

3.48. In the ultimate analysis, the last criterion suggested by the Mahābhārata is acceptable to the Gītā also. But the Gītā, or rather the Gītā-commentators, arrived at that conclusion in a systematic way, by starting with more than one yardstick, and then proceeding through stages. We want to draw attention to what Mahatma Gandhi did by proceeding in this manner. He derived the message of selfless social service, based on non-violence, from the Gītā and justified that by applying two yardsticks—

(i) Non-attachment to the fruits of one's action
(ii) Viewing the inner voice as God's voice

3.49. The first yardstick and its linkage with the good of all is part of the karma-yoga approach, and it occurs in the lokasaṃgraha-section of the Gītā. Chapter eight of the present book will be the right place to explain all that. The second yardstick raises issues of dharma, and so we propose to take it up now. For this purpose, we need to make an in-depth study of verse XIII.22 of the Gītā—

upadraṣṭā'numantā ca bhartā bhoktā maheśvaraḥ
paramātme'ti cā'pyukto dehe'smin puruṣaḥ paraḥ.

Simple Meaning—For a progressive realization of Paramātmā, who is located in the body of every being, it is useful to understand five stages, viz. upadraṣṭā (witness), anumantā (assentor), bhartā (the support), bhoktā (the enjoyer), and Maheśvara (the supreme Lord).

3.50. An important message that Gītā-commentators have derived from this verse is, that God's advice on dharma can be heard as inner voice, and also that this inspires the bhakta to do socially beneficial acts. Acharya Vinoba has explained this in great detail, selected extracts from which are reproduced below—and which also supports Mahatma Gandhi's derivation referred to in paragraph 3.48—

"We learn to experience the Lord progressively. At first, the Lord watches us as an impartial witness. The second stage starts when the life of morality begins and the jīva enters the domain of ethics. Now the Lord does not merely stand aside and watch.... For example, a hungry man comes to your door when you have just sat down to eat. You give your own food to him....Late that night, you hear the still small voice of the Lord saying 'you have done well'...Such a message from the inner voice inspires the bhakta to do selfless service... The third stage starts when the devotee discovers that his own efforts are inadequate to cleanse the subtler impurities of the mind and calls for His help. The Lord who is the Helper of the helpless rushes to his aid as 'bharta'....At the fourth stage, the devotee gives over to the Lord the fruits of action and views Him as 'bhokta'....At the fifth and final stage, the devotee surrenders to Him as 'Maheshvar'..... The seeker goes through these five stages, flying on the twin wings of karma-yoga and bhakti-yoga."[14]

3.51. The above mentioned idea of the Gītā, that the inner voice prompts one to work for the good of all, is exemplified by Tulasīdāsa himself when he wrote the Mānas. Explaining his own source of inspiration for writing Rāma-kathā, and how it helped fulfil his social objective, Tulasī says in Bālakāṇḍa—

jas kachhu budhi vivek bal moren
tas kahihaum hiyan hari ke preren
budh vishrām sakal jan ranjani
ramkathā kali kalush vibhanjani.

Simple Meaning—My heart has received inspiration from God, so I shall write Rama-katha, although I have only limited capability in terms of intellect and knowledge. I feel confident that the Rāma-kathā written by me shall give peace to pandits, and even more importantly, it will bring joy to all the people because it will destroy the evils of kaliyuga.

3.52. We referred to Mahatma Gandhi's idea in paragraph 3.48 and Vinoba's support thereto in paragraph 3.50. In continuation of that, we want to say that, in the opinion of Kishorelal Mashruwala, God's voice and inner voice can be viewed as synonyms. In fact, the objective of satyāgraha is to encourage the opponent to listen to his own inner voice, and this can lead to a resolution of the conflict on reasonable terms, i.e. for the good of all, without the use of physical force.

3.53. Before closing this section, we want to draw attention to Śrī Aurobindo, whose life provides (like that of Mahatma Gandhi) many instances when important decisions were taken on the basis of "God's voice". We present below just one instance, viz. what happened to

Śrī Aurobindo in February 1910. Writing "On Himself", he gives a first-hand account of why he left Calcutta for Pondicherry—

> "Here are the facts of that departure. I was in the Karmayogin office when I received the word, on information given by a highly placed police official, that the office would be searched the next day and myself arrested. (The office was in fact searched but no warrant was produced against me; I heard nothing more of it till the case was started against the paper later on, but by then I had already left Chandernagore for Pondicherry.) While I was listening to animated comments from those around on the approaching event, I suddenly received a command from above, in a voice well-known to me, in three words, "Go to Chandernagore". In ten minutes or so I was in the boat for Chandernagore... Afterwards, under the same "sailing orders" I left Chandernagore and reached Pondicherry on April 4, 1910."[15]

To continue Śrī Aurobindo's account, we must add that during the next forty years, he attained the status of a Pūrṇa-yogin and did immense work (till 1950) for the good of all, many elements of which have been kept going by his followers. The main idea to be stressed for our present purpose is that listening to the inner voice and working for the good of all are inter-related.

CHAPTER FOUR

Call to Participate in God's Work Mat-Karma or Rāma-Kāj

4.1. We recall that chapter two identified ten key words or phrases that convey the message of universal welfare as given in the Gītā and the Mānas. Chapter three then explained the first of these ten expressions. The present chapter carries that process forward by concentrating attention on the second of those words or phrases. More specifically, we shall clarify how the Gītā's expression 'mat-karma', and Tulasī's expression 'Rāma kāj', give the message of the good of all. As in the previous chapters, we start with the Gītā and then move on to the Mānas.

Four Aspects of Mat-Karma

4.2. The literal meaning of 'mat-karma' is 'My work' i.e. God's work because this expression forms a part of the teaching given by Lord Krishna. A detailed study of this topic, as we shall now present, involves giving answers to the following four questions—

(a) Since God's work is of many types, which particular work of His should be understood by 'mat-karma'?

(b) What are the practical components of 'mat-karma' in the Gītā?

(c) A variant of 'mat-karma' is 'nimittamātram bhāva' i.e. consider yourself as an instrument of God. What does that imply?

(d) Another variant of 'mat-karma' is 'karma-samarpaṇam' i.e. dedicate your actions to God. What kinds of actions are suitable for dedication?

We shall consider these four aspects one-by-one.

(a) ***God's Work that Calls for Human Participation***

4.3. Mahatma Gandhi expressed an opinion as to the type of work in which human beings may participate along with God. It is interesting to recall the context in which this opinion was expressed. As is well-known, Gandhi interpreted the Gītā in such a way as to derive his doctrine of non-violence therefrom. He faced opposition from many other Gītā-interpreters. One of the points of dispute was related to the role that Lord Krishna played in the Mahābhārata. Gandhi's opponents argued that since Lord Krishna Himself was indirectly associated with the war, how His teaching in the Gītā could support non-violence. Gandhi replied that the scope of human action has necessarily to be limited, and it would not be appropriate to try to participate in all the work that God Himself does, directly or indirectly. Here are Gandhi's words—

> "I believe in Krishna, but my Krishna is the Lord of the Universe, the creator, preserver and destroyer of us all. He may destroy because He creates."[1]

4.4. We believe that it is reasonable to limit the scope of 'mat-karma' to acts of preservation and sustenance of the universe. Really speaking, it is not a serious limitation because so many useful things can be done by observing this yardstick. We may clarify that our discussion is mainly related to non-governmental actions.

4.5. The following two verses of the Gītā can help us in identifying the general nature of God's work that is suitable for human participation. The first one is verse XV.17 which speaks of sustenance of the universe—

uttamaḥ puruṣas tvanyaḥ paramātme'tyudāhritaḥ
yo lokatrayamaviśya bibhartyavyaya īśvaraḥ.

Simple Meaning—God as Purushottama or Paramātmā or the supreme self is beyond the kṣara and the Akṣara (i.e. the perishable and the imperishable). Paramātmā enters the three worlds and sustains them.

The second verse is from chapter V, but rather than quote the entire verse V.29, we only write below a part thereof which is enough for our present purpose—

suhridaṃ sarvabhūtānāṃ.

Simple Meaning—God is 'suhrid' of all beings, i.e. the Friend who does good to them without expecting any return. (This is the complete meaning of the word 'suhrid' as explained by Shankaracharya.)

(b) ***Practical Components of Mat-Karma***

4.6. In the light of the above, it can be said that the Gītā wants us to be a 'suhrid' of all beings, and that would be a component of 'mat-karma' because God Himself is the 'suhrid' of all beings. Furthermore, since persons in distress (or ārta as mentioned in verse VII.16—reference paragraph 3.6 of our previous chapter) receive priority attention when they pray to God for help, to be a 'suhrid' of 'ārta' would be the most important, practical component of 'mat-karma'. This idea is summarized in the well-known Sanskrit saying—

daridrān bhar kaunteya
mā prayacchesvare dhanaṃ.

Simple Meaning—Help the poor, because it is not so useful if you give money to a rich person.

4.7. Swami Vivekananda coined the famous phrase "Daridra-Nārāyaṇa" which meant that the service of the poor was the service of God. To Shiva-worshippers, he said "Jīva is Shiva", and explained it further—

"He who sees Shiva in the poor, in the weak and in the diseased, really worships Shiva; and if he sees Shiva only in the image, his worship is but preliminary. He who has served and helped one poor man, seeing Shiva in him, without thinking of his caste, or creed, or race, or anything, with him Shiva is more pleased than with the man who sees Him only in temples."[2]

4.8. Vivekananda's ideas about helping the poor bring out three practical components of 'mat-karma'. First, that we need to avoid egotistic feelings as if we are doing something great. Secondly, we should have no desire for any reward, not even 'thank you' from the person whom we have helped. Thirdly, since we view 'sevā' (service) as God's work, we should feel grateful to God that He gave us the privilege to participate in His work. In other words, we are helping ourselves and not the world. Swami Vivekananda explained these ideas in detail in his book entitled "Karma-yoga". We have summarized these ideas in the following Sanskrit verse—

na seva dainyabhāvena nāhmkārat mānecchayā
harirūpadaridrāya matvaivaṃ jñānapreritā.

Simple Meaning—Do not serve the poor with a sense of pity, do not entertain any arrogance while helping others, do not expect any reward or honour, rather view the poor as God, and have the right knowledge that God is looking after the whole world and we are merely participating in His work.[3]

4.9. Verse XI.55 of the Gītā, which, in Shankaracharya's opinion, "is the substance of the whole teaching of the Gītā", lists four practical components of 'mat-karma'. These will be clear from the meaning of the verse (which is the closing verse of chapter XI)—

mat karma krinmat paramo madbhaktaḥ sangavarjitaḥ
nirvairaḥ sarvabhāteṣu yaḥ sa mām eti pāṇḍava.

Simple Meaning—Lord Krishna says—One who does 'mat-karma' looks upon Me as his or her goal, he or she is a bhakta or devotee of God, is also free from attachment and from enmity to all creatures— such a person attains Me.

Shankaracharya explains in his commentary that this person is bereft of the idea of enmity even towards those who might be engaged in doing harm to him or her. In other words, doing 'mat-karma' means doing good to all. Another way of looking at it is that sva-dharma (one's duty), fortified with actions done for the good of all, becomes 'mat-karma'.

We should add that we referred to a part of this verse in paragraph 3.42 in the preceding chapter.

(c) ***Becoming an Instrument of God***

4.10. The Gītā's teaching about becoming an instrument of God occurs in verse XI.33, i.e. in the same chapter (eleventh), the last verse of which we have quoted above in the preceding paragraph. Rather than quote the entire verse XI.33, we write below only the words that contain the teaching—

nimittamātraṃ bhave.

Simple Meaning—Be thou merely an instrument in the hands of God i.e. be free from the egotistic thought as if you are the doer.

4.11. Since we are presenting this teaching as a variant of 'mat-karma', we need not go into metaphysical questions related to this teaching. The main implication of becoming merely an instrument is that we act like a soldier in God's army—not for destructive purposes, but only for the good of the world. Since we are God's instrument, our ultimate victory is certain. This gives us courage and confidence, but no arrogance. Śrī Aurobindo is perhaps the best example of one who actually followed this teaching, therefore his explanation of what it means is very valuable. We reproduce below a few lines from his "Essays on the Gītā"—

> "The highest way appointed for him is to carry out the will of God without egoism, as the human occasion and instrument of that which he sees to be decreed, with the constant supporting memory of the Godhead in himself and man, 'mām anusmaran', and in whatever ways are appointed for him by the Lord of his Nature. 'Nimittamātraṃ bhava'. He will not cherish personal enmity, anger, hatred, egoistic desire and passion, will not hasten towards strife or lust after violence and destruction like the fierce Asura, but he will do his work, 'lokasaṃgrahāya'."[4]

4.12. Three words in the above quotation call for our comment. First, the closing word 'lokasaṃgrahāya'—meaning 'for the good of the world'—provides the purpose of becoming an instrument of God. Chapter eight of this book will explain 'lokasaṃgraha' in detail. Secondly, Śrī Aurobindo mentions 'destruction like the fierce Asura'—that we shall explain in chapter eleven. Thirdly, in the middle of the above quotation, Aurobindo has referred to verse VIII.7 of the Gītā, the first half of which reads as follows—

tasmāt sarveṣu kāleṣu
māmanusmara yuddhya ca.

Simple Meaning—Lord Krishna says—Therefore, at all times, remember Me and fight, i.e. continue doing sva-dharma.

4.13. Obviously, one who becomes an instrument of God, combines bhakti with karmayoga. Even in the face of heavy odds against him, he can maintain his enthusiasm and even-mindedness. In the terminology of the Gītā, he becomes a 'sāttvika-kartā', i.e. a virtuous doer, in accordance with verse XVIII.26—

muktasango'nahamvādī dhrityutsāhasamanvitaḥ
siddhyasiddhyornirvikāraḥ kartā sāttvika ucyate.

Simple Meaning—A sāttvika doer is free from attachment, does not show egotism, is full of resolution and zeal, and is unmoved by success or failure.

He is thus bound to make a significant contribution to the good of the world.

(d) ***Karma-Samarpaṇaṃ or Dedication***

4.14. It was mentioned in paragraph 4.11 that the 'nimittamātram' variant of 'mat-karma' provides, among other things, a safeguard against egotism. A similar consideration lies behind the introduction, in the Gītā, of the technique of karma-samarpaṇaṃ which is the second variant of 'mat-karma'.

4.15. Hiriyanna has sounded a note of caution for ordinary people that they need to avoid a sense of self-importance, arising out of actions done for the good of others—

> "The process of abandoning selfish interest and pursuing only the good of the society is not always conducive to one's spiritual growth. A conscious assumption by an individual, of the role of a social benefactor, is likely to result in a sense of self-importance which is ruinous to all spiritual growth... ."[5]

4.16. In the Gītā itself, the practical problem raised by Hiriyanna is recognized, namely, that a social worker runs the risk of developing egotism. In order to stress this point, Lord Krishna mentions, immediately after the lokasaṃgraha-verses (III. 20-26), that—

> *ahaṃkāra vimūḍhātmā kartāhamiti manyate.*

> ***Simple Meaning***—He whose soul is bewildered by egotism thinks 'I am the doer'.

4.17. As a remedy, to take care of the problem of egotism, Lord Krishna suggests in verse III.30—

> *mayi sarvāṇi karmāṇi saṃnyasyā'dhyātmacetasā*
> *nirāśīr nirmamo bhūtvā yudhyasva vigatajvaraḥ.*

> ***Simple Meaning***—Dedicating all thy works to me, with thy consciousness fixed in the Self, being free from desire and egotism, fight, delivered from thy fever.

We should add that the expression 'fight' means 'continue doing sva-dharma'—as we remarked in paragraph 4.12 also.

4.18. The most well-known verse containing the teaching on dedication of all acts to God, is IX.27—

> *yat karoṣi yadasnasi yajjuhosi dadāsi yat*
> *yattapąsyasi kaunteya tat kuruṣva madarpaṇaṃ.*

Simple Meaning—Lord Krishna says—Whatever you do, whatever you eat, whatever you sacrifice, whatever you give away, whatever austerities you practise, do that as an offering to Me.

4.19. Like the nimittamātram variant, the karma-samarpaṇaṃ variant also is a harmonious combination of karma-yoga and bhakti-yoga, which implies serveral things. The first implication has already been mentioned, viz. freedom from egotism. Secondly, an attitude of samarpaṇaṃ makes it easier to give up the desire for selfish gains. Thirdly, such a person would feel the urge to do only sattvika deeds, because how can impure deeds be dedicated to God?

4.20. Among those who tried to put into practice the method of dedication, names of Gandhi and Vinoba obviously come to mind. Considering, first, the views of Gandhi, we notice that he stressed the value of bhakti which is necessary for karma-samarpaṇaṃ—

> "We learn from the ninth chapter that devotion means attachment to God. This is the royal road to the cultivation of a selfless spirit which inspires us to dedicate all our actions to God. In fact, devotion is the sovereign yoga and easy to practise. It is easy to practise if it takes hold of our heart, but hard going if it does not."[6]

4.21. Vinoba gives the simile of "seed-throwing" and "seed-sowing" to bring home the advantage of combining karma-yoga and bhakti-yoga i.e. of dedicating actions to God—

> "Karmayoga says : perform action but renounce the fruit, do not desire it.... Bhaktiyoga means becoming one with the Lord through devotion....In Rāja-yoga, both karma and bhakti are combined in a beautiful manner. Rāja-yoga says—Do not give up the fruit, do not throw it away, but dedicate it to the Lord. What you throw away is wholly lost. The action dedicated to the Lord is like a seed sown. It fills our life with endless joy and holiness."[7]

4.22. Vinoba also suggests that, although only sattvika actions are worthy of being offered to the Lord, a beginning of the process of dedication could be made with non-sattvika acts as well, with prayers that traces of selfishness in human effort may be eliminated in the process—

> "The ninth chapter speaks of surrendering all actions to the Lord. In the seventeenth chapter, this idea is more fully dealt with. It is specially stressed here that the action which is surrendered to the Lord should be sattvika, for only then will it be worthy of being offered to the Lord....

"But a question arrises : If dedication is only for the pure man, what is the sinner to do? He should also, wishing that his acts should become progressively purer, surrender all his actions to the Lord. Dedication is a mental attitude, and the mere utterance of words of dedication are neither necessary nor sufficient."[8]

Rāma-Kāj in the Mānas

4.23. Like 'mat-karma' in the Gītā, 'Rāma-kāj in the Mānas plays an important role in strengthening the call for the good of all. Questions relating to this topic, that we listed in paragraph 4.2, can all be answered on the basis of the Mānas too. In fact, the relevant material in the Mānas is in greater detail because there are many Rāma-kāj performers of whom the most important ones are—Hanumān, Angad, other monkeys who supported them, and Jaṭāyu. We shall pick up only those references from the Mānas that illustrate the points already raised in connection with 'mat-karma' in the earlier part of this chapter.

God as Bhartā and Suhrid

4.24. Corresponding to the Sanskrit word 'bhartā', Tulasī uses the Hindi equivalent 'bharaṇ poshaṇa', and he repeats this idea by using words like 'jag pālan and 'jag āshraya'. We present below three quotations where these expressions occur—the first two quotations are from Bālakāṇḍa while the third one is from Ayodhyākāṇḍa—

viśva bharaṇ poshaṇ kar joī.

Simple Meaning—God looks after and nourishes the entire universe.

ehi vidhi jag hari āshrit rahaī.

Simple Meaning—In this way, the world is sustained by God.

shruti setu pālak rām tum jagdīsh māya jānakī
jo srijati jag pālati harati rukh pāi kripānidhān kī.

Simple Meaning—O Rāma, You are the Lord of the universe, You maintain it by means of the ideals set forth in the Vedas, and Sītā, Your Shakti, carries out Your plans—she creates the world, maintains it, and destroys it—and this cycle continues.

4.25. Next, about the occurrence, in the Mānas, of Hindi equivalents of 'suhrid', the complete meaning of which (given in paragraph 4.5) is 'a friend who does good to you without expecting any return.' There are many such expressions in the Mānas, but we give below only two—the first one from Ayodhyākāṇḍa, and the second from Uttarakāṇḍa—

rām prāṇ priya jīvan jī ke
svārath rahit sakhā sab hī ke.

Simple Meaning—Rāma is as dear as your own life, in fact, our life is because of Rāma, He is the Friend of all and He has no selfish motive behind this friendship.

hetu rahit jag jug upkārī
tum tumhār sevak asurārī
svārath mīt sakal jag māhiṇ.

Simple Meaning—O Rāma, all worldly friends have selfish motives, but there are two exceptions—You and Your bhakta (like Hanumān) do good to the world without expecting any return.

Practical Components of Rāma-Kāj

4.26. Although the literal meaning of 'Rāma-kāj is 'Rāma's work' which is the same thing as 'God's work', the inner meaning is 'doing good to others'. This can be clarified from the Mānas in five ways. First, Rāma says to Angad in Laṅkākāṇḍa—

kāju hamār tāsu hit hoī.

Simple Meaning—My work and Rāvaṇa's 'hit' (or welfare) go together.

4.27. Secondly, Hanumān, whose life's mission was 'Rāma-kāj' tried his best to do good to Rāvaṇa although the latter did not follow Hanumān's advice. The following extracts from Kishkindhākāṇḍa and Sundarakāṇḍa, respectively, clarify this—

rāma-kāj lagi tav avatārā.

Simple Meaning—O Hanumān, your incarnation is only to do Rāma-kāj.

jadapi kahī kapi ati hit vānī
bolā vihasi mahā abhimānī.

Simple Meaning—Although Hanumān's advice to Rāvaṇa was intended to do immense good to him (i.e. Rāvaṇa), the latter ignored it because of his extreme arrogance.

4.28. Thirdly, Rāma taught Hanumān (and through him to all mankind) that one should serve the world with the feeling that everyone is essentially a form of God. This message of social service is in Kishkindhākāṇḍa (i.e. canto V) and this is the practical technique for doing Rāma-kāj—

main sevak sacharāchar
rūp swāmi bhagwant

Simple Meaning—The best social worker is one who views the whole world as God's form.

4.29. Fourthly, Tulasīdāsa has described Hanumān (whose mission is Rāma-kāj) as one who removes the sorrows of all and who brings about 'sakal kalyāṇ' i.e. the good of all. Here are three quotations from Vinay-Patrikā—

sumirat sankat soch vimochan....
khāni sakal kalyān kī.

Simple Meaning—We pray to Hanumān, he will free us from all difficulties and sorrows, and he will give real happiness and welfare to all.

This quotation reminds us of the popularity of 'sankaṭmochan' as Hanumān's name—

ko nahin jānat hai jag men
kapi sankaṭ mochan nām tihāro.

Simple Meaning—O Hanumān, this is well known that the whole world has named you 'sankaṭmochan' (i.e. one who frees us from all difficulties).

hanumān kalyāṇ kartā....
jagadārti-hartā.

Simple Meaning—Hanumān does good to all, he removes the distress (ārti) of the world.

mangal mūrati māruti nandan
sakal amangal mūl nikandan.

Simple Meaning—Hanumān is the embodiment of mangal (i.e. good). He uproots (i.e. removes completely) all that harms mankind.

4.30. Fifthly Jaṭāyu's sacrifice is glorified in the Mānas by saying that he gave up his life while doing par-hit (i.e. good to others), and also saying that he gave up his life while doing Rāma-kāj. This shows that these two expressions are synonyms. The following two quotations are from Kishkindhākāṇḍa—

parhit bas jinh ke man māhiṇ
tinh kahn jag durlabh kachhu nāhīn

rāmkāj kāran tanu tyāgi
haripur gayau param barabhāgī.

Simple meaning—Jaṭāyu attained Rāma's abode i.e. the highest state that can be attained after death, because his innermost desire was to do parhit, and he fulfilled his desire......He gave up his life while doing Rāma-kāj.

4.31. Jaṭāyu's glorification reminds us of verse III.35 of the Gītā—

svadharme nidhanaṃ śreyaḥ.

Simple Meaning—One who dies while carrying out svadharma (one's duty) attains śreyas (i.e. mokṣa).

And the Mānas speaks similarly in another context too—namely in Bālakāṇḍa—

par-hit lāgi tajai jo dehī
santat sant prasansahi tehī.

Simple Meaning—Saints continuously admire the person who gives up his life for the benefit of others.

4.32. Based on these statements of Tulasīdāsa, we can say, as we did in paragraph 4.9 in the context of the Gītā, that svadharma is elevated to the status of mat-karma or Rāma-kāj when it is oriented to par-hit i.e. the good of others.

Nimittamātram in the Mānas

4.33. We indicated in paragraph 4.23 that next to Hanumān, Angad's contribution to Rāma-kāj is noteworthy. This is particularly so in the present context because Angad explicitly refers to the nimittamātram concept. To understand this clearly, we need to go into some detail which are given in Laṅkākāṇḍa (i.e. canto VI) about Angad. He had a difficult assignment, viz. to go to Laṅkā as a representative of Rāma, and among other things, do good to Rāvaṇa too. He explained his mission to Rāvaṇa in the following words—

main raghubīr dūta daskandhar....
tav hit kāran āyaun bhāī.....
uttam kul pulasti kar nātī
siva viraṇchi pūjehu bahu bhāntī
var pāyau kīnheu sab kājā
jītehu lokpāl sab rājā.......
ab subh kahā sunahu tum morā.

Simple Meaning—O Rāvaṇa, I have come here as Rāma's representative. My mission is to do good to you.... Please remember that you belong to an excellent family. You have worshipped Shiva and Brahmā who granted you special boons. You have made many conquests and have done wonderful things...... Now please listen to my advice which will do good to you.

4.34. Angad's words did have some effect. Rāvaṇa understood that Angad's proposal was to replace enmity with friendship. However, in his arrogance, Rāvaṇa interpreted this as a sign of weakness, and he said—

ripu san prīti karat nahin lājā.

Simple Meaning—In my opinion, it would be a shameful act to make friendship with one's enemy.

4.35. Rāvaṇa's wife, Mandodarī interpreted Angad's mission correctly. She told Rāvaṇa—

jehi jalnāth bandhāyau helā
utre prabhu dal sahit subelā
kārunīk dinkar kul ketū
dūt pathāyau tav hit hetū

Simple Meaning—My dear husband, please do not misinterpret Angad's proposal. Do not think that Rāma has offered peace due to his military weakness. He has immense strength and resources. He got the bridge constructed over the sea, and brought his whole army here. But he is compassionate, so He sent Angad to do good to you.

4.36. More details about Angad need not be told except that he tried all possible ways to make peace, and before leaving, he taught Rāvaṇa a lesson. But Angad remained free from arrogance, because—and this is important for our present discussion—he considered himself merely an instrument in Rāma's hands. He uses the Hindi-equivalent of 'nimittamātram—

svayamsiddha sab kāj
nāth mohi ādar diyau.

Simple Meaning—Rāma-kāj is svayamsiddha' i.e. it is bound to succeed by itself (even without me), because it is backed by Rāma's infinite strength. Although I got the honour as if I did something great, I know that Lord Rāma sent me only for procedural formality, i.e. I am merely an instrument.

4.37. We mentioned in paragraph 4.12 that the nimittamātram attitude is strengthened by thinking of God while doing svadharma. The same message is given in the Mānas by Jaṭāyu's brother, Sampāti, to Hanumān, Angad and other monkeys. Kishkindhākāṇḍa describes how all these monkeys, trying to do 'Rāma-kāj, ran into difficulties. At that critical juncture, Sampāti gave them strength and advice by saying—

pāpiu jākar nām sumirahīn
ati apār bhav sāgar tarahīn
tāsu dūt tum taji kadrāī
rām hridayan dhari karahu upāī.

Simple Meaning—Remember that you are trying to do 'Rāma-kāj. Remember also that you are soldiers in Rāma's army. So there is no need to lose heart. I want to remind you that, by thinking of Rāma, even ordinary people can do great things. So why not you? Keep Rāma in your hearts, give up faint-heartedness, and try your best. (And we all know that this led to success).

4.38. The last point we mentioned in relation to 'nimittamātram', viz. in paragraph 4.13, is that such an attitude makes the concerned person "a sāttvika karta"—in the terminology of the Gītā. The Mānas too provides many illustrations of this, but we shall present here only three of them. The first illustration is from Kishkindhākāṇḍa (i.e. canto IV) which describes the effect of Rāma-kāj on the monkeys—

chale sakal van khojata
saritā sar giri khoh
rām-kāj layleen man
bisrā tan kar chhoh

Simple Meaning—Although the monkeys had a difficult assignment, but Rāma-kāj gave them strength and a strong motivation. They did not mind the difficulties at all, and bodily discomforts did not bother them. Forests, mountains, caves and ponds—none of these could dampen their enthusiasm.

4.39. The second illustration is from Sundarakāṇḍa (i.e. canto V), which gives details of Hanumān's adherence to the principles of karmayoga. The most famous words of Hanumān in the context of Rāma-kāj are—

rām-kāj kīnhe binu
mohi kahān vishrām

Simple Meaning—I am so much dedicated to Rāma-kāj that I do not want to think of 'vishrām' (i.e. rest). This last word 'vishrām' can be interpreted in two ways. First, it denotes a pause for relaxation. Secondly, it denotes 'peace' i.e. jivanmukta state, which is the spiritual goal of many people, but for Hanumān, even that is not important because Rāma-kāj is both the means and the goal for him.

4.40. The third illustration is from Laṅkākāṇḍa (i.e. canto VI) which describes how Hanumān, doing Rāma-kāj, was able to perform superhuman tasks. When Lakshmaṇ was wounded, Hanumān brought the medicinal herb from the Himalayas to Laṅkā within a few hours—

kahā nām giri aushadhī
jāhu pavansut len
rām charan sarsij ur rākhī
chalā prabhanjan sut bal bhākhī

Simple Meaning—The doctor specified the mountain from which the medicinal help was to be brought. It was a long and difficult journey and time was short. But Hanumān (the sāttvika karta) kept Rāma's feet in his heart and expressed confidence that he will do the needful. (And we know that he did).

Karma-Samarpaṇaṃ in the Mānas

4.41. As we mentioned in paragraph 4.19, the technique of karma-samarpaṇaṃ also represents a harmonious combination of karmayoga and bhakti-yoga. We shall present three instances of this on the basis of the Mānas. The first one is Hanumān again, who, as the supreme performer of Rāma-kāj, cannot be left out. Secondly, the poet Tulasīdāsa dedicated the Mānas to the saints, in the true spirit of karma-samarpaṇaṃ. The third instance is provided by Pratāpbhānu, and we shall explain why his karma-samarpaṇaṃ proved to be short-lived.

4.42. Starting with Hanumān, the secret of his success was that he dedicated himself—and not merely his actions—to Rāma. So Hanumān went beyond karma-samarpaṇaṃ to sampūrṇa-samarpaṇaṃ (sampūrṇa meaning all). He says to Lord Rāma in Kishkindhakāṇḍa—

jānaun nahin kachhu bhajan upāī....
sevak sut pati mātu bharose.

Simple Meaning—I do not know any technique like singing of God's praise or observing discipline like yoga, etc. I have simply surrendered myself unto you—like a servant unto master or a son unto mother.

Because of this, Hanumān got immense strength, and he remained completely free from egotism. He even appealed to Rāvaṇa to give up egotism—and this is from Sundarakāṇḍa—

tyāgahu tam abhimān.

Simple Meaning—Hanumān said, give up egotism, it is tamasika i.e. the epitome of badness.

And Hanumān carried out 'sevā' or 'service', remembering all the time that he was merely an instrument in the hands of Rāma. Hanumān told Rāma in Sundarakāṇḍa—

so sab tav pratāp raghurāī
nāth na kachhū mor prabhutāī.

Simple Meaning—O Lord Rāma, all the strength is yours, none of it is mine.

4.43. Secondly, Tulasīdāsa declares repeatedly in Bālakāṇḍa that he is not a poet, and whatever merit there is in the Mānas it is all due to Rāma's grace, and he dedicates the Mānas to saints—

jadapi kavit ras ekau nāhīn
rām pratāp pragat ehi māhīn.....
sujan suchit suni lehu sudhārī

Simple Meaning—Please do not expect any poetic quality in the Mānas, and if you find any, that is Rāma's grace. O saints, please listen to the Mānas with a soft heart and wherever there are errors, please make the necessary corrections, as a guru does to his pupils.

And Tulasī was confident that, since the Mānas would contribute to the happiness of all, the saints would accept his dedication—

rāmcharit rākesh kar
saris sukhad sab kāhu
sajjan kumud chakor chit
hit vishesh bara lāhu.

Simple Meaning—Tulasī says, Rāmakathā (as told in the Mānas) will make all happy (like the rays of the full moon). Saints will find it particularly beneficial (like the lotus and the chakor bird that love the full moon).

4.44. Thirdly, we need to look closely into the story of King Pratāpbhānu as told in Bālakāṇḍa. The story falls into two parts—and they bring out two opposite sides of Pratāpbhānu's mental attitude and performance. In the first part, the king is depicted as a karmayogin who dedicated his actions to God—

> *hridayan na kachhu phal anusandhānā*
> *bhūp vivekī param sujānā*
> *karai je dharam karam man vānī*
> *vāsudev arpit nripa gyānī*

Simple meaning—King Pratāpbhānu was wise and great. He followed the karmayoga principle "Do not hanker after the fruit of your actions." Furthermore, whatever dharmic acts the king performed, by thought, word and deed, he dedicated all of them to God.

No wonder that all the people of his kingdom were happy. So the first part of the story brings out the virtuous mentality as well as actions of the king.

4.45. But the Mānas says in part two of the story that unfavourable circumstances led the king to destruction. He was deceived by a fake sannyāsin who gave him the impossible assurance that he will live for ever—

> *jarā maran dukh rahit tanu.*

Simple Meaning—The fake sannyasin told the king—you will not grow old, will not die, and will always be happy.

In other words, the king strayed away from the earlier practice of karmayoga and karma-samarpaṇaṃ, and fell a prey to excessive desires. He fell into the fake sannyāsin's trap and was destroyed.

4.46. Tulasī's message from Pratāpbhānu's story is that, unless there is a worthwhile purpose in life, like sevā or social service—and unless this purpose is maintained—even the practice of karma-samarpaṇaṃ may prove to be short-lived.

CHAPTER FIVE

Call to Follow the Spiritually Perfect—Yogārūḍha or Sant

5.1. In the preceding chapter we explained how participation in God's work i.e. mat-karma or Rāma-kāj essentially implies performing acts of social service. The basis of this is the realization that God is the sustainer of the universe and also the Friend of all beings who does good to them without expecting any return. So in doing social service as God's work, we follow God's example. In the present chapter, we carry this idea a step further, by extending the list of those whose example we need to follow. Both the Gītā and the Mānas have indicated who these entities are, that is, who, next to God, are setting an example of doing good to all. This is a favourite topic in both the books, so we will have to adopt a selective approach. In terms of the ten key words or phrases that we listed in chapter two, the present chapter deals with the third of those expressions.

5.2. Although social service is the visible, outward characteristic of the above-mentioned entities, they obviously have some extraordinary, inner capability that enables them to give priority to the good of others. Both the Gītā and the Mānas view them as 'spiritually perfect', and, depending on how they attained perfection, various expressions are used to identify them. A related point made by both the books is that the journey to spiritual perfection is, in turn, facilitated by acts of social service. Therefore, besides describing the exemplary nature of those who are perfect, we shall also look into the relationship between social service and spiritual perfection.

Approach to Spiritual Perfection

5.3. We mentioned above that the spiritually perfect are called by many names. Before coming to that topic, we want to say that the state of perfection itself is devoted in the Gītā by several words. One of these words is 'śreyas' which is an Upaniṣadic word meaning 'good' and to which we referred in paragraph 1.11. Dr. Radhakrishnan has made a list of the other words—

> "The end of perfection is called the highest (III.19), mokṣa or emancipation (III.31, IV.15), the eternal state (XVIII.56), the path from which there is no return (V.17), perfection (XII.10), the highest rest (IV.39), the entering into God (IV.9, 10, 24), contact with God (VI.28), rest in Brahman (II.72), transformation into Divine existence (XIV.26), transformation into Godhead (V.24)."[1]

5.4. The popular word 'mokṣa', which occurs in the above list, is one of the four 'puruṣārthas' or values of life. The common belief is that this is an 'afterdeath value', but Mishra warns against any narrow, negativistic interpretation of mokṣa—

> "Mokṣa is not an other-worldly and after-death value, nor is it an individualistic a-social value. The negativistic interpretation of mokṣa found in some sections of the Indian tradition is not correct. The true picture of mokṣa which we find in the Vedas, Upaniṣads and the Gītā is a very positive one... Self-realization is a process of gradual uncovering of the higher or the deeper self, proportionate to self-purification through the means of the cleansing of heart and universal love."[2]

5.5. There is ample evidence in the Gītā to support Mishra's view of mokṣa, namely perfection related to cleansing of heart and to universal love, and the possibility of this being achieved in this world. For example, verse V.23 states very clearly—

śaknotī'hai'va yaḥ soḍhuṃ
prāk śarīravimokṣaṇāt
kāmakrodhodbhavaṃ vegaṃ
sa yuktaḥ sa sukhī naraḥ.

Simple Meaning—He who is able to resist the rush of desire and anger, even here before he gives up his body, he is a yogin, he is the happy man.

5.6. About the yogas or ways by which spiritual perfection can be achieved, three paths are commonly referred to, viz. karma (action), bhakti (devotion), and jñāna (knowledge). However, other possibilities are also mentioned, for example, in verses XIII.24-25—

dhyānenā'tmani paśyanti
kecidātmānamātmanā
anye sāṃkhyena yogena
karmayogena cā'pare.

Simple Meaning—Some perceive the Self in the self by the self through 'dhyāna' (meditation), others by 'Sāṃkhyayoga', and still others by karma-yoga.

anye tvevamajānantaḥ
śrutvā'nyebhya upāsate
te'pi cā'titarantyeva
mrityuṃ śrutiparāyaṇāḥ.

Simple Meaning—Yet others, ignorant of these paths, hearing from others, worship, and they too cross beyond death by their devotion to what they have heard.

5.7. The Mānas uses a simile to point out two things, viz., first, that all the three yogas are important, and secondly, that best results can be achieved if all of them merge into one. In the beginning of Bālakāṇḍa, Tulasī compares saints to Prayāg, the most important centre of pilgrimage. Just as there are three holy rivers in Prayāg (Gaṅgā, Yamunā, Sarasvatī), similarly, says Tulasī, saints teach all the yogas. With this background information, let us look at Tulasī's words—

mud maṅgalmaya sant samājū
jo jag jangam tīrathrājū
rāmabhakti jahan sursari dhārā
sarsai brahma vichār prachārā
vidhi nishedhmaya kalimal harnī
karam kathā ravinandini varnī
harihar kathā virājati venī
sunat sakal mud mangal deṅī.

Simple Meaning—Saints do good to us like Prayāg, but unlike Prayāg (which is fixed in one place) saints move from place to place (and so are more beneficial than Prayāg). Saints teach bhaktiyoga (which is like Gaṅgā in Prayāg), jñānayoga (which is like Sarasvatī), and karmayoga (which is like Yamunā). But the most important point in Prayāg is where the three rivers meet (i.e. Triveṇī). Similarly, when all the three yogas merge into one, and we hear the kathā of Rāma and Shiva, we get 'sakal mangal' i.e. the good of all.

5.8. Another point about spiritual perfection, that is mentioned in the Gītā as well as in the Mānas, is that very few people strive for it. For example, verse VII.3 of the Gītā says—

manuṣyāṇāṃ sahasreṣu
kaścidyatati siddhaye.

Simple Meaning—Among thousands of people, scarcely one strives for perfection.

And the Mānas-words, occurring in Uttarakāṇḍ are similar—

nara sahasra mahn sunahu purārī
kou ek hoi dharma vrat dhārī...
gyānvant koṭik mahn koū
jīvan mukta sakrit jag soū.

Simple Meaning—Among thousands of people, scarcely one takes the path of dharma seriously....Similarly, among many people who acquire knowledge, scarcely one attains the state of 'jīvanmukta' (i.e. liberated while still living).

5.9. Although very few people strive for perfection, both the Gītā and the Mānas contain encouraging words for their success—the underlying idea being that, through genuine efforts spread over several 'births', perfection will be achieved. Verse VI.45 of the Gītā is optimistic—

prayatnādyatamānastu
yogī saṃśuddhakilbiṣaḥ
anekajanmasamsiddhas
tato yāti parāṃ gatiṃ.

Simple Meaning—The yogī who strives and perseveres, will be cleansed of all sins, and perfecting himself through many lives, will ultimately attain to the highest goal.

And similarly, in the Mānas, Kākbhushaṇḍī is the living example of one who attained perfection after many births. He attributes this to God's grace, while addressing Garuḍa in Uttarakāṇḍa—

sudhi mohi nāth janam bahu kerī
siva prasād mati moha na gherī.

Simple Meaning—By the grace of Lord Shiva, I was liberated from delusion after many births, and I am able to recall my experiences in all those births.

Inter-relationship Between Spiritual Perfection and Social Service

5.10. One part of this relationship is usually taken for granted, viz. that spiritually perfect persons are continuously engaged in social service. There are at least six different sections of the Gītā where this aspect of the relationship is described in detail, and similar accounts are even more numerous in the Māṇas. A summary of all these will form part of this chapter.

5.11. The other part of the relationship has received more attention in modern times than in the past. Swami Vivekananda highlighted this relationship when he said that doing good to the world would form an essential part of the spiritual practices of the members of the Rāmakrishna Mission. His ideas and those of Mahatma Gandhi and others will be referred to in chapter thirteen of this book.

5.12. To remove the doubts of those who still prefer the ancient commentaries on the Gītā, rather than the modern ones, we want to point out that there are several verses in the Gītā which link social service to spiritual attainment. For example, verse VI.40 says—

na hi kalyāṇakrit kaścid
durgatiṃ tāta gacchati.

Simple Meaning—One who does 'kalyāṇ' i.e. good to others, can never go down spiritually.

And the same idea is expressed by Tulasī in Uttarakāṇḍa—

kabahun ki dukh sab kar hit tākeṇ.

Simple Meaning—If you try to do good to all, you will never suffer from unhappiness yourself.

5.13. An interesting question arising from the above is the following—if doing good to others helps one become spiritually perfect (and in that perfection you also do good to others), then what is the difference between the perfect state and the one prior to perfection? A simple answer to this question is that, prior to achieving perfection, one does good to others by convincing oneself that this is a part of one's duty, whereas the perfect person does the same thing spontaneously. Dr. Radhakrishnan has derived this idea from verse VI.3 of the Gītā which reads as follows—

āruruksor muner yogaṃ
karma kāranamucyate

yogārūḍhasya tasyai'va
śamaḥ kāranamucyate.

Simple Meaning—An aspirant views acts of social service as a means to perfection. A spiritually perfect person performs such acts as if inspired by serenity i.e. spontaneously.

Further clarification of the meaning of this verse is provided by Dr. Radhakrishnan in a long commentary, a part of which is reproduced below—

"Through work we struggle to obtain self-control; when self-control is attained, we obtain peace. It does not follow that we then abandon all action...The yogin attains complete tranquillity by abandoning the fruit of action. He performs actions with a perfect equanimity. He overflows with a spontaneous vitality and works with a generosity which arises from his own inexhaustible strength."[3]

5.14. The Hindi word for 'spontaneity' is 'sahaj' and this is used in the Mānas to characterize the social service performed by saints, as the following quotation from Uttarakāṇḍa shows—

par upkār vachan man kāyā
sant sahaj subhāu khagrāyā.

Simple Meaning—Kākbhushuṇḍī tells Garuḍa that doing good to others, by thought, word and deed, is 'sahaj svabhāv' of saints i.e. they do this spontaneously and naturally.

5.15. One of the most famous songs about spontaneous acts of service is by Kabīr, and we quote below a part thereof—

sadho sahaj samādh bhalī...
jahn jahn dolon so parikramā
jo kachhu karon so sevā...

Simple Meaning—Kabīr says that he is happy to have arrived at that stage where the distinction between secular and spiritual life has disappeared. For example, ordinary people go to temple to do 'parikramā' (i.e. the ritual of going round the room in which God's image is installed). But, in my case, all my wanderings to help others constitute 'parikramā'. In fact, whatever I do is 'sevā' i.e. service.

Gītā's Descriptions of the Spiritually Perfect

5.16. Six of the eighteen chapters of the Gītā (viz. II, V, VI, XII, XIV, XVIII) contain an account of the characteristics of those who have attained spiritual perfection. One of the reasons why this topic has appeared so many times is, that perfection can be achieved in many ways and the state of perfection has therefore been given many names. It is observed, however, that the characteristics mentioned in the various accounts are broadly similar. This will become clear as we take up the accounts one by one. But, to start with, it will be useful to present some general, background information about the six descriptions—

(a) In chapter II, verses 54 to 72 describe a 'sthitaprajña' i.e. a person of steadfast wisdom.
(b) In chapter V, verses 19 to 29 describe a 'jīvanmukta' i.e. one who is liberated while still alive.
(c) In chapter VI, verses 27 to 32 describe a 'sāmyayogī' i.e. one who has equal vision towards all.
(d) In chapter XII, verses 13 to 20 describe a 'bhakta' i.e. a devotee of God.
(e) In chapter XIV, verses 21 to 27 describe a 'triguṇātīta' i.e. one who has gone beyond the three guṇas (sattva, rajas, tamas).
(f) In chapter XVIII, verses 51 to 56 describe a 'brahmabhūta' i.e. one who has attained Brahman.

5.17. Before moving on to each of the six descriptions, we want to draw attention to three points which are applicable to them as a group. First, since the journey to perfection is accomplished by 'yoga' of one kind or the other, it is relevant to recall the two definitions of 'yoga' given in verses II.48 and II.50. Taking verse II.48 first—

samatvaṃ yoga ucyate.

Simple Meaning—Yoga denotes even-mindedness.

Secondly, verse II.50 says—

yogaḥ karmasu kauśalaṃ.

Simple Meaning—Yoga is skill in action.

Therefore, these two definitional qualities or virtues can be assumed to be part of each of the six descriptions. We shall notice that 'even-mindedness' is referred to in the descriptions themselves, so 'skill in action' can be added thereto in each case, although none of the descriptions contains the word 'kauśalaṃ' as such.

5.18. The second point that is applicable to the six descriptions as a group, is the sameness of their goal, viz. good of the world. Dr. Radhakrishnan has expressed this by a simile—

> "We do not proceed on the same lines but that which we seek is the same. We may climb the mountain by different paths but the view from the summit is identical for all. The liberated souls take upon themselves the burden of the redemption of the whole world."[4]

5.19. The third point relates to the occurrence of the same or similar ideas or expressions in two or more descriptions. The repetitive use of the following nine ideas or expressions provides concrete evidence of the overall similarity between the six descriptions—

(i) Sevā or social service is denoted by the expressions 'sevate' and 'sarvabhūtahite ratāḥ'.

(ii) Steadfast wisdom is denoted by the expressions 'sthitaprajña', 'sthirabuddhi' and 'sthiramati'.

(iii) Even-mindedness towards friends and foes is denoted by the expressions 'samaḥ śatrau ca mitre ca' and 'tulyo mitrāripakṣayoḥ'.

(iv) Equality and friendliness towards all beings, are denoted by the expressions 'samaḥ sarveṣu bhūteṣu', 'sarvatra samaṃ paśyati', and 'adveṣṭā sarvabhūtānaṃ'.

(v) Unselfishness and non-egotism are denoted by the expression 'nirmamo nirahaṃkāraḥ' which has been repeated.

(vi) Purity and sinlessness are denoted by the expressions 'kṣiṇakalmaṣaḥ' and 'vigatakalmaṣaḥ'.

(vii) Freedom from passion, fear and rage is denoted by the expressions 'vītarāgabhayakrodhaḥ' and 'vigatecchābhaya krodhaḥ'.

(viii) Freedom from grief and selfish desire is denoted by the expression 'na śocati na kāṅkṣati' which has been repeated.

(ix) Attainment of Brahman is denoted by the expressions 'brahmanirvāṇa', 'brahmabhūta', 'brahmayogayuktāmā' and 'brahmabhūyāya kalpate'.

5.20. Next, we shall move on to each of the six descriptions. We present in Appendix One all the fifty-seven verses of the Gītā related to this topic—the verses occurring in six different chapters—and we also give a simple meaning of each verse in English. The presentation in this chapter—which follows—will only draw attention to special features of each description.

(a) ***Sthitaprajña***

5.21. Mahatma Gandhi attached special importance to this section of the Gītā. This was recited daily at his prayer meeting. He equated a 'sthitaprajña' and an ideal satyāgrahī i.e. one who is determined to do social service, practise non-violence, and is willing to give up every thing—even one's life—to bring about social justice. He admitted that one who merely translates the relevant words of the Gītā might not find all these points in the sthitaprajña-section. In his opinion, the best way to understand the spirit of the Gītā was to try to put into practice the inner message, and after doing it for forty years he found new meanings which are unique to his commentary. As he put it—

> "I am not aware of the claim made by the translators of enforcing their meaning of the Gītā in their own lives. At the back of my reading there is the claim of an endeavour to enforce the meaning in my own conduct for an unbroken period of forty years."[5]

5.22. The sthitaprajña-section in the Gītā has nineteen verses, out of which Arjuna's question takes up one verse and Lord Krishna's reply consists of eighteen verses. For purposes of our brief presentation here, we confine our attention to ideas contained in only six of them.

5.23. The description of a sthitaprajña begins with the statement that he or she is unselfish—the actual text of verse II.55 being—

prajahāti yadā kāmān sarvān pārtha manogatān.

Simple Meaning—A sthitaprajña puts away all the desires of his or her mind i.e. as Dr. Radhakrishnan puts it, "freedom from selfish desires" is the first characteristic of a sthitaprajña.[6]

Based on this idea, Mahatma Gandhi specified that a satyāgraha movement will not be launched to set right any act of individual injustice—only the removal of social injustice will necessitate such a movement.

5.24. The next verse, viz. II.56 makes it clear that a sthitaprajña, while striving for the happiness of all, does not hanker after personal happiness—

duḥkheṣvanudvignamanāḥ sukhesu vigatasprihaḥ
vītarāgabhayakrodhaḥ sthitadhīr munirucyate.

Simple Meaning—Since personal goals do not have priority for a sthitaprajña, he or she remains even-minded towards one's own sorrows and pleasures. Furthermore, a sthitaprajña is free from passion, fear and rage.

Fearlessness was the basis of the satyāgraha movement because foreign domination had instilled a deep sense of fear in the hearts of common people. At the same time, non-violence necessitated freedom from rage i.e. anger.

5.25. Mahatma Gandhi's disciple, Acharya Vinoba utilized verses II.60-61 to associate all the three yogas—karma, bhakti, jñāna—with a sthitaprajña. Relevant portions of these two verses are—

yatato hyapi kaunteya
puruṣasya vipaścitaḥ...
yukta āsīta matparaḥ.

Simple Meaning—A sthitaprajña is striving (yatataḥ), discerning (vipaścitaḥ) and dedicated to God (mat paraḥ).

5.26. Verse II.69 contains in a nutshell the message that ordinary people need to take an about-turn in regard to their approach to the goal of life—

yā niśā sarvabhūtānaṃ tasyāṃ jāgarti saṃyamī
yasyāṃ jāgrati bhutāni sa niśā paśyato muneḥ.

Simple Meaning—A sthitaprajña serving the society selflessly, and a selfish person caring for none else—these two are diametrically opposite to each other in regard to their goal and approach, like day and night.

5.27. A similar statement (referring to night and day) is made by Tulasīdāsa in Ayodhyākāṇḍa (i.e. canto II of the Mānas)—

moh nisāṇ sab sovnihārā...
ehin jag jāmini jāgahin jogī.

Simple Meaning—Ordinary people are so engulfed in the darkness of narrow-mindedness that they have no idea of what the light of truth is. They differ from the yogis as night differs from day.

5.28. The priority that a sthitaprajña gives to social service is indicated, in verse II.71, by saying that such a person is 'nirmamo nirahaṃkāraḥ' i.e. beyond the sense of I and mine. Acharya Vinoba has explained this in detail, a part of which will be quoted in chapter nine of this book. Here it should suffice to present Vinoba's conclusion that a sthitaprajña lives only to benefit humanity.

(b) ***Jīvanmukta***

5.29. This variant of spiritual perfection is described in eleven verses, viz. V.19-29. A glimpse of that description is conveyed here by referring to four to those verses.

Verse V.19 declares that a person who has equal vision towards all the beings and who acts accordingly, is a jīvanmukta—

> *ihai'va tairjitaḥ sargo*
> *yeṣāṃ sāmye sthitaṃ manaḥ.*

> ***Simple Meaning***—Even while living, a person of equal vision is able to conquer the world i.e. to attain the state of liberation.

The word 'sāmya' used in this verse, conveys the same meaning of 'equal vision' which is referred to as 'samadriṣṭi' in verse V.18. Dr. Radhakrishnan has written a long commentary on these two verses, the concluding part of which is quoted below—

> "This view (i.e. equal vision) makes us look upon our fellow beings with kindliness and compassion. The wise see the one God in all beings and develop the quality of equalmindedness which is characteristic of the Divine."[7]

5.30. Verse V.20 uses the word 'sthirabuddhiḥ' which reminds us of 'sthitaprajña'—

> *na prahriṣyet priyaṃ prapya*
> *no dvijet prāpya cāpriyaṃ*
> *sthirabuddhiḥ...*

> ***Simple Meaning***—There is similarity between a jīvanmukta and a sthitaprajña—for example, both of them are able to maintain their equalmindedness which is not shaken by pleasant or unpleasant experiences.

This verse is similar to verse II.56 which forms part of the description of a sthitaprajña (ref. para 5.24). Their common message is, try for the happiness of all, while remaining even-minded towards your own sorrows and pleasures.

5.31. Verse V.25 contains the most explicit declaration that 'jīvanmukta' persons are 'sarvabhūtahite ratāḥ' i.e. they rejoice in doing good to all. This verse will be taken up in full in chapter seven of this book.

5.32. Verse V.28 says, among other things, that a jīvanmukta person is free from selfishness, fear and rage, which reminds us of verse II.56 where freedom from passion, fear and rage was highlighted as a characteristic of a sthitaprajña.

(c) ***Sāmyayogī***

5.33. The importance given by the Gītā to the concept of equal vision towards all the beings has already been pointed out in the previous section relating to a 'jīvamukta'. So there is obvious similarity between that and the description of a 'sāmyayogī' given in verses VI.27-32. However, a special feature of a sāmyayogī is brought out by extending the scope of 'equal vision'—i.e. beyond the metaphysical standpoint to include behavioural considerations also. To clarify this, it would be enough to look at the last verse of the sāmyayogī's description, viz. verse VI.32—

ātmaupamyena sarvatra samaṃ paśyati yo'rjuna
sukham vā yadi vā duḥkhaṃ sa yogī paramo mataḥ.

Simple Meaning—A sāmyayogī is guided by the philosophy of 'ātmaupamya' which sees the same Ātman in all the beings. Furthermore, this person's sympathetic behaviour towards all reflects this philosophy fully, in the sense that he is happy when others are happy and he is unhappy when others are unhappy.

More on this in chapter ten.

(d) ***Bhakta***

5.34. Eight verses, viz. XII.13-20, describe the characteristics of a bhakta, many of which have already been mentioned in one or other of the proceeding three sections. For example, the expression 'nirmamo nirahaṃkāraḥ' which formed part of the description of a sthitaprajña, occurs as such in verse XII.13 too. Similarly, the ability of viewing all the beings with equal vision, which was highlighted for a jīvanmukta as well as a sāmyayogī, is associated with a bhakta also, by means of the expression 'adveṣṭā sarvabhūtānāṃ'. Both these important concepts are contained in the opening verse, viz. XII.13 which is quoted below—

adveṣṭā sarvabhūtānāṃ maitraḥ karuṇa eva ca
nirmamo nirahaṃkāraḥ samaduḥkhasukhaḥ kṣamī.

Simple Meaning—A bhakta has no ill will towards any being, i.e. even towards those who have ill will towards him (or her). A bhakta is also compassionate and friendly. Furthermore, a bhakta, being 'nirmamo nirahaṅkāraḥ', i.e. beyond the sense of I and mine, gives priority to social service. Although a bhakta tries to make others happy; he or she remains even-minded towards one's own sorrows and pleasures. Besides all this, a bhakta has the quality of forgiveness.

5.35. It is clear that genuine bhakti, according to the Gītā, has a strong social dimension. To be free from ill will is an important part of this. The same idea is repeated in verse XII.18—

samaḥ śatrau ca mitre ca.

Simple Meaning—A bhakta behaves alike to friend and foe.

Dr. Radhakrishnan has summarized the charactristics of a bhakta in the following words—

"A bhakta's life is guided not by the forces of attraction and repulsion, friendship and enmity, pleasure and pain, but by the single urge to give oneself to God, and therefore to the service of the world which is one with God."[8]

5.36. Furthermore, Dr. Radhakrishnan finds a parallel between the Gītā's description of a bhakta and what Tulasī has written in Vinay Patrikā, a translation of which is quoted by Radhakrishnan—we quote below a part of that translation—

"Tulasī prays,
Grant me, O Master, by thy grace
To follow all the good and pure,
To be content with simple things;
To use my fellows not as means but ends,
To serve them stalwartly, in thought, word, deed;
Never to utter word of hatred or of shame,
To cast away all selfishness and pride,
To speak no ill to others......
Thus only shall I please thee, serve thee right."[9]

(e) ***Triguṇātīta***

5.37. The description of a 'triguṇātīta' has a presentational similarity with that of a 'sthitaprajña' in the sense that both of them begin with a specific question by Arjuna. In the present case, Arjuna's question occurs in verse XIV.21, and Lord Krishna's reply thereto is given in verses XIV.22-28.

5.38. We mentioned in the preceding section that the sameness of vision towards friend and foe is an important characteristic of a bhakta. That is true of a triguṇātīta too, as we find in verse XIV—

tulyo mitrāripakṣayoḥ.

Simple Meaning—A triguṇātīta behaves alike to friend and foe.

5.39. Another common charactristic is 'social service' which has been indicated by a variety of expressions. The description of a triguṇātīta contains the word 'sevate' for this purpose, for example, in verse XIV.26—

māṃ ca yo'vyabhicāreṇa
bhaktiyogena sevate.

Simple Meaning—A triguṇātīta's bhakti or devotion to God is unshakeable and it is expressed through social service.

Swami Chinmayananda has explained the relationship between dedicated service and the process of going beyond the three guṇas—

> "Lord Krishna expects his devotees to bring religion from the pūjā-rooms and temples to the fields of their every-day-life of activities and in all their contacts with others around. Such a practice of constant God-awareness and dedicated service removes the agitations of the mind... Tamas and Rajas (guṇas) get more and more reduced, and thereby the proportion of sattva-guṇa in the seeker's subtle constitution increases. And such a seeker is fit to become Brahman."[10]

(f) ***Brahmabhūta***

5.40. This is the sixth and the last description of a person who achieves spiritual perfection. A special feature of the description, and particularly of verses XVIII.54-56, is a clear statement that all the yogas get harmonized when one attains perfection.

5.41. As far as the characteristics of perfection are concerned, it is not surprising that several of the expressions have a parallel in the earlier, five descriptions, as pointed out in the following five examples—

(i) The expression 'nirmamo nirhaṃkāraḥ' has already appeared in verses II.71 and XII.13. Equivalent words in verse XVIII.53 are 'ahaṃkāram vimucya...nirmamaḥ'.
(ii) The concept of 'sāmya' or equal vision has been emphasized in verses V.19 and VI.29. The same idea is conveyed in verse XVIII.54 by the words 'samaḥ sarveṣu bhūteṣu'.

(iii) The words 'na śocati na kāmkṣati', which appeared in verse XII.17, have been repeated in verse XVIII.54.

(iv) The words 'brahmabhūyāya kalpate', which appeared in verse XIV.26, have been repeated in verse XVIII.53.

(v) The expression 'brahmabhūtaḥ' which appeared in verses V.24 and VI.27, has been repeated in verse XVIII.54.

5.42. The message that social service is an essential feature of spiritual perfection, is conveyed in the present description by verse XVIII.56—

sarvakarmāṇyapi sadā
kurvaṇo madvyapāśrayaḥ.

Simple Meaning—Lord Krishna says that a brahmabhūta person takes refuge in Me, that is, he considers himself merely as an instrument of God, while performing all acts of social service.

Swami Chinmayananda's comment on this verse calls for special attention—

"Lord Krishna never wants to receive any devotee at His gate, nor will He give an audience to any one, unless the seeker carries the passport of selfless service to society."[11]

Description of Saints or Bhaktas in the Mānas

5.43. In the Mānas, spiritually perfect persons are referred to either as 'sant' (meaning saints) or 'bhakta' (i.e. God's devotees). Their characteristics are described nearly thirty times, although many of the descriptions are quite short. There is no canto in which this topic does not occur. The fact that these persons are constantly engaged in doing good to others is stated explicitly, and for times without number. As many as twelve persons, who have a role in Rāma-kathā or Shiva-kathā, have sung praises of saints. We present below the main points contained in the statements of each of these twelve persons, although, since only four of them are in detail, the other eight persons are lumped together in subgroups of two each.

Lord Rāma's Views on Saints or Bhaktas

5.44. Lord Rāma talks about saints as many as five times in the entire Mānas, the most important being His dialogue with Bharat. On the other four occasions, the persons who listen to Rāma's words are—Nārad, Lakshman, Sanakādi-Rishis, and Vibhīshaṇ.

5.45. Rāma-Bharat dialogue occurs in Uttarakāṇḍa. Lord Rāma illustrates the contrast between saints and devils by referring to what sandalwood and axe do to each other—

sant asantanh kai asi karnī
jimi kuṭhār chandan ācharnī
kātai parasu malay sunu bhāī
nij gun dei sugandh basāī.

Simple Meaning—A devil is like an axe that cuts the sandalwood into pieces, but a saint is like the sandalwood that imparts its fragrance even to the axe that cuts.

The implication of this for the human world is obvious. A devil tries to harm the sant, but the latter tries to do good even to that devil.

5.46. Other qualities of saints include the following—

sam abhūt-ripu

i.e. they have equal vision towards all so much so that they do not consider any one as their enemy.

par dukh dukh
sukh sukh dekhe par

i.e. they are unhappy when other are unhappy, and they are happy when others are happy.

komalachit dīnanḥ par dāyā
man vach kram mam bhagati amāyā

i.e. they have a soft heart, they have great compassion towards poor people, and they are My true bhaktas, in thought, word and deed.

Obviously, in Tulasī's eyes, a saint and a bhakta are synonyms.

5.47. Rāma-Bharat dialogue also describes the characteristics of devils, which are the opposite of those of saints. While saints do good to others, devils try to harm others so much so that—

jo kar hit anahit tāhū soṇ

i.e. devils harm even those who do good to them.

5.48. The most famous 'chopai' (i.e. the common form of the metre used in the Mānas) occurs in the dialogue between Lord Rāma and Bharat—

par hit saris dharam nahin bhāī
par pīrā sam nahin adhamāī

nirṇaya sakal purāṇ ved kar
kaheun tāt jānahiṇ kovid nar.

Simple Meaning—Lord Rāma says, My dear brother Bharat, there is no dharma as important as doing good to others. Similarly, there is no adharma as bad as doing harm to others. This is the essence of all scriptures. I want to highlight this to you, and this is known to pandits too.

5.49. The second occasion when Lord Rāma talks about saints is described in Araṇyakāṇḍa. Rāma tells Rishi Nārad that saints not only know about dharma, but they also act in accordance with dharma—

dhīr dharama gati param pravīṇā

i.e. saints are experts in the knowledge of dharma, and their gati i.e. conduct too is based on that knowledge.

5.50. As in the Rāma-Bharat dialogue, the Rāma-Nārad conversation too equates a saint with a bhakta, their common characteristic being that they do good to others—as the following words from Araṇyakāṇḍa show—

gāvahiṇ sunahiṇ sadā mam līlā
hetu rahit par hit rat śīlā.

Simple Meaning—Saints recite and listen to Rāma-kathā, i.e. they are bhaktas, and they do good to others, without expecting anything in return.

5.51. The virtue that sustains the saints on the right path is non-egotism—

dambh mān mad karahin na kāū
bhūli na dehiṇ kumārag pāū.

Simple Meaning—Saints are free from arrogance and egotism, and they are extremely careful not to take a single step contrary to dharma.

5.52. The third occasion when Lord Rāma talks about saints is also described in Araṇyakāṇḍa. The conversation between Rāma and Lakshman begins with the difference between Brahman and jīva, but subsequently moves on to Tulasī's favourite topics—bhaktas and saints. Lord Rāma says that spending time in the company of saints and trying to follow in their footsteps, can help in acquiring virtues like unselfishness and thus in becoming a bhakta—

sant charan paṅkaj ati premā....
vachan karma man mori gati
bhajan karahin nihkām.

Simple Meaning—Rāma says that respect for saints will help develop true devotion to God, which involves virtuous conduct in thought, word and deed, and giving up of selfish desires i.e. interest in social service.

5.53. The fourth occasion when Lord Rāma talks about saints is described in Uttarakāṇḍa. Rāma welcomes Sanakādi Rishis as saints, and says that time spent in the company of saints makes life meaningful—

bare bhāg pāib satsaṅgā...
sant saṅg apvarg kar
kāmī bhav kar panth.

Simple Meaning—Rāma says, I consider myself fortunate to spend time in the company of saints like you. Saints can help achieve the highest goal of life—and on the contrary, the company of selfish persons leads to spiritual downfall.

5.54. In their reply, Sanakādi Rishis say that they admire Lord Rāma as the source of 'sakal sukh'—

sevat sulabh sakal sukh dāyak
dīnbandhu samtā vistāraya.

Simple Meaning—Rishis have the highest regard for Rāma because He is easily accessible to all and He gives happiness to all. Above all, He is the poor people's Brother, and He wants that every one should view others with equal vision.

More on 'sakal sukh' in chapter seven.

5.55. The fifth occasion when Lord Rāma talks about saints is described in Sundarakāṇḍa. Vibhīshaṇ, hit by Rāvaṇa's insulting behaviour, leaves Laṅkā and expresses a desire to join Rāma's forces. Rāma welcomes Vibhīshaṇ as a saint—saying that the real motive of Vibhīshaṇ was to bring about the welfare of the people of Laṅkā—

tumh sārikhe sant priya more

dharauṇ deh nahiṇ ān nihore
sagum upāsak parhit nirat...

Simple Meaning—Vibhīshaṇ, saints like you are dear to Me—so dear that the real purpose of My Incarnation is to protect you. I like saints and bhaktas because they are engaged in 'par-hit' i.e. helping others.

Lord Shiva's Views on Saints

5.56. Tulasī views Lord Shiva as the principal narrator of Rāma-kathā, which in turn does good to all. In general too, Lord Shiva, by doing good to all, inspires saints to do likewise. The first step in this process is indicated by Tulasī when he declares in Bālakāṇḍa—

jagadātmā mahesh purārī
jagat janak sab ke hitkārī.

Simple Meaning—Lord Shiva is the Ātmā of jagat, He is the Father of all, He is Maheshwar, He destroys evil and does good to all.

5.57. Secondly, Tulasī is grateful that Lord Shiva inspired him to write Rāma-kathā in common people's language. In this way, by Shiva-Pārvatī's grace, Tulasī's writing can benefit all—

jon har gauri pasāū...
bhāshā bhaniti prabhāu.

Simple Meaning—Tulasī says that only by the grace of Lord Shiva and Pārvatī, my poetry written in common people's 'bhāṣā' or language will have the desired effort of doing good to all.

5.58. While narrating Rāma-kathā to Pārvatī, Lord Shiva makes observations that bring out the great virtues of saints. For example, when Rāvaṇa insulted Vibhīshaṇ, the latter kept on giving the right advice which would have done good to Rāvaṇa. Shiva's comments on this saintly behaviour of Vibhīshaṇ occur in Sundarakāṇḍa—

umā sant kai ihai barāī
mand karat jo karai bhalāī.

Simple Meaning—Lord Shiva says, O Pārvatī, the greatness of a saint lies in that he keeps on doing good to others—even to one who tries to harm the saint.

5.59. Another occasion when Lord Shiva admires a saint or a bhakta for exemplary behaviour in the face of a rebuke or a curse is described in Uttarakāṇḍa. Lomash Muni becomes angry with Kākbhushuṇḍī and, through his curse, turns him into a crow. However, Kākbhushuṇḍī does not lose his temper and maintains his respectful behaviour towards the Muni. Lord Shiva utilizes this incident to point out why a saint like Kākbhushuṇḍī is able to handle a conflict-situation peacefully—

umā je rām charan rat
vigat kām mad krodh
nij prabhumaya dekhahiṇ jagat
kehi san karahin virodh.

Simple Meaning—O Pārvatī, one who is a bhakta or a saint, being free from passion, arrogance and anger, sees God everywhere and therefore maintains a unifying vision. With whom can such a person have any conflict i.e. he returns love even to one who started the conflict.

We recall that the closing words of Lord Shiva 'kehi san karahin virodh' were utilized by us in paragraph 2.16.

Kākbhushuṇḍī's Ideas on Saints

5.60. We saw above how Lord Shiva admired Kākbhushuṇḍī as a saint. In turn, Kākbhushuṇḍī himself, narrating Rāma-kathā to Garuḍa, gives the message that saints are willing to suffer personal loss in order to help others. This message is conveyed by giving the example of a bhoj-tree whose bark is of much use. Contrary to this, a devil is compared to a hemp-plant which ends up in the form of a rope that is used to strangle people. Kākbhushuṇḍī's words occur in Uttarakāṇḍa—

bhūrj taru sam sant kripālā
par hit niti sah vipati visālā
san iva khal par bandhan karaī
khāl karhāi vipati sahi maraī.

Simple Meaning—Saints are compassionate like a bhoj-tree, ready to make sacrifices (like the bhoj-tree giving its bark) in order to do good to others. Devils are just the opposite—they are like a hemp-plant which undergoes self-destruction in order (to become a rope) to strangle people.

5.61. Another famous statement of Kākbhushuṇḍī in Uttarakāṇḍa is that, for purposes of carrying on God's work in the world, saints play a more visible role then God Himself—

rām sindhu ghan sajjan dhīrā

chandan taru hari sant samirā...
rām te adhik rām kar dāsā.

Simple Meaning—If God is ocean, then saints are clouds that spread the ocean's water as rain. If God is a sandalwood plant, then saints are the winds that spread its fragrance all around. These examples show that saints or bhaktas (although they are God's servants) have a more visible role than God Himself.

Views of Yājñavalkya and Vālmīki

5.62. Yājñavalkya Muni says in Bālakāṇḍa that saints' willingness to suffer personal loss for the benefit of others is so well-known that people in need can themselves approach the saints with such a request—we omit details here which showed that this particular saint turned out to be a fake—

as kahi gahe naresh pad swāmi hohu kripāl
mohi lāgi dukh sahia prabhu sajjan dīn dayāl.

Simple Meaning—The king fell at the feet of the saint and said, "You are compassionate and helpful, so may I make a request to help me, although I know that this will cause difficulties to you."

5.63. Rishi Vālmīki's conversation with Lord Rāma, as described in detail in Ayodhyākāṇḍa, is well-known for specifying the numerous qualities of bhaktas or saints, but for our present purposes, the following three, brief quotations should suffice—

sab ke priya sab ke hitkārī...
je harshahin par sampati dekhī.....
jāti-pānti...taji....tumahi ur lāī.

Simple Meaning—Bhaktas or saints do good to all, and are loved by all.... They rejoice when others prosper...... They do not attach any importance to caste-divisions because they know that Lord Rāma lives in the heart of all, just as He lives in their hearts.

Views of Hanumān and Vibhīshaṇ

5.64. Both these are saints and their conduct plays an important role in Rāma-kathā. Hanumān deserves special credit for having identified Vibhīshaṇ who was living in the midst of demons. Hanumān was on a mission to do Rāma-kāj i.e. good to all, and when he heard Vibhīshaṇ saying 'Rāma, Rāma', he guessed correctly that here was a saint. Then

Hanumān took the initiative to talk to Vibhīshaṇ because he argued as described in Sundarakāṇḍa—

sādhu te hoi na kāraj hānī

i.e. a saint can promote Rāma-kāj, but never prove to be an obstacle to it.

5.65. Subsequent events proved that Vibhīshaṇ did promote Rāma-kāj. He tried his best to persuade Rāvaṇa to give up the path of evil—this too is described in Sundarakāṇḍa—

jo kripāl pūchhihu mohi bātā
mati anurūp kahaun hit tātā.

Simple Meaning—Vibhīshaṇ said to Rāvaṇa, my dear brother, you have kindly asked for my opinion, so I shall say what I think will do good to you.

5.66. Vibhīshaṇ continued to give good advice to Rāvaṇa, in spite of stiff opposition. He even gave a warning—

jahāṇ sumati tahn sampati nānā
jahāṇ kumati tahn vipati nidānā.

Simple Meaning—O Rāvaṇa, please listen to good advice and not to bad one, because good advice will bring you happiness while bad advice will put you into serious trouble.

And we know that Rāvaṇa insulted a saint like Vibhīshaṇ and brought about his own downfall—

sādhu avagyā turat bhavānī
kar kalyān akhil kai hāni.

Simple Meaning—Insulting a saint is bound to result in disaster.

Views of Brihaspati and Garuḍa

5.67. Brihaspati is the guru of gods and in Ayodhyākāṇḍa, he gives them the right advice when they were planning something inappropiate. In Ayodhyākāṇḍa, gods are depicted as trying to put an obstacle in the way of Bharat so that he may not see Lord Rāma at all—gods were afraid that Bharat may be able to persuade Rāma to come back to Ayodhyā. In that case, argued the gods, how would Rāvaṇa be killed? At this point, Brihaspati advises gods not to do anything contrary to Bharat's wishes because Bharat is a bhakta or saint—

jo aprādh bhagat kar karaī
rām rosh pāvak su jaraī.

Simple Meaning—Rāma gets extremely angry with those who oppose a bhakta or saint.

5.68. Continuing his advice to gods, Brihaspati utters words that glorify bhaktas or saints for their social service—words that are counted among the most famous sayings of the Mānas—

rām bhagat par hit nirat
par dukh dukhī dayāl.

Simple Meaning—A bhakta or saint is constantly engaged in doing good to others—he or she is compassionate, and becomes unhappy when others are unhappy.

5.69. Another famous saying about the qualities of saints occurs in Uttarakāṇḍa—and it is attributed to Garuḍa—

sant hridaya navnīt samānā
kahā kavinh pari kahai na jānā
nij paritāp dravai navnītā
par dukh dravahin sant supunītā.

Simple Meaning—Poets have compared the heart of a saint to butter, but, says Garuḍa, this simile is imperfect, because butter melts when heat is applied to itself, whereas a saint's heart melts when heat (i.e. pain) is experienced by others (i.e. not by the saint himself).

Views of Kāmadev and Laṅkiṇī

5.70. The story of Kāmadev giving up his life for helping others is told by Tulasī in Bālakāṇḍa. Gods requested Kāmadev to go and awaken Lord Shiva who was in deep meditation—gods wanted Shiva to marry Pārvatī. Kāmadev knew that this was the most challenging assignment, because he might even lose his life at the hands of an angry Shiva. But fear of death did not weaken Kāmadev's determination to help the gods—

tadapi karab main kāj tumhārā
shruti kah param dharam upkārā
parhit lāgi tajai jo dehī
santat sant prasansahiṇ tehī.

Simple Meaning—Kāmadev tells the gods, in spite of the great risk involved, I shall help you because the Vedas have specified 'helping others' as the highest dharma. Saints always admire the person who is willing to give up his life for the sake of others.

5.71. The story of Laṅkini, a female demon, is narrated by Tulasī in Sundarakāṇḍa. To start with, she tried to block Hanumān's entry into Laṅkā, but she soon realized that Hanumān is Lord Rāma's bhakta, i.e. a saint, and therefore unstoppable. She then told Hanumān how fortunate she was to have the opportunity to spend some time in the company of a saint—

tāt svarga apvarg sukh dharia tulā ek ang
tūl na tāhi sakal mili jo sukh lav satsang.

Simple Meaning—A single moment spent in the company of a saint gives more happiness than what one can hope to get in heaven or even in mokṣa.

Tulasī's Views—As a Writer and As a Saint

5.72. Although all the views expressed in the Mānas can be called Tulasī's views, we have, in the above paragraphs, attributed them to various persons because, in the text, the relevant words were spoken by them. In addition, before closing this chapter, we want to draw attention to two more aspects. First, what others characteristics of saints (i.e. other than those specified so far) did Tulasī mention as a writer, and secondly, what type of ideal did Tulasī exemplify as a saint?

5.73. First, as a writer, Tulasī depicts saints as pure in heart and working constantly for the good of the world—and the following words are from Bālakāṇḍa—

sant saral chit jagat hit.

Simple Meaning—Tulasī emphasizes both internal and external qualities that together make a saint—internally, saints are pure-hearted, and externally, since they have no selfish desires, they act spontaneously for the good of the world.

5.74. Other qualities of saints mentioned by Tulasī include (i) tolerance in regard to their own criticism, and (ii) firmness in regard to principles. Of the two relevant quotations given below, the first one is from Kishkindhākāṇḍa, and the second one is from Laṅkākāṇḍa—

būnd aghāt sahahin giri kaise
khal ke vachan sant sah jaise

.....

koṭi vighna te sant kar
man jimi nīti na tyāg.

Simple Meaning—In the matter of tolerance, saints are like mountains who remain calm even when they are hit by torrential rain. Similarly, saints remain calm even when evil-minded critics try to find fault with them... But tolerance of criticism does not mean that they yield on principles. Even if they face a million difficulties, saints remain steadfast to ethical standards i.e. in their resolve to do good to all.

5.75. Secondly, as a saint, Tulasī set an example of humility, respect for all, and whole-hearted desire to do good to all as 'Rāma-gulām' i.e. as a servant of Lord Rāma. For example, Tulasī says in Bālakāṇḍa repeatedly—because of his humility—that he is not a poet and so his poetry is full of faults—

kavi na houn nahìn chatur kahāvauṇ.....
kavit vivek ek nahiṇ more......
bhaniti mori sab gun rahit.

Simple Meaning—Tulasī says, I am not a poet, no one calls me learned, I do not possess a single qualification in the field of poetry-writing, and so it is obvious that my poetry has no quality worth the name.

5.76. Tulasī not only prays to Lord Rāma, Sītā, Saraswatī, and other divine entities, but he also bows down respectfully to all mankind, because, as a real saint, he views everyone—even the demons—as pervaded by God. Some of the ways he shows respect for all will be clear from the following quotations from Bālakāṇḍa—

sarvaśreyaskarīṃ sītāṃ nato'haṃ....
siyārāmamaya sab jag jānī
karaun pranām jori jug pānī.....
bandaun kinnar rajnichar
kripā karahu ab sarva.

Simple Meaning—Tulasī says, I bow to Sītā who does good to all.... I pray to everyone with folded hands because I know that Lord Rāma and Sītā reside in their hearts..... . I bow to all categories of beings, including the demons, and I pray that all of them may be kind to me.

5.77. The ideal that Tulasī exemplified was not that of a saint aiming to achieve only personal salvation or mukti, but rather it was that of a saint or a bhakta who wants to do Rāma-kāj, that is, God's work for the good of all. In Uttarakāṇḍa, Tulasī declares that, for a bhakta, there is no charm in mukti—

as vichāri hari bhagat sayāne
mukti nirādar bhagati lubhāne.

Simple Meaning—It is the considered opinion of wise bhaktas that they want to continue as bhaktas even if it means disrespect towards mukti i.e. giving up the desire for mukti.

5.78. Vinay-Patrikā contains several prayers where the above-mentioned ideal is explicitly stated by Tulasī. For our present purposes, two quotations from Vinay-Patrikā would suffice—

kabahunk hon yahi rahani rahongo
......sant....subhāv gahongo.....
par-hit nirat nirantar.....bhagati lahongo.

Simple Meaning—O Rāma, will there be a time when I shall acquire the nature of a saint, that is, I shall be such a bhakta who is constantly engaged in doing good to others.

ko jāne ko jaihai jampur ko surpur pardhām ko
tulsihi bahut bhalo lāgat jag jīvan rāmgulām ko.

Simple Meaning—Who knows who will go to hell or heaven or even param-dhām i.e. mukti? Tulasī is perfectly happy to remain in the world as 'Rāma-gulām' (i.e. Rāma's servant) doing Rāma-kāj for the good of all.

CHAPTER SIX

Call to Adapt to Changing Needs—Desh-Kāla-Pātra

6.1. The subject of this chapter is related to that of chapter three in which the dharma, enunciated by the Gītā as well as the Mānas, was linked to the Avatāra declaration. Attention was drawn in that chapter to several crucial issues that form part of the Avatāra doctrine as envisaged in the Vedic tradition. One of these issues was the role of the Avatāra for bringing the practice of dharma in tune with the changing needs of the society. Because of the importance given to this issue by the Gītā as well as the Mānas, further light thereon will be thrown in the present chapter. In terms of the ten key words or phrases that were identified in chapter two for conveying the message of universal welfare, the contents of the present chapter is related to item number four, viz. "desh-kāla-pātra" which literally means "place, time and the worthiness of the cause". This expression is from the Gītā—and the question pertaining to the corresponding Mānas-expression has been raised and answered in paragraphs 2.15-17.

Yuga-Dharma—Another Name for Avatāra-Dharma

6.2. As a part of the Avatāra declaration, Lord Krishna says in verse IV.8 of the Gītā—

> *sambhavāmi yuge yuge*

i.e. God appears as an Avatāra in every yuga. This suggests the equivalence of the two expressions—'Avatāra-dharma' and 'Yuga-dharma'. The latter expression occurs in the Mānas too, for example, in Uttarakāṇḍa—

> *budh jug dharma jāni man māhīṇ*
> *taji adharma rati dharma karāhīṇ*

Simple Meaning—Wise people understand the importance of 'yug-dharma' which helps in distinguishing dharma from adharma.

6.3. If we interpret the expression 'yuga-dharma' literally, we can associate a particular variant of dharma with each of the four yugas—satya, tretā, dvāpar and kali. This meaning is conveyed by the following verse which occurs in the Mahābhārata as well as Manusmṛti—

> *anye kritayuge dharmās tretāyāṃ dvāpare'pare*
> *anye kaliyuge nriṇāṃ yugarhāsānurūpataḥ*

Simple Meaning—The shape of dharma changes from yuga to yuga, therefore, we need to recognize that each of the four yugas—satya, tretā, dvāpar and kali—has its own specific dharma.

6.4. However, since the duration of each yuga is very long, it is doubtful whether a single variant of dharma can fulfil the needs of the individuals and the society for the whole of each yuga. It is advisable, therefore, to envisage that, even before the end of a yuga, some of the elements of dharma may need to be modified. This can be considered as a practical interpretation of 'yuga-dharma'—to distinguish it from the literal interpretation mentioned above.

Doctrine of Change Brought Out from Avatāra Declaration

6.5. K.M. Panikkar is of opinion that in the days prior to Lokamanya Tilak, both yuga-dharma and Avatāra-dharma were interpreted so narrowly that even the need for human initiative to bring about changes was not recognized. Tilak characterized this as a 'perverted interpretation' and blamed the scholars of the school of renunciation, who were known as 'jñānins' or followers of the jñānayoga. Here is a part of the long argument put forward by Tilak—

> "It is totally improper for a jñānin to give up universal welfare, and say that "Parameshwara will maintain the world the way He likes; that is no part of my duty," because, whatever Parameshwara has to do, He will get it done through the medium of human beings."[1]

6.6. Panikkar gives credit to Tilak for putting an end to the narrow, anti-social interpretation of yuga-dharma which had come in the way of innovation and change. Furthermore, the time of the publication of Tilak's revolutionary commentary on the Gītā was also significant because the Indian society was in a mood to listen to new ideas in the beginning of the twentieth century. This is how Panikkar assesses the significance of Tilak's *Gītā-Rahasya*—and this is relevant to what we want to say in the present chapter—

> "To a static society held down by custom and tradition and suffocated by the accretions of ages, *Gītā-Rahasya's* teaching that change is divinely ordained when society has decayed, came as a life-giving revelation. There it was provided in the most authoritative text (i.e. the Gītā) that dharma requires to be restated in every age and society must be reorganized to suit new needs. No stronger weapon could have been put in the hands of those who desired to reshape Indian society and give it purpose and vitality."[2]

6.7. In the remainder of this chapter, we shall discuss the doctrine of change, by proceeding from particular examples and then going on to general issues. More specifically, we shall explain how the Gītā changed the Vedic form of yajña and also the Upaniṣadic concept of sannyāsa. Then we shall take up the key words of the Gītā, viz. desh-kāla-pātra. As we have done in the previous chapters, the material from the Mānas will follow that from the Gītā.

How the Gītā Changed the Vedic Form of Yajña

6.8. Yajña is a Vedic term and it denoted a particular type of ceremonial act in those days. But with the passage of time, the need for bringing about a change in the form of yajña was felt. The Gītā did that, but still retained the term 'yajña' to denote new forms thereof. Since this is the most important illustration of modifying an element of dharma to suit changing social needs, it will be useful to present some details relating thereto.

6.9. The first point to note is the early recognition in Indian thought of two streams of religious practice. In fact, a clear distinction was made in the Vedas, Brāhmaṇās and Upaniṣads, between karmakānḍa and jñānakānḍa, or the path of work and the path of knowledge. The Vedic yajña was the most important element of karmakānḍa. The famous Purusha Sūkta of Rigveda attributed the creation of the universe itself to yajña. Every desired object could be achieved if the specified yajña was performed correctly.

6.10. Every yajña had four components—dravya or sacrificial matter, tyāga or the relinquishing of the object sacrificed, a devatā or deity to be addressed as the recipient, and mantra or Vedic hymn to be chanted. The closing words of every mantra were 'idaṃ na mama' i.e. it is not mine. We shall explain in chapter nine how the Gītā utilized the spirit behind these words to give the message of selfless service.

6.11. At the time of the Upaniṣads, the emphasis shifted from karmakāṇḍa to jñānakāṇḍa, and the faith of the people in Vedic yajña was shaken. The Upaniṣads taught that a genuine release from the bondage of karma was possible, not through yajña, but only through knowledge. However, with the lapse of time, pursuit of knowledge was delinked not only from yajña but from karma as such. How the Gītā modified the Upaniṣadic concept of sannyāsa will be explained in paragraphs 6.20-22.

6.12. Coming back to yajña, the main change that the Gītā introduced was to remove the element of selfish desire. For example, through a Vedic yajña, householders wanted to obtain children, grandchildren, cows, horses or other wealth in this life and a happy state after death. According to the Gītā, selfish desires lead to attachment i.e. āsakti or sanga, which in turn causes bondage. Verse III.9 contains this new idea of the Gītā—

tadarthaṃ karma kaunteya
mukta saṅgaḥ samācara

Simple Meaning—Lord Krishna tells Arjuna, working for yajña is good provided that the doer of the yajña is free from attachment.

Although it may look like a simple change suggested by the Gītā, it transforms the entire concept of Vedic yajña. As Dr. Radhakrishnan says, "The religious duty to the Vedic gods here becomes service of creation in the name of the supreme."[3]

6.13. In verses III.14-16, the Gītā presents a world-wide chain of interdependence which involves yajña, performance of other acts, food production, all human beings, all creation, nature and God. It can be called "a wheel of yajña or karma" because yajña as well as karma constitutes an important link in this chain, and the wheel conveys the idea of continuity and preservation of the creation because God Himself is intimately connected therewith. The importance of keeping the wheel in motion is stressed by Lord Krishna in verse III.16—

evaṃ pravartitaṃ cakraṃ
nā'nuvartayatī'ha yaḥ

Simple Meaning—It will create problems if any one does anything to put an obstacle in the turning of this wheel which has been going on.

Upadhyaya calls it the "wheel of the world" and emphasizes that the Gītā's concept of yajña involves selfless service to world—

> "As the origin of the world is traced to God, and God Himself is engaged in the work of maintaining the world-order, it becomes the duty of man to live in the world and promote its welfare. The wheel of the world, according to the Gītā, goes on by means of sacrifice or renunciation, and one who does not discharge his selfless service to the world lives only in vain."[4]

6.14. Verses IV.23-33 give the message that yajña can be performed in many ways, including, for example, the yogic breath control (prāṇāyāma), controlling the senses so that they function within limits, and doing tapas i.e. discipline and austerities. In fact, the process of realizing the supreme through one's acts, by dedicating them to God, is also yajña. Although 'dravya' or sacrificial matter was an important component of a Vedic yajña (reference para 6.10), the Gītā did not attach much value thereto, as we find in verse IV.33—

> *śreyān dravyamayādyajñāj*
> *jñānayajñah paramtapa*

Simple Meaning—Lord Krishna says, in comparison to a yajña based on 'dravya' (material), a yajña based on jñāna (knowledge) is superior.

Gītā's Approach to Yajña Carried Further

6.15. Modern interpreters of the Gītā—Tilak, Aurobindo, Gandhi, Vinoba—encouraged by the new approach, found new forms of yajña, in tune with the changing needs of the society. For example, Tilak argued that it is better to offer animal tendencies like desire, anger, egotism, etc. by way of sacrifice into the fire of mental control, than to offer commodities or animals into sacrificial fire. In his view, yajña meant working for 'lokasaṃgraha' i.e. good of the world. (More on lokasaṃgraha in chapter eight). The most important component of 'lokasaṃgraha' at that time was to obtain 'swarāj' (self-rule). So Tilak became a pioneer in interpreting Gītā-concepts (including yajña) from a political angle.

6.16. Aurobindo further strengthened the link between yajña and the freedom movement. Just as offerings put into the sacrificial fire bear fruit only if they are pure and dedicated to the deity with full faith and devotion, Aurobindo wanted his countrymen to be ready to sacrifice their all—even lives—in the struggle for freedom—

> "Liberty is the fruit we seek from the sacrifice, and the Motherland, the Goddess to whom we offer it; into the seven leaping tongues of the fire of the yajña we must offer all that we are and all that we have, feeding the fire even with our blood and lives and happiness of our nearest and dearest; for the Motherland is a Goddess who loves not a maimed and imperfect sacrifice, and freedom was never won from the gods by a grudging giver."[5]

6.17. Gandhi carried further the task of modifying the meaning of yajña so as to make it increasingly relevant to current conditions. This was a twofold process. On the one hand, it meant identifying new approaches and productive activities (like khādī and village industries) which if undertaken in a spirit of yajña could help the society. Secondly, Gandhi also suggested the abandonment of the traditional way of performing a yajña, for example, burning of wood. Although fire was the symbol of yajña in Vedic times, the Gītā (verse IV.24) envisaged the possibility of using fire in a symbolic sense. Gandhi wanted public opinion to be created in favour of subjecting every religious practice to the test of relevance in modern times—

> "I cannot understand the idea that one can perform yajña by lighting a few sticks. It does not do to say that doing so purifies the air. There are many other ways of purifying the air. Why should we at all pollute the air? But this is not the aim behind a yajña... There were big forests in those days, and it may have been regarded as every one's duty to help in clearing these forests, for it was a social necessity.... In burning wood in this age, we misuse the capital of our forefathers, or we show ourselves witless pedants by understanding the thing in a literal sense."[6]

6.18. Gandhi also suggested during the freedom struggle that the wheel of yajña (reference paragraph 6.13) should in today's conditions mean the spinning wheel—

> "Whereas in old days, cutting down trees and burning wood had become a yajña, at the present time, spinning and other village industries have become a yajña. If water was scarce and we had to fetch it from a distance of two miles, fetching water would be a yajña."[7]

6.19. Vinoba carried further the above approach and argued that chapter XVII of the Gītā, in which yajña, dānaṃ and tapas are viewed as 'triple duty', should be interpreted with reference to three levels of creation, viz. nature, society, and body. According to this interpretation, yajña represents the effort made to replenish nature's loss. Afforestation, tree-planting and improvements in agriculture thus constituted yajña.

How Gītā Modified the Upaniṣadic Concept of Sannyāsa

6.20. Bṛhadāranyka Upaniṣad presents a picture of wandering mendicants who give up their homes to concentrate attention on the search for Brahman. A glimpse of this picture is provided by the words—

prajāṃ na kāmayante

i.e. they do not desire progeny.

6.21. Since the main teaching of the Gītā is 'karmayoga' (not karmakāṇḍa of paragraph 6.9), it does not envisage the giving up of one's duties and social obligations, by any person at any stage. Bondage, according to the Gītā, is not caused by karma, but by attachment to the fruits of one's action. A brief summary of Gītā's ideas on bondage, attachment, and sannyāsa is contained in verses IV.22, III.19 and III.4, parts of which are quoted below in that order—

samaḥ siddhāvasiddhau ca
kṛtvā'pi na nibadhyate...

asakto hyācarankarmu
paramāpnoti pūruṣaḥ....

na ca sannyasanādeva
siddhiṃ samadhigacchati

Simple Meaning—Actions do not cause any bondage to a karmayogin because he or she performs them without attachment, staying even-minded in success or failure....Such a person attains the highest state i.e. liberated while still alive.... On the other hand, it is inadvisable to think that physical renunciation will lead to liberation. In other words, what is important is mental renunciation, accompanied with performance of one's duties without attachment to the fruits thereof.

6.22. D.S. Sarma is of opinion that the emphasis on jñāna in the

Upaniṣads had encouraged karma-sannyāsa (i.e. giving up of karma), but the problem was set right by the Gītā—

"The Gītā supplied a much needed corrective to the over-emphasis on jñāna and renunciation, which had led to more quietism. It may be said that the whole Gītā is a long and sustained protest against the dangers of quietism."[8]

Gītā's Approach Supported by Tulasī Too

6.23. Modifications suggested by the Gītā in regard to yajña and sannyāsa have been generally supported by Tulasīdās also, although he did not go into the same type of details. Taking yajña first, the mere fact that Rāvaṇa and his son Meghnād performed yajñas did not make them good in the opinion of Mānas (or sāttvika in the terminology of the Gītā). The purpose for which yajñna is done and the manner in which it is done have to be appropriate, both morally and socially.

6.24. Why was Meghnād's yajña considered bad? Mahatma Gandhi's comment on 'animal sacrifice' is relevant to this question—

"It is possible that, in the age prior to that of the Gītā, offering of animals as sacrifice was permissible. But there is not a trace of it in the sacrifice in the Gītā sense."[9]

Tulasī says in Laṇkākāṇḍa that 'animal sacrifice' done by Meghnād for his yajña made it unholy—

meghnād makh karai apāvan...
āhuti det rudhir aru bhainsā

Simple Meaning—The yajña of Meghnād was impure because he made offerings of blood and buffalo.

6.25. Subsequently, but in the same canto, Tulasī finds fault with the yajña of Rāvaṇa too because its purpose was bad—

uhāṇ desānan .... karai kachhu yajña......
rām virodh .... haṭh bas ... svārath man rātā

Simple Meaning—There, i.e. in Laṅkā, Rāvaṇa performed some sort of yajña, but his motive was bad—he was antagonistic to Rāma (i.e. dharma), he was obstinate in sticking to a wrong cause because he was utterly selfish.

6.26. The above illustrations relate to what makes a yajña bad i.e. the negative aspect. However, the Gītā and Tulasīdās agree on the positive aspect too, i.e. which yajña is good. First, we have verse X.25 of the Gītā—

yajñānāṃ japayajno'smi

Simple Meaning—Lord Krishna says, among yajñas, I am japayajña, i.e. repetition of God's name is an excellent yajña.

Parallel to this, we have Tulasī glorification of japa in Vinay Patrika—

rām japu ..... sānurag re
kali māhin....jīvan-adhār re

Simple Meaning—Perform yajña in the form of reciting of Rāma's name with genuine devotion in heart—this will sustain you in kaliyuga.

Tulasī's views on yajña will be referred to again in chapter nine.

6.27. Next, in regard to sannyāsa, we mentioned in paragraph 6.21 that the Gītā values mental renunciation without any outward show. Tulasīdās, looking at conditions in kaliyuga, not only accepted Gītā's view, but even went a step further. He warned that sannyāsins of kaliyuga misused the outward appearance of renunciation for immoral purposes of deceiving and cheating innocent people. Here is a glimpse of what the Mānas says in Uttarakāṇḍa—

jākeṇ nakh aru jatā visālā
soi tāpas prasiddha kalikālā
soi sayān jo pardhan hārī

Simple Meaning—Sannyāsins in kaliyuga become famous by their appearance—long hair, nails, etc., but their real intentions are bad—they want to cheat people.

More on kaliyuga in chapter eleven.

Quotations about Desh-Kāla-Patra

6.28. So far we concentrated our attention on two particular instances, viz. yajña and sannyāsa, to highlight the importance of adjusting religious practices to changing social needs. From the particular, we now move on to the general suggestion made in verses XVII.20-22 of the Gītā—and we feel that the presentation will be more effective if we look at these three verses in the reverse order, i.e. 22, 21 and 20. So here is verse XVII.22—

adeśakāle yaddānaṃ apātrebhyaśca dīyate
asatkṛtamavajñātaṃtattāmasamudāhṛitaṃ

Simple Meaning—That gift which is made at a wrong place or time or to an unworthy person, without proper respect or with contempt, that is declared to be tāmasika or bad.

6.29. The main message of this verse is that even the act of giving—which is normally considered be a good act—may become bad under the circumstances indicated in the verse. Wrong place, wrong time, improper way of giving—all these are certainly matters of concern, but perhaps the most damaging to the welfare of the society is the unworthiness of the recipient. Swami Chidbhavananda has explained who these unworthy recipients could be—

"Persons unworthy of charity and gifts are they who are of questionable character, who are devoid of self-control, who do not engage themselves in the welfare of beings, and who squander away money."[10]

6.30. Next we look at verse XVII.21—

yat tu pratyupakārārthaṃ phalamuddiśya vā punaḥ
dīyate ca parikliṣṭaṃ taddānaṃ rājasaṃ smṛtaṃ

Simple Meaning—That gift which is made with the hope of a return or with the expectation of future gain or when it hurts to give—that is rājasi i.e. of average quality.

6.31. Finally, we have verse XVII.20—

dātavyamiti yaddānaṃdīyate'nupakāriṇe
deśe kāle ca pātre ca taddānaṃ sāttvikaṃ smṛtaṃ

Simple Meaning—That gift which is made to one from whom no return is expected, with the feeling that it is one's duty to give and which is given in proper place and time and to a worthy person—that is held to be sāttvika i.e. good.

We feel that although the words 'desh-kāla-pātra' occur in this verse in the context of dānam (gift), they are applicable to religious practices in general—and they point out the importance of adapting these practices to changing social needs.

Other Gītā-Quotations that Support Adjustment

6.32. Besides the verses quoted above, there are several others in the various chapters of the Gītā which draw attention to the need for adjustment. We shall draw attention to only four of them. First, Lord Krishna implicitly tells Arjuna at the very outset, viz. in verse II.2, that your faintheartedness might have been excusable under non-critical circumstances, but they have no place "in this hour of crisis"—

viṣame samupasthitaṃ

i.e. remember that you are face-to-face with a crisis-situation. That is why Klostermaier has called the Gītā "a book of crisis".[11]

6.33. A similar suggestion is implicitly associated with the words that Lord Krishna speaks towards the end of his teaching, viz. in verse XVIII.63—

vimṛśyaitadaśeṣeṇa yathecchasi tathā kuru

Simple Meaning—Reflect fully on what I have said, and then do what you think is the best for you.

The implication is that nothing is imposed upon Arjuna. He must take into account his own situation before deciding upon the action that he need to do.

6.34. The above two verses refer respectively, to the beginning and the end of Lord Krishna's teaching. During the course of the teaching too, when the example-setting role of great personalities of the past is depicted, Krishna sounds a note of caution not to follow them blindly, for example, in verse IV.15-16—

kuru karmaiva tasmāttvaṃpūrvaiḥ pūrvataraṃ kṛtaṃ
kiṃ karma kimakarmeti kavayo' pyatra mohitāḥ

Simple Meaning—Lord Krishna says, O Arjuna, noble persons from times immemorial have set an example for others to follow, but everyone has to choose and decide carefully because it is not easy to determine what is karma and what is akarma.

6.35. Obviously, the question that underlies the need for careful consideration is, "How far are old ideas still relevant?" The Sanskrit word 'naṣṭaḥ' used by Lord Krishna in verse IV.2, although literally meaning 'destroyed', should really be interpreted as 'became irrelevant', because the yoga taught to the sun is 'avyaya' i.e. imperishable, and so cannot be destroyed. With this explanation, let us look at verses IV.1-2—

imaṃ vivasvate yogaṃproktavānahamavyayaṃ...
sa kāleneha mahatā yogo naṣṭaḥ paraṃtapa

Simple Meaning—Lord Krishan says, I proclaimed imperishable yoga to the sun...but through long lapse of time, even that yoga became partially irrelevant.

Dr. Radhakrishnan says that the imprishable yoga is "for the welfare of humanity"[12], and to serve that purpose, it has to be readjusted from time to time.

Corresponding Quotations from the Mānas

6.36. Tulasīdās fully supports the 'desh-kāl-pātra' view of the Gītā, and we shall give several illustrations from the text of the Mānas. However, before doing that, we want to point out the significance of the fact that Tulasī called the Mānas as—

sakalkalikalushvidhvansan

i.e. a remover of all the evils of kaliyuga for the benefit of all. That is why he modified Vālmīki Rāmāyaṇa and presented a version which he thought would solve the problems of kaliyuga.

6.37. Now the Mānas-quotations. Both Lord Rāma and Guru Vashishṭh gave suggestions after taking into account time, place and other considerations. First, we consider the role of Rāma. Ayodhyākāṇḍa describes the background as well as how Rāma responded—

nidharak baithi kahai kaṭu bānī
sunat kaṭhintā ati akulānī...
desh kāl avasar anusārī
bole vachan vinīt vichārī

Simple Meaning—Kaikeyī had created a difficult situation, by speaking bitter words that deeply hurt King Dashrath...Rāma tried to find a way out of the difficulty, and he spoke softly, words that were appropriate to time, place and occasion.

6.38. Again, a delicate situation arose in Chitrakūṭ and it was difficult to decide what would be best. Tulasī says in the latter part of

Ayodhyākāṇḍa that Rāma took into account time, place, occasion and society—

desh kāl lakhi samay samājū....
bole vachan vāni sarvasu se
hit pariṇām sunat sasi rasu se

Simple Meaning—Words that Rāma spoke were sweet like nectar and they were aimed to achieve the good of all... it was clear that Rāma had taken into account time, place, occasion and society.

We recall that a reference to these Mānas-words was made by us in paragraph 2.16—and we remarked there that the use of the word 'samāj' (meaning society) shows that Tulasī not only supported 'desh-kāl-pātra' doctrine of the Gītā, but even went a step further.

6.39. Many more instances like the above could be cited, but we feel that we can end this chapter by giving only one more quotation, viz. that relating to Guru Vashishṭh. The occasion is the arrival of King Janak in Chitrakūṭ to help resolve the problem created by Kaikeyī. About the important role of Guru Vashishṭh, Tulasī says in Ayodhyākāṇḍa—

gaye janak raghunāth samīpā...
samay samāj dharam avirodhā
bole tab raghuvansh purodhā

Simple Meaning—King Janak joined the assembly which had gathered around Rāma...Guru Vashishṭh took into consideration the gravity of the occasion, and also the expectations of the assembly, but he also realized that maintenance of dharma was his priority too. Tulasī says that the words that Guru Vashishṭh spoke were the most appropriate under these circumstances.

CHAPTER SEVEN

Call for the Good of All— Sarvabhūtahitaṃ or Sakal-Mangal

7.1. The process of explaining the ten key words or phrases, that we began in chapter three, has now arrived at the mid-way point because the subject of the present chapter is the fifth of these ten expressions. But apart from the positional significance, the expression that we are going to explain now—i.e. sarvabhūtahitaṃ—has attracted special attention because it conveys most explicitly the message of the good of all. In the early years of the twentieth century, a common criticism (of course, uninformed) of the Vedic literature was that it was difficult to locate therein a direct statement of the social message expressed in a non-ambiguous manner. It was on the basis of the expression 'sarvabhūtahitaṃ' that Gītā-scholars were able to give the most effective answer to such criticism. The corresponding expression in the Mānas too, i.e. sakal-mangal, has provided to readers the most convincing proof of the existence therein of the message of the good of all.

Sarva—The Most Frequently Used Word in the Gītā

7.2. The fact that the word 'sarva'—meaning 'all'—occurs so many times in the Gītā, has, in our opinion, not only linguistic significance but also philosophical importance. One of the messages that we get from this is that God cares for all beings. For example, verse V.29 (already referred to by us in paragraph 4.5) says—

suhridaṃ sarvabhūtānāṃ

i.e. God is the Friend of all beings, doing good to them without expecting anything in return.

7.3. A related message is that the simplest way to attain God is to try to do good to all. This is the sarvabhūtahitaṃ message which is contained in two verses (V.25 and XII.4)—

labhante brahmanirvāṇaṃ riṣayaḥ kṣīṇakalmaṣāḥ
chhinnadvaidhā yatātmānaḥ sarvabhūtahite ratāḥ.

Simple Meaning—Rishis whose sins are destroyed, whose doubts or dualities are cut asunder, whose minds are disciplined and who rejoice in doing good to all beings—they attain brahmanirvāṇa

saṃniyamye'ndriyagrāmaṃ sarvatra samabuddhayaḥ
te prāpnuvanti māmeva sarvabhūtahite ratāḥ.

Simple Meaning—Lord Krishna says, those who restrain and discipline all the senses, who are even-minded in all situations, and who rejoice in doing good to all beings—they attain Me.

Practical Steps Towards Sarvabhūtahitaṃ

7.4. The most feasible way to proceed to the high goal of sarvabhūtahitaṃ, which the Gītā has repeatedly suggested, is 'svadharma' i.e. to carry on one's duty. In terms of the sattva-rajas-tamas classification, the first practical step is to avoid tāmasika i.e. bad karma, in accordance with verse XVIII.25—

anubandhaṃ kṣayaṃ himsāṃ anavekṣya ca pauruṣaṃ
mohādārabhyate karma yattattāmasamucyate.

Simple Meaning—Lord Krishna says, a tāmasika karma is that which is undertaken through ignorance, without taking into account four things, viz. consequence, loss, violence, and the capability of the doer.

7.5. In day-to-day life, we can avoid being tāmasika by doing only those things which are socially useful and which promote non-violence. But these are external considerations. In addition to these, the last item in the above verse draws attention to an internal factor, viz. the capacity of the doer. In other words, the Gītā wants everyone to try to do only that much of sarvabhūtahitaṃ which is within the doer's capacity, and so can be done efficiently, because otherwise it will not come up to the desired standard of 'yogaḥ karmasu kauśalaṃ' (which means that yoga is skill in action).

Serve According to Capacity—Story from Mahābhārata

7.6. The Mahābhārata has illustrated, by means of the story of a mongoose, that even a small help given by a poor person is more praiseworthy than a big one given by a king. We first state the conclusion of the story, in the form of the following verse from the Mahābhārata—

sahasraśaktiśca śatam śataśaktirdaśāpi ca
dadyādāpaśca yaḥ śaktyā sarve tulyaphalāḥ smritāḥ.

Simple Meaning—A person who owns a thousand giving a hundred, or a person who owns a hundred giving ten, or a person giving only a drink of water according to one's capacity—all these acts are equally praiseworthy.

7.7. The message about 'giving only a drink of water', as stated in the above verse, reminds us of verse IX.26 of the Gītā—

pattraṃ puṣpaṃ phalaṃ toyaṃ yo me bhaktyā prayacchati
tadahaṃ bhaktyuparhitaṃ aśnāmi prayatātmanaḥ.

Simple Meaning—Lord Krishna says, whosoever offers to Me with devotion a leaf, a flower, a fruit, or water—that offering of love, of the pure of heart, I accept.

7.8. Now the mongoose story in brief. When Yudhishthira ascended the throne after the defeat of the Kauravas, food was served to thousands of people who, in turn, admired his generosity. But a half-golden mongoose expressed disagreement with such admiration, and he explained this in the following words—A poor brahrmin, with his wife and children, who had not eaten for many days, finally got some food. However, just then a hungry mendicant came. The poor family made a sacrifice by giving all the food to the hungry visitor. When I rolled about in the remnants of food in that house, half of my body became golden. Now, although I rolled about in the remnants of food in this vast canopy of Yudhishthira, the remaining half of my body has not become golden.

Journey from Sva to Sarva—Views of Commentators

7.9. The question as to how the Gītā encourages everyone to orient one's capabilities to the goal of the good of all has been studied by many scholars and social workers. We summarize below the findings of only four of them, viz. Donald Bishop, Kashinath Upadhyaya, Lokmanya Tilak, and Mahatma Gandhi.

7.10. Bishop views the Gītā as a book which not only offers practical directions for people to follow in the battle of life but also has a big appeal, providing encouragement towards every one's participation and purification—

> "In life we are constantly engaged in a struggle both within and without between the forces of good and evil.... The Gītā gives us guidance or a set of beliefs to help us in that battle... It is a source of inspiration... The message of the Gītā is that the tendency of the universe is toward consolidation through purification. That consolidation consists of the harmony of man with man and with nature on the Maya level and the union of man with Brahman on the absolute level. That union is accomplished through participation on the part of both man and God, man becoming purified in the process. The Gītā, as a synthesis of Indian thought, describes different ways of joining with Brahman. It does not declare one to be better than the other, for each leads the sojourner to his true destination, God."[1]

7.11. Upadhyaya has put together in one place as many as eight Gītā verses (or parts or sets thereof), to document his statement that 'the general tone of the Gītā is one of encouragement...in carrying on one's worldly duties with a purity of purpose as far as possible'. Upadhyaya's study is basically a comparison between early Buddhism and the Gītā. He says that early Buddhism prescribed disinterested action only after the attainment of perfection, but that the Gītā wanted the practice of nishkāma karma from the very beginning without first realizing the infallible stage of perfection. The Gītā says that 'abhyāsa' i.e. long practice will bring perfection. In other words, nishkāma karma for serving humanity is suggested all the way. We referred to this in paragraph 5.13, but it is interesting to see Upadhyaya's interpretation too, expressed in the following words—

> "The Gītā speaks of two stages of disinterested action—the one which is performed by the aspiring saint (āruruksa) with a view to reaching perfection, and the other which is performed by the perfect or accomplished saint (siddha or yogārūḍha) with a view to serving humanity with perfect equanimity."[2]

7.12. Upadhyaya says that apart from recommending 'abhyāsa' (which has been done six times in the Gītā), the message of encouragement has been strengthened by Lord Krishna by an assurance—

mā śucaḥ

i.e. grieve not. In fact, verse XVI.5 (where these words occur) contain such an assurance, not only for Arjuna, but also for all mankind—

> *mā śucaḥ sampadaṃ daivīṃ*
> *abhijato'si pāṇḍava.*

Simple Meaning—Grieve not because your inherent nature has divine endowments.

7.13. Upadhyaya draws attention to the fact that the assurance "mā śucaḥ" occurs again towards the end of Lord Krishna's teaching (i.e. in verse XVIII.66)—

> *ahaṃ tvā sarvapāpebhyo*
> *mokṣayiṣyāmi mā śucaḥ.*

Simple Meaning—Grieve not, I shall free you from all sins.

7.14. Furthermore, says Upadhyaya, even in regard to the attainment of jñāna, the Gītā gives encouragement in verse IV.38—

> *tat svayaṃ yogasaṃsiddhaḥ*
> *kālenā'tmani vindati.*

Simple Meaning—He who acquires perfection in nishkāma karma, attains jñāna, in his self, by himself, in course of time.

7.15. We do not want to prolong this section by trying to cover all the verses which Upadhyaya used to discover messages of encouragement in the Gītā. However, we reproduce below the closing arguments of Upadhyaya, based on the closing verses of chapter VI of the Gītā—

> "When Arjuna, referring to the highly difficult process of yoga, asks Krishna about the fate of those who, though endowed with faith, fail to follow the yoga to perfection, and being careless fall from it, Krishna at once encourages him by saying 'There is no destruction (setback) for him, either here or elsewhere. One who has done good can never tread the path of woe.' Then it is pointed out how after having spent a happy life in heaven for long, he is born in the family of those who are pure and prosperous, or in the family of glorious yogins themselves and ultimately 'perfecting himself' through many lives, he reaches the supreme goal."[3]

7.16. Tilak's statements about the journey from 'sva' to 'sarva' are perhaps more explicit than those of Upadhyaya. Tilak's reasoning is elaborated in two stages. First, he interpreted the Gītā in such a way as to assert that its main message is lokasaṃgraha-centred karmayoga. Secondly, he emphasized that, everyone, small or big, should, by performing svadharma, contribute to one or the other aspect of lokasaṃgraha i.e. the good of the world.

7.17. We feel that the next chapter of this book (dealing with lokasaṃgraha) will be the right place for presenting the first stage of Tilak's reasoning. However, the present section is appropriate to summarize Tilak's views for encouraging all members of the society to contribute to social causes. These views themselves cover the subject from two angles—one related to coördination between the inner and outer development of each person, and the second related to the inter-connected nature of the society.

7.18. Tilak believes that the process of achieving inner purity of mind should go hand-in-hand with the outer process of performing svadharma oriented to the good of the society—

> "It is the highest ideal of everybody to make his mind pure like that of a sthitaprajña...However, one need not wait for performing action until that ideal has been reached. While efforts for inner purity are made, one should perform all actions with as much unselfishness as possible. Thereby the reason will become purer and purer, and the society need not wait to receive the contribution of each and every person."[4]

7.19. Finally, Tilak based his appeal for universal participation in social work, on the inter-connected nature of the society—

> "Every human being...acquires by birth, the high or low qualification of maintaining and uplifting society according to his or her own powers, and proportionately with whatever capacity is either naturally possessed by him, or can be acquired by him, having regard to his status in life. Just as extremely small wheels are necessary along with large wheels in order that any machine should work properly, so also is it necessary that the authority of common-place persons should be exercised properly and fully in the same way as the authority of superior persons like Vyasa and others, in order that the immense and ponderous activity or mechanism of the cosmos should continue to work in a properly regulated manner...If the potters do not manufacture pots or weavers do not weave cloth, the maintenance of society cannot be satisfactorily carried out, even if the king protects the society properly."[5]

7.20. Although Gandhi, like Tilak, also wanted mass-scale participation in socio-political activities, he (Gandhi) prescribed certain minimum standards for all such participants. The most obvious condition to be observed by all satyāgrahīs (the ideal for whom was the sthitaprajña of the Gītā), was that they could not cause physical injury to the opponent. Although non-violence ideally meant no injury by thought, word, and deed, it was obviously too much to expect that millions of ordinary people would come up to that lofty standard. Nevertheless, when cases of physical violence against the British officials or their supporters were brought to the attention of Gandhi, he suspended the movement itself.

7.21. Standards of self-discipline and purity, which Gandhi prescribed for the Ashram-residents, were broadly patterned so as to come as close as possible to the sthitaprajña-ideal. However, for ordinary participants in the Satyāgraha movements, certain feasible standards were indicated from time to time. For example, a list of seven qualifications, which Gandhi considered essential for every satyāgrahī in India, reads as follows—

(i) He must have a living faith in God, for He is his only Rock.
(ii) He must believe in truth and non-violence as his creed and therefore have faith in the inherent goodness of human nature which he expects to evoke by his truth and love expressed through his suffering.
(iii) He must be leading a chaste life and be ready and willing for the sake of his cause to give up his life and his possessions.
(iv) He must be a habitual khadi-weaver and spinner. This is essential for India.
(v) He must be a teetotaller and be free from the use of other intoxicants in order that his reason may be always unclouded and his mind constant.
(vi) He must carry out with a willing heart all the rules of discipline as may be laid from time to time.
(vii) He should carry out the jail rules unless they are specially devised to hurt his self-respect.

The above qualifications are not to be regarded as exhaustive. They are illustrative only.[6]

Journey from Sva to Sarva—Success by God's Help

7.22. Just as an Avatāra helps when righteous human effort is not adequate to overpower the unrighteous forces, similarly, the journey from sva to sarva is, according to the Gītā, facilitated by God's help.

The success achieved by social workers in the face of heavy odds provides support to this view. Textual support to this can be derived from verses XI.3 and 8—

draṣṭumicchāmī te rūpaṃ aiśvaraṃ puruṣottama....
na tu māṃ śakyase draṣṭuṃ anenaiva svacakṣuṣā
divyaṃ dadāmi te cakṣuḥ paśya me yogamaiśvaraṃ.

Simple Meaning—Arjuna said, O Purushottama, I have a keen desire to see Your Cosmic Form. Since this desire of Arjuna was sattvika, Lord Krishna replied, your own eyes (sva-cakṣu) have only limited capability, but I shall give you divine eyes (ḍivya-cakṣu) so that your desire may be fulfilled.

In this case, God helped take Arjuna from sva to divya which symbolizes sarva.

Journey from Sva to Sakal—Tulasī's View

7.23. All that we have written above, in this chapter, explaining Gītā's views, has been accepted by Tulasīdāsa, and he has illustrated these ideas by means of many examples. We shall summarize Tulasī's views in four sections, namely—

(a) 'Sakal'—Tulasī's favourite word for 'sarva'
(b) 'Mati' and 'Bal' correspond to Gītā's 'paurush'
(c) Sakal-mangal and sakal-sukh correspond to sarvabhūtahitaṃ
(d) Journey from sva to sakal—by Rāma's help.

Next, the presentation of each of these four sections, one by one.

(a) ***Sakal—Tulasī's Favourite Word for Sarva***

7.24. Just as the word 'sarva'—meaning all—occurs so many times in the Gītā, the corresponding word 'sakal' occurs again and again in Tulasī's writings. He called the Mānas as—

sakalkalikalushvidhvansan

i.e. the remover of all the evils of kaliyuga for all the people.

In Vinay-Patrikā, Tulasī prays to Rāma as

patit pāvan...rām kiye pāvan sakal

i.e. Lord Rāma purifies those who are down-trodden. In other words, He purifies all.

In Sanskrit verses of the Mānas, although Sītā is addressed as 'sarvaśreyaskarī' i.e. the doer of good to all, Hanumān is addressed as—

sakalguṇanidhānaṃ

i.e. the abode of all the virtues.

More instances of the use of the word 'sakal' will be given in (c).

(b) ***'Mati' and 'Bal' Correspond to Gītā's 'Paurush'***

7.25. Gītā's advice "serve according to paurush or capacity" has been given in the Mānas too. Tulasī himself declared in the beginning of the Mānas—

kavi na houṇ nahin vachan pravīnū
sakal kalā sab vidyā hīnū....
mati anurūp rām guṇ gāvaun.

Simple Meaning—Tulasī says, I am not a poet, I am not an expert in the use of words, in fact, I am devoid of 'sakal' i.e. all the training that makes a poet. Even so, I am singing and narrating the virtues of Lord Rāma, in accordance with what little 'mati' i.e. intellect that I have.

In Kishkindhākāṇḍa Lord Rāma tells Sugrīva what a sincere friend should do—

bal anumān sadā hit karaī

i.e. a friend should always help according to his or her 'bal' i.e. capacity.

(c) ***Sakal-mangal and Sakal-Sukh Correspond to Sarvabhūtahitaṃ***

7.26. We mentioned above that 'sakal' is Tulasī's favourite word for 'sarva'. Similarly, 'mangal' (meaning good) is his favourite word for 'hitaṃ.' In the opening verse of the Mānas, there is a joint prayer for Saraswatī and Ganesh, addressing them, in Sanskrit, as

mangalānāṃ kartārau

i.e. they both bring about 'mangal'.

In the body of the Mānas, the most popular prayer for Rāma, which occurs in Bālakāṇḍa, is

mangal bhavan amangal hārī

i.e. Lord Rāma is the abode of 'mangal', and He takes away all 'amangal' (which is the opposite of 'mangal').

7.27. In Sundarakāṇḍa, Tulasī says—

jāsu sakal mangal maya kītī

i.e. Lord Rāma's glory brings about 'sakal mangal', and the closing words of the same canto are—

sakal sumangal dāyak
raghunāyak guṇ gān

i.e. all those who sing about the virtues of Lord Rāma are sure to attain 'sakal mangal.'

7.28. Tulasī's famous prayer addressed to Hanumān in Vinay Patrikā begins with the words—

mangal mūrati māruti nandan
sakal amangal mūl nikandan.

Simple Meaning—Tulasī says, Hanumān is the embodiment of 'mangal'—and he also uproots and removes 'sakal amangal.'

7.29. 'Sakal-sukh' (meaning 'happiness of all') is another expression used in the Mānas for 'sarvabhūtahitaṃ' Bālakāṇḍa describes how Manu and Shatrūpā pray to God—

sevat sulabh sakal sukh dāyak.

Simple Meaning—O God, You are easily attainable to those who 'serve' mankind, and You are the giver of happiness to all.

As a follow-up of this prayer, Manu and Shatrūpā were later born as Dashrath and Kaushalyā, and God came to them in the form of their son, Rāma.

7.30. In Uttarakāṇḍa, Lord Rāma Himself tells all the citizens who had assembled to hear Him—

bhakti sutantra sakal sukh khānī

i.e. all those who want 'sakal sukh' should follow the path of bhakti.

And in the same canto, Kākbhushuṇḍī describes the smiling face of Rāma—

sakal sukhad sasi kar sam hāsā

i.e. Rāma's smile (like the soft moonlight) brings about 'sakal sukh'.

7.31. Ayodhyākāṇḍa gives a detailed account of Lord Rāma's stay in

Chitrakūṭ, along with Sītā and Lakshman. So Tulasī sings the glory of Chitrakūṭ—

jahn sukh sakal sakal dukh nāhīṇ

i.e. the place where Lord Rāma stayed not only gave 'sakal sukh' but it also removed 'sakal dukh' (i.e. unhappiness of all).

The use of both 'sukh' and 'dukh' in the same line points to its similarity with the expression 'mangal bhavan amangal hārī' which was referred to in paragraph 7.26.

7.32. More instances relating to the significance of 'sakal sukh' will be presented in the next section. However, before moving on to that, we want to say that the expression 'sarvabhūtahit' itself has been used by Tulasī in Vinay-Patrikā—

sarvabhūtahit...hoi tabahin jab dravai īsh

i.e. only by God's grace, a bhakta is able to work for and achieve sarvabhūtahit (i.e. the good of all beings).

In the Mānas, the closest that Tulasī comes to 'sarvabhūtahit' is by using the expression 'sarvahit'. Bharat's suggestion relating to that is made in the assembly at Chitrakūṭ, and it is given in Ayodhyākāṇḍa—

sab ke sammat sarvahit kariya prem pahichāni.

Simple Meaning—Bharat says, I suggest that we should do what is acceptable to all, and what is good for all, and we can find this out by appealing to Rāma's love that exists in every one's heart.

(d) ***Journey from Sva to Sakal—by Rāma's Help***

7.33. The idea that Lord Rāma or Lord Shiva helps a bhakta in progressing from personal goals to larger goals, is not only expressed in words by Tulasīdāsa, but is also effectively illustrated by what happened to him in his own life. His biographers have pointed out that, initially, Tulasī started writing in Sanskrit, but on the eighth day, he received a message from Lord Shiva in a dream, following which he wrote in the language of the common people. This event represented not merely a change of language, but more importantly, a widening of the purpose of Tulasī's writings. This is clear from the Mānas too. For example, the initial goal of Tulasī, as expressed in Sanskrit, was focused on 'sva', as the following words from Bālakāṇḍa show—

svāntaḥsukhāya tulasī raghunāthagāthā....

i.e. I am writing Rāma-kathā for my own inner happiness.

7.34. Very soon this personal goal became a part of the wider goal viz. the happiness of all, as the following quotation from Bālakāṇḍa—expressed in Hindi—shows—

rāmcharit rākesh kar
saris sukhad sab kāhu

i.e. the Rāma-kathā, which I am going to write, will give happiness to all (like the pleasant light of the moon).

7.35. Tulasī tells us that this act of wisdom (switching from Sanskrit to Hindi and from sva to sarva) was inspired by Hari-Har i.e. Lord Rāma and Lord Shiva—

tas kahihaun hiyan hari ke preren.....
budh vishrām sakal jan ranjani......
sambhu prasād sumati hiyan hulsī.

Simple Meaning—Tulasī says, I shall write in accordance with the inspiration that I have received in my heart from Lord Rāma. Therefore, my Rāma-kathā will not only give peace to scholars, but, more than that, it will give pleasure and happiness to 'sakal jan' i.e. all people...This act of wisdom, I must say, became possible by the grace of Lord Shiva.

7.36. Bālakāṇḍa also declares a direct linkage between 'Hari-Har-kathā' and 'sakal mangal'—

hari har kathā virājati benī
sunat sakal mud mangal denī.

Simple Meaning—Listening to Hari-Har-kathā brings about 'sakal mangal'—just as the confluence of three rivers—Triveṇī—does so at Prayāg.

7.37. Another illustration of the journey from 'sva' to 'sakal' is provided by Hanumān and the other vānaras i.e. monkeys. At the time, Hanumān first meets Lord Rāma, as described in Kishkindhākāṇḍa, he (i.e. Hanumān) is depicted as—

hridaya agyān....bahu avagun

i.e. Hanumān says, ignorance and other vices prevail in my heart.

But Lord Rāma accepts Hanumān as his bhakta and instructs him to serve all beings—

tain mam priya.... so ananya jākeṇ asi

mati na ṭarai hanumant
main sevak sacharāchara rūp swāmi bhagvant.

Simple Meaning—Lord Rāma says to Hanumān, you are dear to Me, and you will always remain dear to Me, but remember my teaching and serve all beings, because they are My own forms.

And we saw in paragraph 7.28 that Hanumān became 'sakal amangal mul nikandan'.

7.38. Tulasī further describes in Kishkindhākāṇḍa how ordinary monkeys by Lord Rāma's grace, became karmayogins and devoted themselves whole-heartedly to Rāma-kāj—

chale sakal van khojat saritā sar giri khoh
rām kāj laylīn man visrā tan kar chhoh.

Simple Meaning—'sakal' i.e. all the monkeys started looking for Sītā, in hills, caves and forests, and they gave up attachment to 'sva' i.e. personal physical comforts, because all their energies were devoted to Rāma-kāj.

7.39. Tulasīdās says at the end of Kishkindhākāṇḍa that Lord Rāma's glory converted ordinary monkeys into a disciplined army devoted to the cause of righteousness—

trailok pāvan sujas....
kautuk lāgi sang kapi senā.

Simple Meaning—Rāma is the Lord of the three worlds, and He utilized the army of the monkeys, only to give honour to them—and this aspect of Rāma-kathā purifies all.

7.40. Tulasī has repeatedly said that, by becoming a Rāma-bhakta, one easily moves up from 'sva' to 'sakal', another expression for which is 'doing good to others'. Just as in the beginning of the Mānas, 'svāntaḥ sukh' became 'sakal sukh', practically the same idea occurs in the closing words of the Mānas. The Sanskrit verse at the end says—

svāntastamaḥ śāntaye

i.e. my goal was to remove the darkness of my own inner self, but by God's grace, the Mānas became—

puṇyaṃ pāpharaṃ sadā shivakaraṃ

i.e. an embodiment of virtue, remover of sins and one that will always do 'Shiva' i.e. 'good' to all.

CHAPTER EIGHT

Call for the Good of the World—Lokasaṃgraha or Jag-Mangal

8.1. From the viewpoint of explicitness in conveying the message of the good of all, the high point was reached in the preceding chapter where we explained the expression 'sarvabhūtahitaṃ' of the Gītā, and the corresponding expression 'sakal-mangal' of the Mānas. But Gītā-commentators from Tilak onwards have given the pride of place to 'lokasaṃgraha' and Mānas-commentators have done the same to 'jag-mangal'—the meaning of both these expressions being 'the good of the world'. There are technical and literary reasons why the term 'lokasaṃgraha' rose to such prominence, and these will form a part of the discussion that constitutes the present chapter. Of course, parallel material on 'jag-mangal' will also be presented. In terms of the ten key words or phrases that we listed in chapter two, 'lokasaṃgraha' or 'jag-mangal' occupies the sixth place.

How the Stage is Set for the Lokasaṃgraha Message

8.2. One of the reasons underlying the prominence of lokasaṃgraha is that Lord Krishna chose the most appropriate moment for introducing this topic, on His own initiative, without a specific question about it having been put to Him by Arjuna. To understand this statement clearly, we have to look into the essence of the first two chapters of the Gītā and also the early part of the third chapter, prior to verses III.20-26 which can be called the seven lokasaṃgraha-related verses.

8.3. The first chapter of the Gītā depicts Arjuna in a state of confusion, anxiety and argumentation. Out of twenty-two verses that contain words spoken by him, the following two, viz. I.31 and I.37, are particularly important. So let us look closely at what Arjuna says in these two verses—

na ca śreyo'nupaśyāmi hatvā svajanamāhave....
svajanaṃ hi kathaṃ hatvā sukhinaḥ syāma mādhava.

Simple Meaning—Arjuna says, śreyas (meaning good) is my goal, but I feel that I will not get it if I kill svajanaṃ i.e. my own people. In fact, after killing svajanaṃ, how can we be happy?

8.4. In the light of the first chapter, Arjuna's goal is twofold viz., first, śreyas (his own good), and second, svajana-hit (i.e. the good of his own people). 'Śreyas' is an Upaniṣadic term, referred to by us in paragraph 1.11.

8.5. Although the word 'svajana' as such is not repeated in the Gītā, the word 'śreyas' occurs twice in Arjuna's statements made in chapter two, and it occurs for the third time in what he says in the beginning of chapter three. These three verses, viz. II.5, II.7 and III.2 are quoted below, in that order—

śreyo bhoktuṃ bhaiksyamapīha loke.

Simple Meaning—Arjuna says that in his search for śreyas, it may be better for him to survive by begging.

yacchreyaḥ syānniścitaṃ brūhi tanme.

Simple Meaning—Arjuna requests Lord Krishna to show him the way that is sure to lead him to śreyas

tadekaṃ vad niścitya
yena śreyo'hamāpnuyām.

Simple Meaning—Arjuna says to Lord Krishna, you have mentioned two paths, viz. Sāṅkhyayoga and Karmayoga. Out of these two, please specify the one by which I can definitely attain śreyas.

8.6. Next, a brief look at Lord Krishna's reply. He explains Sāṅkhyayoga in verses II.11 to II.38, the last eight of these verses being devoted to svadharma. Verse II.39, that paves the way for Karmayoga, then declares—

eṣā te'bhihitā sāṅ khye
buddhiryoge tvimāṃ śriṇu

Simple Meaning—Lord Krishna says, O Arjuna, what I spoke so far was about Sāṅkhyayoga, but now I shall talk about Karmayoga.

8.7. The fact that Lord Krishna's preference is for Karmayoga becomes clear when he says in verse II.40—

> *svalpamapyasya dharmasya trāyate mahato bhayāt.*

> ***Simple Meaning***—O Arjuna, practice of Karmayoga can save one from disaster, even if the karma appears to be quantitatively small, i.e. what counts is the quality and purity of purpose.

8.8. In the rest of chapter two of the Gītā, and also in the early part of chapter three, Lord Krishna continued to talk about Karmayoga, keeping in mind the questions posed by Arjuna. He then summarizes his teaching in verse III.19—

> *tasmādasaktaḥ satataṃ kāryaṃ karma samācara*
> *asakto hyācaran karma paramāpnoti pūruṣaḥ.*

> ***Simple Meaning***—Lord Krishna says, keep on doing your duty without attachment to the fruits of your action. This will lead you to your goal i.e. 'param' or śreyas.

8.9. As far as Arjuna was concerned, he got the answer to his question. However, Lord Krishna wanted to talk about lokasaṃgraha too, and He began doing so in verse III.20. So we can say that, whatever He had said so far, set the stage for the lokasaṃgraha-message.

The Message with Comments that Made it Famous

8.10. The word 'lokasaṃgraha' occurs twice in the Gītā and it gives the message of the good of the world. It was unfortunate, not only for India but also for the whole world, that the great importance of the lokasaṃgraha-message contained in the seven verses of the Gītā (III.20-26) was not brought out by the commentators prior to the twentieth century. The first writer to try to set things right in this matter was Lokmanya Tilak. Thereafter Śrī Aurobindo also declared—

> "There are few more important passages in the Gītā than these seven striking couplets."[1]

8.11. Once the ice was broken by Tilak and Aurobindo, there was no dearth of scholars and social workers to bring out more and more meanings from the lokasaṃgraha-verses. Mahatma Gandhi, Acharya Vonoba, D.S. Sarma, Dr. Radhakrishnan, and many others made useful contributions. In the following paragraphs, we present, one after another, the seven verses (starting from III.20) along with a brief selection of the comments thereon, because of which the word 'lokasaṃgraha' became so popular—

> *karmaṇaiva hi saṃsiddhiṃ āsthitā janakādayaḥ*
> *lokasaṃgrahamevāpi sampaśyan kartumarhasi.*

Simple Meaning—Lord Krishna tells Arjuna, in order to determine the right course of action, take into account 'lokasaṃgraha' also. Perfect karmayogins like Janaka did this, and they attained 'saṃsiddhi' i.e. śreyas too.

8.12. The word 'lokasaṃgraha' is generally interpreted as 'the good of the world', or action performed with that end in view. Tilak has said that, although this is adequate for common purposes, a broader meaning based on standard dictionaries should also be recognized. Here is an English translation of a part of what Tilak wrote in Marathi—

> "Lokasaṃgraha means binding men together, and protecting, maintaining and regulating them in such a way that they might acquire that strength which results from mutual cooperation, thereby putting them on the path of acquiring merit while maintaining their good condition...(After looking at Śaṅkara's definition—weaning people from the tendency to take to the path of wrong) it will be clear that my interpretation of lokasaṃgraha as 'making wise, those persons who behave recklessly as a result of ignorance, and keeping them together in a happy state, and putting them on the path of self-amelioration' is neither strange nor without authority."[2]

8.13. The reference to Janaka in verse III.20 provides support to the wider interpretation of 'lokasaṃgraha' if we recall from Mahābhārata the relevant details about this famous king. For example, the most commonly quoted statement of Janaka, as a firm indication of his non-attachment, is—

> *mithilāyāṃ pradīptāyām na me dahyati kincana*

i.e. even if the capital of my kingdom is burnt, there is nothing in it that is mine that is burnt. But Tilak says that this only tells half the story, and he completes the story in the following words—

> "From the point of view of lokasaṃgraha, the main question is why Janaka was still carrying on the activities of ruling, though he had no selfish interest or advantage and had become perfectly non-attached to his kingdom. Janaka himself says in the Mahābhārata—

devebhyaśca pitribhyaśca bhūtebhyo'tithibhiḥ saha
ityartham sarva evaite samārāmbhā bhavanti vai

i.e. all these activities are for the benefit of the gods, the ancestors, all created beings, and my guests, but not for my own self."[3]

8.14. In the light of the preceding two paragraphs, Lord Krishna's words, addressed to Arjuna, could be interpreted so as to convey the following message, maybe implicitly—

"You wanted a definite answer from me to your questions. I have given that, but now I want to add something on My own initiative because it is very important. Your vision is limited—you want śreyas i.e. your own good, and svajanahitam i.e. the good of your own people. I want you to have a still broader vision so that you also want loka-hitam i.e. the good of the world."

8.15. We now move on to verse III.21—

yadyadācarati śreṣṭhas tattadeve'taro janaḥ
sa yat pramāṇaṃ kurute lokastadanuvartate.

Simple Meaning—Whatever a great person does, the same is done by others as well. Whatever standard he or she sets, the world follows.

The main idea behind this verse is God's advice to every individual to set an example to others by his or her own good conduct. Mahatma Gandhi had taken this advice to heart, and therefore, he believed in practising a virtue (like truth, non-violence, social service) before preaching it.

8.16. In the next verse, viz. III.22, Lord Krishna, as an Avatāra, gives His own example—

na me parthāsti kartavyaṃ triṣu lokeṣu kincana
nānavāptamavāptavyaṃ varta eva ca karmaṇi.

Simple Meaning—God (Lord Krishna) says, I work for lokasaṃgraha all the time, as My spontaneous activity. There is not for Me any work in the three worlds which has to be done, nor anything to be obtained which has not been obtained, yet I am engaged in karma.

8.17. This verse contains a strong warning to those who have a narrow view about the purpose of karma, namely that it will help them obtain something which they do not have and want to obtain. In fact, Arjuna himself had taken this stand when he argued that since he was willing to give up his claim on the kingdom, he saw no harm in withdrawing from the battle and in taking up sannyāsa. Lord Krishna emphasizes in this verse that the real purpose of karma is not to satisfy any narrow, selfish desire, because if it had been so, then He need not have performed any karma.

8.18. Mahatma Gandhi has written a long commentary on this verse. He sees here a reference to God's karma as preserver of the universe which includes the unceasing movement of the sun, the moon, the earth, etc. as also nature's processes and laws which are guided by divine intelligence and will. Furthermore, says Gandhi, the actions of Lord Krishna as an Avatāra also present an ideal of service—

> "Krishna served the people all his life, a real servant of the people. He could have led the forces at Kurukshetra, but He preferred to be Arjuna's charioteer. His whole life was an unbroken Gītā of karma... As a child He was a cowherd and we still know Him by the name of Gopāl....Krishna knew no sleep nor idleness. He kept a sleepless vigil over the world."[4]

8.19. Writing in a similar vein, Vinoba presents further details of what Lord Krishna did as a karmayogin—

> "In the Mahābhārata war, everybody at sunset leaves the field for evening prayer, but Lord Krishna unyokes the horses from the chariot, gives them water, rubs them, removes the burrs from their bodies, and feeds them from his yellow garment which he has filled with grain...
>
> "At the Pāṇḍavas' Rājasūya sacrifice, Lord Krishna clears the leaf-plates after the feast...

"So the saints have pictured a karmayogi God who rubs horses, takes cows out to graze, drives a chariot, cleans dishes and mops up floors."[5]

8.20. Verse III.23, continuing the ideal-establishing role of an Avatāra, emphasizes the avoidance of tāmasika vices—

> *yadi hyaham na varteyaṃ jātu karmaṇyatandritaḥ*
> *mama vartmānuvartante manuṣyāḥ pārtha sarvaśaḥ.*

Simple Meaning—Lord Krishna says, I work for lokasaṃgraha without a trace of weariness, because otherwise men in every way would follow My path.

8.21. The next verse (III.24) is important for purposes of deriving a practical definition of 'lokasaṃgraha'—

> *utsīdeyurime lokā na kuryāṃ karma cedahaṃ*
> *sankarasya ca kartā syāṃ upahanyāmimāḥ prajāḥ.*

Simple Meaning—Lord Krishna says, if I do not work for lokasaṃgraha, all these worlds would perish, and I would be held responsible for creating confusion and for destroying the people.

In the light of this, we can define 'lokasaṃgraha' as any work that, on the one hand, prevents world's destruction and social confusion, and, on the other hand, contributes to world's protection and social development.

8.22. D.S. Sarma believes that if you ignore the lokasaṃgraha-message, you may not find social service in the Gītā, because other expressions for this message are not so effective. Here is Sarma's conclusion—

> "Unsympathetic critics of Hinduism have often ignored it (i.e. lokasaṃgraha), and said that social service forms no integral part of our religion."[6]

8.23. J.G. Arapura is of opinion that, in the light of verse III.24, the scope of lokasaṃgraha-activities can be widened so as to include environmental protection, afforestation, and proper handling of wastes of all types. Dandekar finds in the same verse the principle of ethical interdependence of the various constituents of the society, which implies that "man must have an active awareness of his social obligations."[7]

8.24. The next verse, viz. III.25, specifies the desire for lokasaṃgraha as an important characteristic of learned people—

> *saktāḥ karmaṇyavidvānso yathā kurvanti bhārata*
> *kuryādvidvānstathāsaktaś cikīrsurlokasaṃgrahaṃ.*

Simple Meaning—Lord Krishna says, those who act from attachment (which is a sign of their selfish desires) are devoid of learning. On the other hand, learned people are those who act with the desire for lokasaṃgraha, and without attachment.

8.25. P.T. Raju interprets this verse to assert that both 'lokasaṃgraha' and individual salvation constitute the 'double aim' of the Gītā. Sustaining the world through the satisfaction of desires according to the laws of the Cosmic Person is lokasaṃgraha, says Raju, and action without any self-centred motive leads one to salvation.

Dr. Radhakrishnan says that liberated souls, who act with the desire for lokasaṃgraha, take upon themselves the burden of the redemption of the whole world.

8.26. Since lokasaṃgraha means bringing about a unity of purpose and cooperative effort in the society for a just cause, Lord Krishna asks wise men not to be content with their own effort, but also to encourage others to do likewise. This message is contained in verse III.26 which is the final verse in the lokasaṃgraha section—

> *na buddhibhedaṃ janayed ajñānāṃ karmasanginām*
> *joṣayet sarvakarmāṇi vidvān yuktaḥ samācaran.*

> ***Simple Meaning***—Lord Krishna says, let the men of knowledge not unsettle the minds of the ignorant who are attached to action. The enlightened man, doing all works for lokasaṃgraha in the spirit of yoga, should set others to act as well.

8.27. The word 'joṣayet' (meaning to encourage or induce) occurring in this verse led Śrī Aurobindo to find much support for his doctrine of Pūrṇa-yoga (according to which a person, after achieving perfection, helps others to achieve the same goal). We give below a part of his long commentary on this subject—

> "Liberated oneself, to live in this oneness, to help mankind on the path that leads towards it and meanwhile to do all works for God and help man also to do with joy and acceptance all the works to which he is called, kritsnakarmakrit, sarvakarmani josayan, no greater or more liberal rule of divine works can be given."[8]

8.28. Dr. Radhakrishnan suggests that the word 'buddhibhedaṃ' (meaning to unsettle the mind) occurring in verse III.26 gives a warning to developmental enthusiasts—

> "We must approach the followers of simple faiths with reverence and not heedlessly disturb them, for the simple faiths have practical value and spiritual appeal. Modern anthropologists advise us that we should not, in our anxiety to 'uplift' the aborigines, deprive them of their innocent joys, their songs and dances, their feasts and festivals. Whatever we should like to do for them, we should do with love and reverence."[9]

Lokasaṃgraha's Prominence due to Literary Support

8.29. Gītā-commentators have strengthened the lokasaṃgraha-message by pointing out that several important Sanskrit-texts contain the same or similar words. This process is still going on. We present here only four such instances.

(a) ***Chāndogya and Bṛhadāraṇyaka Upaniṣads***

8.30. Prior to 1973, it was commonly believed that Upanisads have neither the exact word 'lokasaṃgraha' nor any other similar expression. Acharya Vinoba's research findings, published in that year, linked 'lokasaṃgraha' to—

> *lokānāṃ asambhedāya...setuḥ...*

which occurs in two Upaniṣads viz. Chāndogya and Bṛhadāraṇyaka, and which he translated as follows—

> This Ātman is like a bridge to keep people united.

(b) ***Mahābhārata***

8.31. The word 'lokasaṃgraha' occurs, as such several times in the Mahābhārata, but here we present only one such verse from Śānti-parva—

> *lokasaṃgrahasaṃyuktaṃ vidhātrā nihitaṃ purā*
> *sūkṣmadharmārthaniyataṃ satāṃ caritamuttamaṃ.*

> ***Simple Meaning***—Brahmā created the excellent lives of saints in order to explain which path of duty should be followed on critical occasions, so as to promote lokasaṃgraha.

(c) ***Manusmṛti***

8.32. Manusmṛti has used the expression 'loka-vivsiddhi' which means 'growth or prosperity of the people'. This is supposed to have been the criterion for the establishment of the varṇa-system. Manusmṛti also suggests the abandonment of those elements of dharma which are 'loka-vikruṣṭa' i.e. disliked by the people.

(d) ***Yoga-Vāsiṣṭha***

8.33. Yoga-Vāsiṣṭha uses the word 'loka-parāmarśa' to convey an idea similar to 'lokasaṃgraha'. Here is the relevant verse of Yoga-Vāsiṣṭha—

> *yāvallokaparāmarśo nirūḍho nāsti yoginaḥ*
> *tāvad rūḍhasamādhitvaṃ na bhavatyeva nirmalaṃ.*

> ***Simple Meaning***—So long as the need for looking after other people remains, to howsoever small an extent, it cannot be said that the state of the person, who wants to concentrate on yoga, is free from blame.

Jag-Mangal in the Mānas

8.34. The word 'jag-mangal' occurs six times in the Mānas. Although, numerically speaking, the expression 'sakal-mangal' (discussed in the preceding chapter) occurs more often than that, yet the verses in which jag-mangal occurs are linked more intimately with the purpose for which Tulasī wrote the Mānas. For example, we have the famous declaration made in the beginning of Bālakāṇḍa—

rām kathā jag-mangal karnī

i.e. Tulasī says, I am writing Rāma-kathā with the purpose of bringing about jag-mangal i.e. the good of the world.

8.35. A similar declaration, linking jag-mangal with the purpose of Rāma's Avatāra, is made by Guru Vasiṣṭha in Ayodhyākāṇḍa—

rām janam jagmangal hetū

i.e. Guru Vasiṣṭha says, Lord Rāma has appeared as an Avatāra with the purpose of establishing jag-mangal.

Link with Rāma's Coronation, the Beginning of Rāma-Rājya

8.36. It is well-known that Mahatma Gandhi attached special significance to the 'Rāma-rājya' section of the Mānas, in which Tulasī has given a detailed description of an ideal society based on the principle of jag-mangal. A summary of that will be given by us in chapter twelve. For our present purposes, we want to point out how the topic of Rāma's coronation is closely associated in the Mānas with 'jag-mangal'.

8.37. The original plan of King Dashrath to declare Rāma as heir-apparent is described in Ayodhyākāṇḍa. When Dashrath asked his advisers for their opinion about his plan, they replied—

jag-mangal bhal kāj vichārā begia nāth na lāia bārā.

> ***Simple Meaning***—The advisers said, O King, what you have thought of is excellent, because Rāma's assumption of powers as heir-apparent will bring about jag-mangal. And an excellent plan like this should be acted upon immediately, without any delay.

8.38. However, delay could not be avoided, and it was only after fourteen years that Rāma's rule i.e. Rāma-rājya actually began. King Dashrath was then no more alive, but Guru Vasiṣṭha performed the ceremony as described in Uttarakāṇḍa. The words that advisers spoke on this occasion are similar to what they had used fourteen years earlier—

ab munivar vilamb nahin kīje.... jag abhirām rām abhishekā.

Simple Meaning—The advisers said, O Guru Vasiṣṭha, please do not cause any more delay, and declare Rāma as King. Rāma's rule will bring about 'jag-abhirām' i.e. happiness of the world.

The close similarity between 'jag-abhirām' and 'jag-mangal' is obvious.

Link with Rāma's Virtues which Made Him Maryādā-Puruṣottama

8.39. Tulasī has drawn repeated attention to Rāma's virtues. Among the many verses where this has been done, two have pointed out the linkage between Rāma's virtues and jag-mangal. The first of these two verses is in Bālakāṇḍa—

jag-mangal gun grām rām ke.

Simple Meaning—Tulasī says, I want to call the attention of everybody to the great virtues and qualities of Lord Rāma—virtues that can bring about jag-mangal.

Obviously, these are the virtues and the high ideals because of which Rāma is called 'maryādā puruṣottama' i.e. the lord of the universe who laid great emphasis on 'maryādā' i.e. social norms and social values.

8.40. The second verse linking Rāma's virtues with jag-mangal is in Ayodhyākāṇḍa, and the words are spoken by Bharat—

jag-mangal hit ek upāū.... prabhu āyasu....sir dhari karihī....

Simple Meaning—Bharat says, in my opinion, jag-mangal can be brought about only, if all of us follow Lord Rāma's ideals and instructions.

Prominence Strengthened by Use of Synonyms

8.41. We saw above that great personalities of the Mānas like Guru Vasiṣṭha and Bharat have contributed to the popularity of the word 'jag-mangal'. Furthermore, slight variations of this word have been used by other great entities like Anasūyā, and also by Lord Shiva. For example, Anasūyā, wife of Rishi Atri, says in Araṇyakāṇḍa—

kahiun kathā saṅsār hit

i.e. whatever kathā I have said, the purpose of all that is 'saṅsār hit' i.e. the good of the world.

8.42. Rishi Yājñavalkya, describing the conversation between Lord Shiva and His wife Pārvatī, says in Bālakāṇḍa—

kathā jo sakal lokhitkārī soi pūchhan chah shailkumārī.

Simple Meaning—Yājñavalkya says, Pārvatī expressed a keen desire to listen to Rāma-kathā which is 'sakal-lok-hit-kārī' i.e. which brings about the good of all the lokas (lokas meaning both 'worlds' and 'the people').

8.43. Lord Shiva Himself, admiring Pārvatī for having put a question about Rāma-kathā, uses a similar expression, as described in Bālakāṇḍa again—

pūñchheu raghupati kathā prasaṅgā
sakal lok jag pāvani gaṅgā...
kīnhiu prasna jagat hit lāgī.

Simple Meaning—Lord Shiva replies to Pārvatī, by asking me to narrate Rāma-kathā to you, you have helped the cause of 'jagat-hit' i.e. good of the world, because Rāma-kathā, like the holy river Gaṅgā, purifies 'sakal lok' i.e. all the worlds or all the people.

8.44. In the last three paragraphs, we drew attention to several synonyms of 'jag-mangal' that have been used in the Mānas. Another synonym of 'jag-mangal' is 'lok-vishrām' which means 'giver of peace to the world'. This expression is significant because it represents the widening of the personal goal of 'vishrām', which, says the Mānas, any individual can obtain from Rāma-kathā. We are emphasizing the wider goal 'lok-vishrām' because Bālakāṇḍa links this expression with the purpose of Rāma's Avatāra—

jag-nivās prabhu pragate akhil lok vishrām.

Simple Meaning—Tulasī says, God is 'jag-nivās' i.e. He supports the world and pervades it. He took Avatāra as Rāma to give peace and happiness to 'akhil lok' (which is similar to 'sakal lok' i.e. the entire world).

8.45. Obviously, the expression 'akhil lok vishrām' is Tulasī's favourite because he used it again in Bālakāṇḍa. At the time of the naming ceremony, Guru Vasiṣtha explains why the name 'Rāma' was chosen—

jo ānand sindhu sukh rāsī sīkar ten trailok supāsī

so sukhdhām rām as nāmā akhil lok dāyak vishrāmā.

Simple Meaning—Guru Vasiṣṭha says, the name 'Rāma' was chosen because He is the abode of happiness, He is like an ocean of joy (a single drop of which can make the three worlds happy). He is 'akhil lok vishrām' (the simple meaning of which has been written in the preceding paragraph).

Special Importance of Bālakāṇḍa

8.46. In the early portion of Bālakāṇḍa, Tulasīdāsa has declared repeatedly that the purpose of his writing is 'jag-mangal' or 'sab kahn hit' (the latter expression meaning 'good of all'). In order to cover that portion in greater detail than what has been done in the present and the preceding chapters, we give in Appendix Two the original words of the Mānas along with a simple meaning thereof in English. For a detailed discussion on 'jag-mangal' in Hindi, we refer the reader to the author's books entitled *"Tulasī-Rāmāyaṇa:Jag-Mangal-Parāyaṇa,"*[10] and *"Mānas Evaṃ Gītā: Lok-Mangal-Guñjitā."*[11]

Chapter Nine

Call to Avoid Self-Centred Attitudes—Nirmamo Nirahaṅkāraḥ

9.1. In religious and spiritual matters, Vedic scriptures have adopted an integrated approach, in the sense that adherence to a practicable idea, say lokasaṃgraha (or doing good to the world), is considered complete only if it is 'manasā vācā karmaṇā' i.e. by thought, word and deed. Gītā-verses XVII.14-17, by using the expression 'tapastattrividhaṃ' speak simultaneously of the importance of the three tapas, of body, speech and mind. Similarly, in Mānas too, Kākbhushuṇḍi says in Uttarakāṇḍa—

man vach kram mohi nij jan jānā

i.e. Lord Rāma calls only that person 'My own' who practices dharma by mind, speech and actions.

9.2. In the present chapter, we examine the first of the trio i.e. 'mana', by asking what type of mental attitude is viewed, by the Gītā and the Mānas, as conducive to the goal of the good of all. In terms of the ten key words or phrases that we listed in chapter two, the topic that we are now covering occupies the seventh place. The corresponding discussion relating to 'vacana and karma' will form a part of the next chapter which is devoted to behavioural issues.

Sense of Mine-ness Linked with Three Desires

9.3. Bṛhadāraṇyaka Upaniṣad speaks of three types of desires—

putraiṣaṇā vittaiṣaṇā lokaiṣaṇā

i.e. desire for son, wealth and honour in the world. In the Gītā, the sense of mine-ness of the Kauravas is linked with these three desires. For example, verses I.1, I.7 and I.9 contain either the word 'mama' (meaning mine) or other words that convey the same meaning—

(a) Verse I.1 is spoken by Dhṛtarāṣṭra who uses the word 'māmakāḥ' for his sons, of whom the eldest and the chief is Duryodhana, and also for the other Kaurava-supporters.
(b) Verse I.7 is spoken by Duryodhana who boasts of 'mama sainya' i.e. my army, which is linked with possession of wealth.
(c) Verse I.9 is also spoken by Duryodhana who uses the expression—

madarthe tyaktajīvitāḥ

i.e. I am so great that many warriors are willing to give up their life for my sake.

9.4. In the Mānas too, Kākbhushuṇḍī says in Uttarakāṇḍa—

sut vit lok ishnā tīnī
kehi kai mati inh krit na malīnī.

Simple Meaning—Desires for son, wealth and honour in the world lead to perverted thinking.

Dhṛtarāṣṭra's Infatuation with His Wicked Son

9.5. Since the Gītā gives only a glimpse of the sense of mine-ness which Dhṛtarāṣṭra had for his son, we need to look into the Mahābhārata to understand the serious mistake that this represented. It was the wicked Duryodhana who blocked the peace proposal which Lord Krishna Himself took to Hastināpur, on behalf of the Pāṇḍavas. Krishna and Vidura both tried their rest to avert the war, but Dhṛtarāṣṭra was too infatuated with his greedy son to listen to anyone else. Vidura then gave the following advice to Dhṛtarāṣṭra which also contained a warning—

tyajedekaṃ kulasyārthe grāmasyārthe kulaṃ tyajet
grāmam janapadasyārthe ātmārthe prithivīṃ tyajet.

Simple Meaning—Vidura says, O king, it is better to give up one person (i.e. Duryodhana) for the sake of the family, similarly, give up the family for the village, and the village for the state. For the sake of Ātman (i.e. truth and high principles), even the whole world could be given up.

9.6. Vidura's statement was a warning to Dhṛtarāṣṭra that his fondness for Duryodhana (in spite of the latter's wickedness) may cause the destruction of the family. For the topic that we are discussing in the present chapter, Vidura's message is that for the sake of universal welfare, the sense of narrow-minded mine-ness will need to be given up.

Duryodhana's Attachment to Army, at the Cost of Krishna

9.7. Again we have to turn to the Mahābhārata to show that attachment to the army made Duryodhana completely lose his sense of priorities. The occasion where this self-destructive aspect of Duryodhana's mentality becomes clear, is dramatically depicted in the epic. When peace proposals were turned down by Duryodhana, preparations for war had to be intensified, by the Kauravas as well as the Pāṇḍavas. Help from the respective allies was sought.

9.8. In order to seek help from Lord Krishna, Arjuna and Duryodhana travelled separately to Dvarikā. Duryodhana arrived there first. He was admitted to the room where Lord Krishna was taking a nap. There were two chairs for visitors, one near His head and the other near His feet. Duryodhana, out of arrogance, occupied the chair near Lord Krishna's head. Shortly thereafter, Arjuna arrived, and, out of respect for Krishna, he was glad to occupy the chair near His feet.

9.9. When Krishna got up, He first saw Arjuna and started talking with him. Duryodhana intervened and said that he was the first to arrive there. After listening to both of them, Lord Krishna said, "I want to help both of you. I shall divide into two parts whatever I have. In part one, I include myself, alone without any army, and with my further declaration that I will not fight. In part two, I include my army, ready to fight. Out of these two options, tell me, Arjuna, what is your preference?"

Arjuna immediately replied, "Krishna, I choose you. Whether you fight or not, I want you."

Duryodhana felt happy and said, "I accept the second option, i.e. the army."

9.10. After Duryodhana had left with the army, Lord Krishna spoke to Arjuna, "It seems that you did not think properly while making your choice. Since I will not fight, what use shall I be to you? Perhaps you ought to have chosen the army instead."

Arjuna smiled and said, "I have thought out the entire strategy. You will not fight, but you can still be my charioteer."

And the Mahābhārata describes how Lord Krishna played a crucial role for ensuring Arjuna's victory. In fact, the Gītā shows that Arjuna not only placed the reins of his horses in Lord Krishna's hands, but he also became His disciple, in thought, word and deed.

9.11. The message that we get from the above for our present discussion is that Duryodhana's attachment to the army, even at the cost of losing Lord Krishna, gave a clear indication, in advance, that he was following the path of self-destruction.

Contrast Between Duryodhana and Bharat

9.12. As we explained above, both Dhṛtarāṣṭra and Duryodhana—i.e. father and son—were victims of the perverted sense of mine-ness. So it was impossible to prevent the tide of destruction from taking its full toll on the family of the Kauravas. Vidura had already given such a warning.

9.13. A similar sequence of events could have taken place in the family of Dashrath—and this obviously relates to the Mānas—if Bharat would not have stopped the tide set in motion by his mother Kaikeyī. The Mānas makes it clear that Kaikeyī was a victim of the sense of mine-ness. Because of that, she wanted her own son, Bharat to be the king, instead of Kaushalyā's son, Rāma. Kaikeyī neither appreciated Kaushalyā's desire for family unity, nor did she consult Bharat, when she declared in Ayodhyākāṇḍa—

jas koshilā mor bhal tākā
tas phal unhahi deun kari sākā.

Simple Meaning—Kaikeyī says, why should I not protect the interests of myself and my son? Kaushalyā had planned to hurt my interests, so why should I not play the game of tit-for-tat?

9.14. Kaikeyī's narrow-mindedness dragged Ayodhyā along the path of family disunity, sorrow and likely destruction. Rāma, Sītā and Lakshman went to the forest for fourteen years and Dashrath could not survive. The future looked bleak.

9.15. But Bharat changed the course of events. He refused to accept the throne, because he said it was Rāma's entitlement, not his. He went beyond the sense of mine-ness, and revolted against his own mother, Kaikeyī. He went to Chitrakūṭ and tried to persuade Rāma to return to Ayodhyā. After a long discussion, Bharat agreed to carry on the affairs of the kingdom, but only as Rāma's nominee, and for fourteen years only. Ayodhyā was saved from destruction because of Bharat's large-heartedness. Tulasīdāsa says in Ayodhyākāṇḍa that Bharat was guided, not by a sense of mine-ness, but by the desire to do good to all—

sab ke sammat sarva hit kariya prem pahichāni.

Simple Meaning—Bharat says, addressing the assembly at Chitrakūṭ, please devise a plan which is based on mutual love and love for Rāma, which is acceptable to all, and which will do good to all.

9.16. Tulasī says in Vinay-Patrikā that for the sake of 'mangal', it might be necessary to make personal sacrifice, and he cites several examples including that of Bharat—

tajyo pitā prahlād, vibhīshan bandhu,
bharat mahtārī.... bhaye mud mangal-kārī.

Simple Meaning—Tulasī says, although, Prahlād had to oppose his father (Hiraṇyakashyap), Vibhīshaṇ had to leave his brother (Rāvaṇa), and Bharat had to disown his mother (Kaikeyī), the result was 'mangal' (i.e. good) because these persons placed Rāma (God) above personal relationships.

Giving up of Mine-ness Glorified as the Essence of Yajña

9.17. The topic entitled "journey from sva to sarva" was discussed in chapter seven of this book. Another topic "yajña" was similarly discussed in chapter six. It is interesting to see how the present topic "nirmama" can be viewed as another variant of these two topics—thus illustrating the inter-connected nature of the various components of the social message of the Gītā and the Mānas.

9.18. Anyone who, like Bharat, goes beyond the narrow mentality of mine-ness or sva (i.e. one's own), and feels happy in the wider framework of sarva (i.e. all) or God or Brahman (the universal self), is admired by the Gītā as a performer of yajña. In a poetic style, the Gītā says that one who cooks only for oneself eats only sin, i.e. he or she cannot be called a good person or a saint. On the other hand, saints are those who first feed others and then eat only what is left—such food is like nectar and so they attain Brahman. Verses III.13 and IV.31 are put together to convey this message—a variant of which was described in chapter six—

bhunjate te tvaghaṃ pāpā ye pacantyātmakāraṇāt
yajñaśiṣṭāśinaḥ santo mucyante sarvakilbiṣaiḥ
yajñaśiṣṭāmritabhujo yānti brahma sanātanaṃ.

Simple Meaning—Since these verses occur in the yajña-related sections of the Gītā, the glory of yajña forms the background. The essence of yajña (as already mentioned in paragraph 6.10) is the mental determination "idaṃ na mama", i.e. giving up of mine-ness. Those who cook merely for their own sake, eat but sin. Saints eat only what remains after others have been fed, so all their sins are destroyed. They eat nectar and attain Brahman.

9.19. Swami Chinmayananda, commenting on the above verses, interprets the yajña-spirit as the spirit of self-dedicated activities, with no attachment or sense of mine-ness. Here is a portion of his long commentary—

> "The Gītā is obviously against the principle of arrogation of wealth, and of hoarding the same, motivated by lust of profit, meant mainly for selfish enjoyment, utterly regardless of the privations and poverty of the unfortunate folks in the community....The Gītā wants the yajña-spirit, instead, that is, the spirit of self-dedicated activities....All causes for the sorrows in social life would be removed if the good and socially-conscious members of the community were to feel satisfied in enjoying the remnants of their co-operative work performed in the true yajña-spirit."[1]

Mānas Condemns Formal Yajña if Mine-ness not Given Up

9.20. The fact that Tulasī disapproved the yajñas performed by Rāvaṇa and his son Meghnād was already stated by us in chapter six. Reasons for Tulasī's disapproval were, firstly, that Rāvaṇa's purpose was rooted in unrighteousness, and, secondly, that Meghnād took recourse to animal sacrifice for his yajña. One more factor which, in Tulasī's view, makes a yajña tāmasika is related to the topic of this chapter, and that is what we shall explain now, using the story of Daksha for illustration.

9.21. Daksha's story is related by Tulasīdās in Bālakāṇḍa. He was the father of 'Satī' the first wife of Lord Shiva. Daksha had administrative skills which led to his nomination by Brahmā, as the chief of Prajāpati's. But assumption of power aroused egotism in Daksha's mind, and he adopted a disrespectful attitude towards his son-in-law, i.e. Lord Shiva.

9.22. With a view to demonstrating his powerful position, Daksha organized a grand yajña. He invited all the gods, but none of the top three, i.e. Brahmā, Vishnu, Shiva—this was part of Daksha's plan to insult Lord Shiva. Obviously, Daksha had fallen prey to a tāmasika sense of mine-ness as well as arrogance.

9.23. Daksha's daughter, Satī heard about this grand yajña and expressed her desire to go and see it, but her husband (Lord Shiva) tried to dissuade her from going, by arguing like this. He said, Daksha wants to insult me, and so he has not invited even his own daughter i.e. you. If you go uninvited, you will not be welcome and there will be opposition to your visit, even in your father's home. Lord Shiva added—

tadapi virodh mān jahn koī tahān gaye kalyān na hoī.

Simple Meaning—If you go into a situation marked by opposition, then the result will not be good.

9.24. But Satī ignored Lord Shiva's advice and went to her father's home. As soon as she reached there, it became clear to her that she was not welcome, because the main purpose behind Daksha's yajña was to insult Lord Shiva. If Satī is welcomed in that house, argued Daksha, it might reduce the intensity of insult towards Shiva.

9.25. Tulasī explains that this yajña, in spite of being grand, was tāmasika because Daksha was not guided by the mantra 'idaṃ na mama' (meaning, this is not mine). How can, asks Tulasī, such a yajña contribute to the good of any individual or the family or the society?

9.26. Satī declared that she could not tolerate this type of insult to Lord Shiva (who does good to all), and she did not want to remain alive any longer as Daksha's daughter—

jagadātmā mahesh purārī
jagat janak sab ke hitkārī
pitā mandmati nindat tehī
daksha shukra sambhav yah dehī
tajihaum turat deh tehi hetū.

Simple Meaning—Satī said, my father has fallen prey to tāmasika buddhi (perverted thinking), and so he is insulting Lord Shiva in spite of the fact that Shiva does good to all. I am therefore putting an end to my relationship with Daksha (my father), jumping into the fire of the yajña.

9.27. Satī's sacrifice resulted in the destruction of Daksha's yajña which was tāmasika (bad). Satī was reborn as Pārvatī, and was re-united with Lord Shiva, but Daksha's evil designs failed—

bhai jagvidit daksha gati soī
jasi kachhu sambhu vimukh kai hoī.

Simple Meaning—Tulasī says, Daksha suffered defeat, like all those who are so arrogant as to oppose Lord Shiva.

Tulasī's message is that performing a grand yajña, without giving up mine-ness and egotism, brought no benefit to Daksha—rather it became a cause for his downfall.

Nirmamo Nirahaṅkāraḥ—Another Name for Social Service

9.28. Acharya Vinoba has explained that the phrase 'nirmamo nirahaṅkāraḥ' (literally meaning 'going beyond the sense of I and mine) conveys the message of social service. Vinoba's explanation forms part of his long commentary on verse II.71, which is one of the verses describing a sthitaprajña (reference paragraphs 5.21-28)—

vihāya kāmān yaḥ sarvān pumāṇścarati niḥsprihaḥ
nirmamo nirahaṅkāraḥ sa śāntimadhigacchati.

Simple Meaning—Lord Krishna says, a sthitaprajña does not have selfish desires—since he is free from longing, his actions are spontaneous—he has gone beyond the sense of I and mine, and he attains peace i.e. he is liberated while still living.

Now we quote a part of Vinoba's commentary—

"Nirmamo means that a sthitaprajña karmayogin has no selfish desires. Nirahaṅkāraḥ means that he has dedicated all his actions to God and does not regard himself as the doer. But still he puts in his best effort in whatever he does. What can he do other than lokasaṃgraha? In fact, he lives only in order to benefit humanity."[2]

9.29. The phrase 'nirmamo nirahaṅkāraḥ' is a favourite expression of the Gītā. As we saw above, it is first used in the description of a karmayogin (verse II.71). Its second use is in verse XII.13 which describes a bhakta—we have quoted this verse in paragraph 5.34. Finally, let us look at verse XVIII.53—which describes a jñānin worthy of becoming one with Brahman—

ahaṅkāraṃ balaṃ darpaṃ kāmaṃ krodhaṃ parigrahaṃ
vimucya nirmamaḥ śānto brahmabhūyāya kalpate.

Simple Meaning—Lord Krishna says, a jñānin who is worthy of becoming one with Brahman is tranquil in mind, 'nirmamaḥ' and he casts aside 'ahaṅkār', force, arrogance, desire, anger and possessiveness.

It is clear that the phrase 'nirmamo nirahaṅkāraḥ'—although not occurring as such in verse XVIII.53—does describe a jñānin too, for practical purposes.

So, perfection achieved through any yoga—karma, bhakti, jñāna—is depicted by 'nirmamo nirahaṅkāraḥ' and it gives the message of social service.

Mānas Associates Par-hit with the Giving Up of 'Main Aru Mor'

9.30. We already mentioned in paragraph 2.16 that the Mānas does not have a short and straightforward translation of the Gītā-expression 'nirmamo nirahaṅkāraḥ'. However longer expressions do exist to convey the message of 'par-hit' i.e. doing good to others. The Mānas takes the view that holding on to the sense of I and mine goes on because of lack of bhakti and jñāna. For example, Tulasī says in Laṅkākāṇḍa—

main aru mor mūdhtā tyāgū mahāmoh nishi sūtat jāgū.

Simple Meaning—Give up the arrogance of I and mine (main aru mor). You are sleeping in the darkness of extreme ignorance. Arise and see the light of jñāna.

The same appeal is continued in Uttarakāṇḍa and Araṇyakāṇḍa where bhakti and par-hit are brought in too—

gat mamtā mad moh.... mam gun grām nām rat....
gāvahiṇ sunahiṇ sadā mam līlā hetu rahit par hit rat śīlā.

Simple Meaning—Tulasī says, once you have given up ignorance, and the sense of I and mine, then you will sing glories of Rāma and His virtues, and like Rāma, you will help others without expecting anything in return.

9.31. In paragraphs 9.12-16, we spoke of Bharat through whom Tulasī has given the message of 'nirmamo nirahaṅkāraḥ'. Ayodhyākāṇḍa describes the dialogue between Bharat and Guru Vasiṣṭha. The latter tells Bharat, do not feel too sad over the death of Dashrath because he performed good deeds when he was alive. Vasiṣṭha then indicates who are the persons who do not do good deeds and why—

nij tanu poshak nirdaya bhārī
sab vidhi sochia par apkārī.

Simple Meaning—Those who feed and maintain merely their own body and have no compassion for others—i.e. they are victims of 'main aru mor'—they harm others, and when they die, their well-wishers ought to feel sad (because they did not do good deeds when they were alive).

CHAPTER TEN

Call for Even-minded Vision—Samadriṣṭi

10.1. This chapter is a continuation of the preceding one in which we started discussing the role of the trio 'mana-vacana-karma' i.e. thought, word and deed. We examined there as to what type of mental attitude is viewed, by the Gītā and the Mānas, as conducive to the goal of the good of all. Now we focus attention on 'vacana and karma' i.e. the type of vision, speech and behaviour that go hand-in-hand with social harmony and social service. Obviously, the Vedantic philosophy of viewing the same Ātman in every being provides the starting point for our discussion, but we will also need to look into the bhakti-based variant of this (which is highlighted in the Mānas too) and practical applications of both of them. The subject is of great importance because social workers all over the world are battling against discriminatory practices based on race, colour, creed, sex, socio-economic status and so on, and we want to present the spiritual approach in support of all such workers. In terms of the ten key words or phrases that we listed in chapter two, the topic that we are now covering occupies the eighth place. It is also interesting to recall paragraph 2.17 where we stated that the expression 'samadriṣṭi' is the only one (out of ten) which has been commonly used in the Gītā as well as the Mānas.

Message of Equal Vision in Jñānayoga or Vedantic Philosophy

10.2. The Gītā says in verse VI.29 that a jñānayogin, seeing the same Ātman in all beings, attains 'samadriṣṭi' i.e. equal vision—

sarvabhūtasthamātmānaṃ sarvabhūtāni cā'tmani
īkṣate yogayuktātmā sarvatra samadarśanaḥ

Simple Meaning—Lord Krishna says, he whose self is harmonized by yoga, sees the Self abiding in all beings and all beings in the Self—he has equal vision everywhere.

Dr. Radhakrishna explains this verse in the following words—

"Though, in the process of attaining the vision of Self, we had to retreat from outward things and separate the Self from the world, when the vision is attained, the world is drown into the Self. On the ethical plane, this means that there should grow a detachment from the world and when it is attained, a return to it, through love, suffering and sacrifice for it....The sense of a separate finite self with its hopes and fears, its likes and dislikes, is destroyed."[1]

10.3. Swami Ranganathananda has attached the highest importance to what he calls 'the message of same-sightedness' or 'removing the delusion of separateness'—

"Vedantic philosophy proves to us that the sense of separateness is not true, it imparts to us the knowledge of oneness, and with this knowledge comes also morality and ethics, and we discover our true kinship with every man and woman and with the whole of nature.... The purpose of spiritual knowledge is to remove the delusion of separateness.... The Gītā gives, through several of its verses, the message of same-sightedness."[2]

Parallel Message of Seeing God Everywhere, in Bhaktiyoga

10.4. The Gītā recognizes that the message of equal vision based on Ātman (which is formless) is not easily grasped by common people. Verse XII.5, by stating this difficulty, prepares the ground for giving the same message based on Īshwara (who has form)—

avyaktā hi gatirduḥkhaṃ dehavadbhiravāpyate

Simple Meaning—Lord Krishna says, for embodied human beings, the goal or high ideal expressed in terms of the unmanifested Ātman is difficult to grasp.

10.5. The message of equal vision based on bhakti-yoga is given by Lord Krishna in verse VI.30—that is, immediately after He gave it in terms of jñānayoga—

yo māṃ paśyati sarvatra sarvaṃ ca mayi paśyati
tasyā'haṃ na praṇaśyāmi sa ca me na praṇaśyati

Simple Meaning—Lord Krishna says, he who sees Me (i.e. God) everywhere and who sees all in Me (i.e. in God), I am never away from him and similarly he is never away from Me.

10.6. Lokmanya Tilak has explained the significance of this verse for those who combine karmayoga and bhaktiyoga—

> "The technique of performing action, but abandoning the desire for its fruit, now becomes the technique of performing action with he idea of dedicating it to Parameshwar....As both one's self, and everyone else, has been included in the Parameshwar, and the Parameshwar is included in one's self and everyone else, both one's interest and other's interest are merged in the highest goal in the shape of dedication to Lord Krishna....Obviously such dedicated souls work only for the benefit of the world."[3]

Equal Vision Needs to be Reflected in Behaviour

10.7. Swami Vivekananda used the expression "Practical Vedanta" to convey the message that a true knowledge of Vedanta must be reflected in compassionate behaviour. He was pained to see that many of the orthodox scholars who knew Vedantic scriptures by heart were as much guilty of unkind treatment towards the low-caste, poor countrymen as other high-caste persons who were not scholars. "Practical Vedanta", according to Vivekananda, meant theoretical knowledge as well as practice—

> "Raise once more that mighty banner of Vedanta for on no other ground can you have that wonderful love until you see that the same Lord is present everywhere. The nation is sinking, the curse of unnumbered millions is on our heads—the unnumbered millions to whom we have talked of Vedanta and whom we have hated with all our strength, to whom we have talked theoretically that we are all the same and all are one with the same Lord, without even an ounce of practice...Throw away everything, even your own salvation, and go and help others. Ay, you are always talking bold words, but here is practical Vedanta for you. The first part of this is that you should go to the sinking millions of India, and take them by hand, remembering the teaching of Lord Krishna."[4]

10.8. The teaching of Lord Krishna to which Swami Vivekananda drew our attention is contained in several well-known verses of the Gītā. Perhaps verse VI.32, to which we referred in paragraph 5.33, summarizes most clearly the teaching of practical Vedanta—

ātmaupamyena sarvatra samaṃ paśyati yo'rjuna
sukhaṃ vā yadi vā duḥkhaṃ sa yogī paramo mataḥ.

Simple Meaning—A sāmyayogī is guided by the philosophy of 'ātmaupamya' which sees the same Ātman in all the beings. Furthermore, his sympathetic behaviour towards all reflects this philosophy fully, in the sense that he is happy when others are happy and he is unhappy when others are unhappy.

10.9. Dr. Radhakrishnan, quoting Shankaracharya and adding his own commentary, has explained this verse in the following words—

"Atmaupaṃya means equality of others with oneself. Even as he desires good to himself, he desires good to all. He embraces all things in God, leads men to divine life and acts in the world with the power of spirit and in that luminous consciousness. He harms no creature as, in the words of Shankaracharya 'he sees that whatever is pleasant to himself is pleasant to all creatures, and that whatever is painful to himself is painful to all beings.' He does not any more shrink from pleasure and pain. As he sees God in the world, he fears nothing but embraces all in the equality of the vision of the Self."[5]

Equal Vision Supplemented by Even-mindedness Towards Situations

10.10. The word 'sama' (meaning equal or same) is a favourite word of the Gītā. In fact, two variants of 'samatva' are described there, viz. (i) samatva towards situations and (ii) samatva towards people. In the preceding paragraphs we have discussed the second variant because of its close connection with the message of the good of all which is the topic of this book. However, within the Gītā itself, chapter II introduces samatva towards situations (i.e. the first variant), and chapter V introduces samatva towards people (i.e. the second variant). It will be useful to understand how the Gītā has explained the first variant (to supplement what we have written above about the second variant), and also to appreciate the subtle difference between the two variants.

10.11. The background for the introduction (in chapter II) of the first variant of samatva has already been provided by us in paragraphs 8.3-5. Arjuna requested Lord Krishna to show him the way to 'śreyas' (i.e. good). About svajanam (own people), Arjuna's concern was two-fold—i.e. either to avoid killing them (if possible) or at least to avoid the sin (pāpam) in killing his own people. Closely connected with these goals was Arjuna's request to Lord Krishna to show the way to obtain release from śokaṃ (sorrow).

10.12. While answering Arjuna's question, Lord Krishna recommends the technique of 'samatva', the first reference to which is made in verse II.15—

samaduḥkhasukhaṃ dhīraṃ so'mritatvāya kalpate

Simple Meaning—Lord Krishna says, O Arjuna, pain and pleasure (i.e. dualities) are part of life, and only by remaining 'sama' i.e. the same in pain and pleasure, you can make yourself fit for eternal life.

10.13. Lord Krishna refers to 'samatva' for the second time in verse II.38, in the context of 'svadharma'. The message here is that if Arjuna could perform his traditional svadharma according to the new Gītā-technique of samatva, then he need not have the fear of incurring sin, even if he killed his svajanam—

sukhaduḥkhe same kritvā lābhālābhau jayājayau
tato yuddhāya yujyasva nai'vaṃ pāpamavāpsyasi

Simple Meaning—Lord Krishna says, O Arjuna, remain 'sama' (i.e. even-minded) in pleasure and pain, gain and loss, victory and defeat. With this attitude if you fight, you will not incur sin.

10.14. In verse II.48, Lord Krishna elevates 'samatva' to be synonymous with yoga—

siddhyasiddhyoḥ samo bhūtvā samatvaṃ yoga ucyate

Simple Meaning—Lord Krishna says, O Arjuna, perform your svadharma without attachment to the fruits of your action, i.e. with an even mind in success or failure. In fact, 'samatva' is called yoga.

10.15. Since Arjuna was keen to know the way to 'śreyas', Lord Krishna assured him that 'samatva' (i.e. the first variant) was the way. Several verses in the Gītā convey this message, but it should suffice to look at verse IV.22—

samaḥ siddhāvasiddhau ca kritvā'pi na nibadhyate

Simple Meaning—Lord Krishna says, O Arjuna, one who is even-minded in success or failure, attains śreyas i.e. even though he performs all (doable) actions as svadharma, he is still liberated (not bound).

10.16. The way we have explained 'samatva' (first variant), also clarifies its difference from 'samadriṣṭi' (i.e. second variant of samatva), viz. that the first variant is closely linked with śreyas, while the second one is closely linked with lokasaṃgraha. Verses VI.8-9 refer to these two variants, one after the other, in two consecutive verses which, admiring both, view the second as 'excellent'—

yukta ityucyate yogī samaloṣṭāśmakāñcanaḥ

Simple Meaning—One to whom a clod, a stone, and piece of gold are the same, is said to be firm in yoga.

sādhuṣvapi ca papeṣu samabuddhirviśiṣyate.

Simple Meaning—One who is equal-minded (i.e. has equal vision) towards saints and sinners, he excels.

10.17. Dr. Radhakrishnan too, explaining the difference between the two variants of samatva, views the second as God-like. For example, the yogī who has samatva (first variant), says Radhakrishnan, "is unperturbed by things and happenings of the world and is therefore said to be equal-minded to the events of this changing world."[6] And about the second variant of samatva, he writes, "This view makes us look upon our fellow beings with kindliness and compassion. The wise see the one God in all beings and develop the quality of equal-mindedness which is characteristic of the Divine."[7]

Sāmya or Equality Given Special Importance in Modern Times

10.18. We already mentioned the pioneering role of Swami Vivekananda (in paragraph 10.7) who brought out the distinction between the 'monastery-based Vedānta' and 'practical Vedānta'. The latter concept provided a spiritual basis for setting aside all distinctions based on caste, creed, sex, race, socio-economic status, etc. Another famous term coined by Vivekananda was 'Daridra-Nārāyaṇ' which meant that serving the poor constituted service to God. Social unity and harmony and selfless service were stressed by him in his final message to the disciples in 1902—

"It is not easy to establish social unity and harmony in India but you can make a significant contribution.... Your duty is to serve the poor and the distressed, without distinction of caste and creed. What business have you to consider the fruits of your action?... Let the reading of the Vedānta and the practising of meditation and the like be left to be done in the next life! Let this body go in the service of others—and then I shall know you have not come to me in vain."[8]

10.19. Mahatma Gandhi placed great emphasis on "constructive programme" through which the message of serving the poor and raising their status was carried far and wide. For our present purposes, it will be useful to give some details on three components of this programme. First, he was keen to remove 'untouchability'. He coined a new term 'Harijan'—meaning God's men—for the so-called 'untouchables'. Orthodox people opposed Gandhi, but he was able to achieve considerable success. Betai believes that this was because of the support of the Gītā's message of 'equal vision'—

> "The Gītā told him that all men are equal, all men deserve the supreme blessings of God, the Gītā bars no one from divine attainment that he calls self-realization. This spirit that he derived from the Gītā made him a life-time servant of and upholder of the rights of the untouchables in particular and the down-trodden of the society in general."[9]

10.20. 'Uplift of women' constituted another important plank in Gandhi's constructive programme. The fact that the Gītā makes no distinction between man and woman strengthened Gandhi's belief in the need to provide equal opportunities to women...He encouraged women to play a leading role in the Satyagraha movements and in the reconstruction of the country, and he achieved success too.

10.21. The third important cause (and the last for our present discussion) for which Gandhi fasted several times, and ultimately faced the assassin's bullet, was inter-religious harmony, in general, and Hindu-Muslim unity in particular. In his prayer meetings, verses from various scriptures—including the Gītā and Koran—were recited. The partition of India was a setback, but Indian society does carry on Gandhi's legacy to maintain inter-religious harmony.

10.22. Acharya Vinoba highlighted the message of 'sāmya' or equality by suggesting that the Gītā should be called 'sāmya-yoga'.

> "I have named the Gītā 'sāmya-yoga' which is both the art and the philosophy of equality, equanimity and identity. Other commentators have given other names....It is possible that the present age or the nature of the work that I have undertaken might have been the influencing factor behind my decision to name the Gītā as 'sāmya-yoga'."[10]

Beneficial Speech as Part of Non-Violent Behaviour

10.23. The Vedāntic basis of even-mindedness obviously implies non-violent behaviour, because violence can thrive only on the notion of separateness. If the other party does not reciprocate properly and carries on with evil design, then matters need to be set right with non-violent non-cooperation. This is not an easy thing to do but to return evil for evil is unlikely to provide a better alternative, as demonstrated by actual experience of activists in many situations.

10.24. The Gītā considers the use of 'right speech' as a component of tapas i.e. self-discipline. Verse XVII.15 lists four important characteristics of such speech—

> *anudvegakaraṃ vākyaṃ satyaṃ priyahitaṃ ca yat*

> ***Simple Meaning***—Right speech gives no offence, is truthful, pleasant and beneficial.

10.25. Tilak suggests that these words of the Gītā should be read along with similar messages given in Manusmṛti and the Mahābhārat. Here is a part of Tilak's commentary on this verse—

> "The words, 'satya', 'priya', and 'hita', used in this verse seem to refer to the dictum of Manu—
>
> *satyaṃ brūyāt priyaṃ brūyāt*
> *na brūyāt satyamapriyaṃ*
> *priyaṃ ca nānritaṃbrūyāt*
> *esa dharmaḥ sanātanaḥ*
>
> i.e. one should speak what is true, one should speak what is pleasant, one should not speak what is true if it is not pleasant, nor what is pleasant if it is not true—this is the ancient religion. But Vidura has told Duryodhana in the Mahābhārata—
>
> *apriyasya ca pathyasya*
> *vaktā śrotā hi durlabhaḥ*
>
> i.e. of what is unpleasant and beneficial, the speaker as also the listener is hard to find."[11]

10.26. A follower of the Gītā's message gives priority, while speaking, to the good of all, which includes the good of the opponent too. Lord Krishna told Arjuna in verse X.1—

> *vakṣyāmi hitakāmyayā*

i.e. underlying all my words is the desire to do good to you. Of course, Arjuna was a disciple, not an opponent, but Arjuna's good—and the good of mankind—was the goal of Lord Krishna in the Gītā. Another useful advice of Lord Krishna, pertaining to speech, is to avoid dogmatism, for example, verse II.42 disapproves of a closed mind—

nā'nyadastīti vādinaḥ

i.e. only non-discerning people insist that their way is the only way.

Gītā's Warning Against Divisive Behaviour Based on Biased Vision

10.27. We discussed in paragraphs 10.18-22 how social reformers have tried to realize in practice the vast potential that exists in the Gītā's message of equal vision, and 'karma' (deeds) based thereon. Because of the crucial importance of this message in the modern world, we want to draw attention to what can be called 'the other side or denial of the message', viz. how much harm can be caused, according to the Gītā, if the vision is unequal i.e. biased. Verse XVI.9 lists both personal and social harm—

etāṃ driṣṭimavaṣṭabhya naṣṭātmāno'lpabuddhayaḥ
prabhavantyugrakarmānaḥ kṣayāya jagato'hitāḥ

Simple Meaning—People with biased vision not only destroy themselves because of their narrow-mindedness, but they also commit cruelty, and they behave like enemies of the world, bent upon destroying it too. (Insult of Draupadi by the Kauravas was one such act of barbarity, leading to destruction).

Those who are interested in protecting the world and in bringing about 'equal' vision and cooperative 'karma' in the society would obviously try so that the strong warning of the Gītā effectively reaches the ears of all narrow-minded persons.

Parallel Message and Ideals in the Mānas

10.28. Like the other expressions discussed in the earlier chapters, 'samadriṣṭi-related' messages and ideals of the Gītā have their parallels in the Mānas also. These will be presented under four sections.

(a) ***Mānas Promotes Equal Vision and Racial Equality***

10.29. When Tulasī started writing the Mānas, he prayed not only to Rāma, Sītā, and other divine entities, but also to demons and all the beings—because he saw Rāma and Sītā in all of them, because of his equal vision—

siyārāmamaya sab jag jānī
karaun praṇām jori jug pānī....

bandaun kinnar rajanichar
kripā karahu ab sarva

Simple Meaning—Tulasī says, I know that Rāma and Sītā pervade the whole universe, so I bow to everyone with folded hands. I pray to all beings, including demons, and seek their blessings.

10.30. Mānas-scholars in Trinidad, belonging to different races, find in the Rāma-Hanumān relationship, a clear and powerful message of racial equality and mutual cooperation for a great cause. Again, in the beginning of Mānas i.e. in Bālakāṇḍa, Tulasī draws attention to this relationship—using the word 'samān', which corresponds to 'sama' in the Gītā—

prabhu taru tar kapi dār par
te kiya āpu samān

Simple Meaning—Tulasī says, glory to Lord Rāma who made the monkeys equal to Himself, inspite of the big difference between the two. (In poetic style, Tulasī says, Rāma lived on earth, under the tree, while monkeys jumped from one branch of tree to another).

10.31. The Gītā-word 'samadarshī' (meaning one who sees with equal vision) occurs several times in the Mānas. For example, in Kishkindhākāṇḍa, Lord Rāma tells Hanumān—

samadarshī mohi kah sab koū

i.e. all the people know and say that I am 'samadarshī'. And, similarly, in Sundarakāṇḍa, Lord Rāma welcomes Vibhīshaṇ by saying that I like saints like you who are 'samadarshī'—

samadarshī ichchhā kachhu nāhīṇ....
tum sārikhe sant priya moreṇ.....

i.e. although you expressed a doubt whether, being Rāvaṇa's brother, you would be accepted by Me, I want you not to have any fear or hesitation, because in My opinion you are a saint, 'samadarshī' and free from any selfish desires.

10.32. An in-depth study of both the above-mentioned contexts (where the word 'samadarshī' occurs) shows that Lord Rāma explained the significance of 'equal vision' by linking it with the message of social service. For example, the relevant words of Kishkindhākāṇḍ are—

maiṇ sevak sachrāchar
rūp swāmi bhagwant

Simple Meaning—Lord Rāma tells Hanumān, you are dear to Me but do remember My instruction, viz. think and act like a servant whose goal is to serve the whole world, which is nothing but a form of God.

And, similarly, in Sunarakaṇḍa too, Lord Rāma, immediately after saying the words of welcome to Vibhīshaṇ (quoted in the preceding paragraph), gives the message of 'par-hit' i.e. doing good to others—

sagun upāsak par-hit
nirat nīti driḍh nem

Simple Meaning—Lord Rāma tells Vibhīshaṇ, I welcome you as a saint, and I want to clarify that a saint is a bhakta, always doing good to others, and firm on principles and morality.

(b) ***Even-mindedness Towards Situations in Mānas too***

10.33. Lord Rāma Himself set a great example of even-mindedness when He showed no effect of coronation or exile. Tulasī draws attention to this in the following Sanskrit verse in the beginning of Ayodhyākāṇḍa—

prasannatāṃ yā na gatābhiṣekatas
tathā na mamle vanavāsaduḥkhataḥ

Simple Meaning—Tulasī says, I pray to Lord Rāma for 'mangal'—He is so great that He neither rejoiced at the news of coronation nor did He feel sad when (in stead of coronation) He was sent to forest for fourteen years.

10.34. Rāma's mother, Kaushalyā also admired the even-mindedness of her son Rāmā. In the same canto (i.e. Ayodhyākaṇḍa), Kaushalyā told Bharat—

pitu āyasu bhushan vasan
tāt taje raghuvīr
vismaya harsha na hridayan kachhu
pahire valkal chīr

Simple Meaning—Kaushalyā said, O Bharat, you are asking me to tell you what happened when you were not here. In my opinion, the main thing to tell is this—Rāma interpreted the events of that day as if his father (Dashrath) cancelled the coronation and ordered exile instead. So he (Rāma) discarded the royal clothes and ornaments, and covered his body with leaves and barks—and in so doing, he showed no signs of sadness or joy.

10.35. Apart from the particular instance of Rāma's even-minded behaviour, the general philosophic statement glorifying 'samatva' also occurs in the Mānas in several contexts. We want to quote only one of them here, viz. the one spoken by Sumantra (Prime minister) to King Dashrath in Ayodhyākāṇḍa—

sukh harshahiṇ jaḍa dukh bilakhāhīṇ
dou sam dhīr dharahiṇ man māhīṇ
dhīraj dharahu vivek vichārī
chhāriya soch sakal hitkārī

Simple Meaning—Sumantra says to Dashrath, O great King, joys and sorrows come and go. Only unwise persons celebrate their joys and cry at the sorrows. But wise person remain 'sam' (i.e. even-minded) under both the situations. You are wise and are devoted to 'sakal hit' (i.e. the good of all). Therefore you should be able to take things calmly, unperturbed by the sad event (of Rāma's exile).

Through this statement of Sumantra, Tulasī also wants to give the message that even-mindedness and 'sakal-hit' (i.e. doing good to all) go together.

(c) ***Norms of Behaviour and Karma Glorified as 'Maryādā'***

10.36. The Mānas has depicted Rāma as 'maryādā-purushottam', i.e. one who set exemplary standards of good conduct with the idea of developing social norms. Guru Vashishṭh indicated in Ayodhyākāṇḍa the underlying object of these norms—

sab kar dharam sahit hit hoī

i.e. doing only such karma which is consistent with dharma and which contributes to 'sarva-hit' i.e. the good of all.

Tulasī says in Uttarakāṇḍa that all the citizens followed these norms in Rāma-rājya—

sab nar karahiṇ paraspar prītī
chalahiṇ svadhana nirat shruti nītī...
sab udār sab par upkārī...
sakal param gati ke adhikārī...

Simple Meaning—In Rāma-rājya, all the people loved one another. Everyone followed sva-dharma, and observed norms established by the Vedas. All were broad-minded. Since they helped others, all were entitled to 'param gati' i.e. spiritual perfection.

10.37. Rāma had equal vision towards all, but special sympathy for the poor. He visited the Ashram of Shabrī, an old woman neglected by many. She offered berries to Rāma—after eating a part of each berry to ensure that it was sweet. Tulasī says in Araṇyakāṇḍa—

prem sahit prabhu khāye
bārambār bakhāni

Simple Meaning—In eating berries (partly eaten by Shabrī) Rāma showed no hesitation, rather He enjoyed eating them, repeatedly saying 'How sweet'.

10.38. Ayodhyākāṇḍa describes how Kevaṭ, the poor boatman took Rāma, Sītā and Lakshmaṇ across the river Gangā. The affection showed by Rāma and Sītā towards Kevaṭ set an example of ideal behaviour. Tulasī says in the same canto that Kevaṭ wàs no exception because all the villagers were blessed with Rāma's love—

hohiṇ prem bas log imi
Rąm jahāṇ jahāṇ jāhiṇ
gāoṇ gāoṇ as hoi anandū.....
mag loganh sukh det

Simple Meaning—Wherever Rāma went, He established bonds of love. Every villager was thrilled with joy....In fact, Rāma gave happiness to all the people on the roadside too.

(d) ***Beneficial Speech as Part of 'Par-Hit'***

10.39. On the subject of 'right speech', the following words of the Mānas (from Ayodhyākāṇḍa) resemble those of the Gītā (referred to by us in paragraphs 10.24 and 10.26)—

kahahin satya priya vachan vichārī.....
sab ke priya sab ke hitkāri.....
muni udveg na pāvai koī

Simple Meaning—Tulasī says, bhaktas of Rāma do not speak thoughtlessly—they speak what is true and pleasant.... Since they want to do good to all, their words establish bonds of love with all....They also want to make sure that their speech gives no offence to good people.

10.40. Tulasī describes in the same canto (i.e. Ayodhyākāṇḍa) two critical occasions which Rāma handled superbly by his appropriate speech. The first one relates to the crisis that Kaikeyī created by her selfish demands, aggravated by her poisonous words—

bolī ashubh bharī shubh chhūnchhī....
pratham dīkh dukh sunā na kāū
tadapi dhīr dhari samaya vichārī
pūchhi madhur vachan mahtārī

Simple Meaning—Tulasī says, Kaikeyī's words were mean, with no trace of goodness in them. For Rāma, this was the first experience of getting involved with an unhappy situation face to face. Even so, he remained cool and made a quick assessment of what needed to be said and done. He addressed Kaikeyī as 'mother', and spoke sweet words, to find out what the problem was.

10.41. The second critical occasion relates to Chitrakūṭ. Bharat wanted Rāma to return to Ayodhyā, and there were several suggestions given by Vashishṭh, Janak and Kaushalyā. Rāma did not want to offend any one but he also wanted to protect the interests of the society—

bole vachan vāni sarvas se
hit pariṇām sunat sasi ras se

Simple Meaning—Tulasī says, Rāma's words were (in poetic language) blessed by goddess Saraswati, they were sweet as nectar, and above all, they helped take a decision beneficial to all.

10.42. Before closing this chapter, we want to present one more instance of beneficial speech, described in Sundarakāṇḍa. Hanumān had gone to Laṅkā to do 'Rāma-kāj'. His goal was to do good to Rāvaṇa, by persuading him to take an about-turn from the path of evil that he had followed so far. But Rāvaṇa was too arrogant to listen to anyone. Even so, Hanumān tried his best—

bintī karauṇ jori kar rāvana
sunahu mān taji mor sikhāvan
rishi pulasti jasu vimal mayankā....
lankā achal rāj tum karhū....
jadapi kahī kapi ati hit vānī

Simple Meaning—Hanumān said, O Rāvaṇa, I pay respects to you with folded hands. Please give up arrogance and listen to my suggestion. Remember that you belong to the noble family of Rishi Pulastya. My suggestion will not adversely affect your sovereign rule over Laṅkā, but you need to undo the evil that you have done.... Tulasī says, Hanumān's advice was 'beneficial speech'.

Chapter Eleven

Call not to Succumb to Evil—Āsurī Sampat or Kaliyug

11.1. In chapters three to ten, we have summarized the advice of the Gītā and the Mānas about putting into practice their common call for the good of all. In other words, we have discussed what our role could be in bringing about an improvement in the society. At this stage, it is necessary to recognize that there are some elements in the society who might be trying to do just the opposite. This can be viewed as a clash between the good and the evil forces. Such a clash has been going on from times immemorial, and a consideration thereof is an essential part of the social message of the Gītā and the Mānas. This is what we plan to do in the present chapter. However, only a part of our presentation will adopt a two-way classification of branding individuals as 'good' or 'bad'. For the rest, we shall view each individual as a mixture of good and bad, raising the possibility that evil tendencies might gain the upper hand in any person's heart when self-discipline becomes lax. Both of these interpretations will be illustrated by quotations from the Gītā and the Mānas. In terms of the ten key words or phrases that we listed in chapter two, the topic that we are now covering occupies the ninth place.

Terminology to Denote Anti-social Elements

11.2. Warning against anti-social tendencies is given in the Gītā in four different contexts, viz.

(a) Āsurī sampat, i.e. demoniac forces;
(b) Adharma, i.e. unrighteousness;
(c) Ahaṃkāra-mūla dveṣa-śrinkhalā, i.e. chain of hatred rooted in egotism; and

(d) Tāmasika varieties of buddhi, tapas, etc.

11.3. Besides containing parallels to these, the Mānas has a special feature called 'kaliyuga' which provides an alarming picture of a society which has fallen prey to unrighteous thoughts and practices. We present in Appendix three the full text of the relevant Mānas-section which occurs in Uttarakāṇḍa, accompanied with a simple English language meaning thereof. A gist of the same will be given in this chapter too.

Two Ways of Looking at the Good-Bad Dichotomy

11.4. Verse XVI.6 speaks of two types of beings—

dvau bhūtasargau loke'smin daiva āsura eva ca

Simple Meaning—There are two types of beings that exist in this world, viz. the divine and the demoniac.

However, Mahatma Gandhi took the view that the real struggle between the good and the bad goes on in the heart of each individual. Explaining this, Mahadev Desai wrote—

"Let no one misunderstand these labels (of good and bad) and misapply them. We may only say that when particular characteristics predominate us, we are of God, and when the opposite ones do so, we are of the devil."[1]

11.5. The idea that our real enemy is within ourselves and not outside, is supported by verse VI.5 which says—

ātmai'va ripurātmanaḥ

i.e. Oneself is verily one's own enemy.

Swami Vivekananda, quoting this verse, said, "This is a great lesson. There is no other enemy but this self of mine."[2]

Next we take up the four Gītā-descriptions of anti-social elements, one by one.

Description of Anti-Social Elements in the Gītā

(a) ***Āsurī Sampat i.e. Demoniac Forces***

11.6. There are sixteen verses in chapter sixteen of the Gītā which describe in detail the demoniac forces. Pandit Ram Kinkar Upadhyay has suggested that if we make a group of vices that go together, then they can present a picture of the wicked trio of the Mahābhārata, viz. Duryodhana-Duhshāsan-Shakuni. The three vices that can be viewed as a group are, kāma-lobha-anyāya, i.e. lust-greed-injustice, and these are mentioned in verses XVI.10, 12, 13—

kāmamāśritya duṣpūraṃ...
bhaviṣyati punardhanaṃ....
anyāyenārthasaṃcayān

Simple Meaning—Desires of the demoniac persons are insatiable, so they become greedy, anxious to increase their wealth, even if they have to employ unjust means for that purpose.

Pandit Upadhyay comments—

"Duryodhana is an embodiment of greed and his brother Duhshāsan is an embodiment of lust. Their uncle Shakuni won the game of dice by foul means. Thus this trio constituted a clearly visible group of demoniac forces in the Mahābhārata."[3]

(b) ***Adharma, i.e. Unrighteousness***

11.7. Adharma too is a comprehensive term that includes many vices. Parallel to the group of vices referred to in the preceding paragraph, Upadhyay has suggested another group consisting of ajñāna-darpa-asatya-anīti, i.e. ignorance-arrogance-falsehood-impropriety, to present a picture of Karṇa in the Mahābhārata. These vices are mentioned in verses XVI.4, 7, 10—

ajñānaṃ ca.....darpaśca....
aśucivratāḥ....āsadgrāhān.....
na satyaṃ teṣu vidyate

Simple Meaning—Demoniac persons suffer from ignorance and arrogance, they have impure resolves and they hold wrong views, and no truth is found in them.

Pandit Upadhyay comments—

"Ignorance was the first problem with Karṇa. For a long time, he did not even know that he was the son of Kunti. Lord Krishna removed this ignorance of Karṇa, but the latter said that he had already joined hands with Duryodhana, the enemy of the Pāṇḍavas.

"Karṇa's second problem was 'arrogance'. Because of that he picked up a quarrel with Bhīshma and declared that, so long as Bhīshma was alive, he (i.e. Karṇa) would not participate in the war.

"The third problem with Karṇa was falsehood. He went to Paraśurāma and became his disciple by telling him a lie (that he i.e. Karṇa was a Brāhmin). But Karṇa's lie was ultimately detected. Paraśurāma in his anger pronounced this curse on Karṇa, "Since you deceived your guru, the weapon you have learnt shall fail you at the fated moment. You will be unable to recall the mantra when your hour comes."

"The fourth problem with Karṇa was 'impropriety'. He joined the Kauravas in conspiracies, but during his last battle, he appealed to Arjuna to observe 'dharma'. Lord Krishna told him that an appeal to dharma can be made only by one who had himself observed it."[4]

11.8. To continue with another aspect of 'adharma', Acharya Vinoba has interpreted verse III.12 to identify 'theft-mentality' as an anti-social element which widens the gap between the rich and the poor. To understand this, let us first look at the verse III.12—

tairdattānapradāyai'bhyo yo bhuṅkte stena eva saḥ

Simple Meaning—A thief is one who takes and consumes but does not give.

Based on this, Vinoba presents a four-way categorization of an individual's economic relationship with the society, namely:

(i) Theft,
(ii) Begging,
(iii) Earning one's livelihood, and
(iv) Dānam (sharing)

First, Vinoba defines theft as a situation in which an individual takes from the society goods and services but gives nothing in return. The second category is begging when an individual takes more from the society than what he or she gives in return. The third category represents a state of equality of what one takes and what one gives. Fourthly, dānam (sharing) refers to a situation in which one is apparently giving more to society than what one is currently receiving in return, but Vinoba says, this should be viewed as discharging old debts.

11.9. What Vinoba calls 'theft-mentality', can also he viewed as 'lack of social responsibility'. Swami Vivekananda put it this way, "Ask yourself what will be the impact of my action or inaction on the society." He illustrated this by pointing out the responsibility of mothers to ensure that, by leading a pure life, they would give birth to healthy babies. "So long as you live in society," said he, "it is your responsibility to prevent the very birth of evil."[5]

11.10. Vivekananda also pointed out that the richer sections of the society are failing in their 'dharma' if they do not recognize that they are at least partly responsible for the misery of the masses. Of course, on the positive side, he saw therein a challenge for social workers. For their guidance, he outlined the purposes of rendering service—

> "to struggle unto life and death to bring about a new state of things—sympathy for the poor and bread to their hungry mouths, enlightenment to the people at large, and struggle unto death to make men of them who have been brought to the level of beasts by the tyranny of the forefathers of the rich and powerful."[6]

(c) ***Chain of Hatred Rooted in Egotism***

11.11. The chain of hatred rooted in egotism is mentioned twice in the Gītā, first as a part of the 'āsurī sampat' and then as a part of process of elimination needed for attaining spiritual perfection. From the point of view of the good of all, this chain has special significance because hatred between different members of the society is a serious threat to social harmony. We quote below verse XVI.18 where the components of the chain are specified—

> *ahaṃkārṃ balaṃ darpaṃ kāmaṃ krodhaṃ ca saṃśritāḥ*
> *māmātmaparadeheṣu pradviṣanto 'bhyasūyakāḥ*

> ***Simple Meaning***—Demoniac persons suffer from the vice of egotism, then they take recourse to force, arrogance, lust, anger and malice, and then they despise God dwelling in the bodies of themselves and others i.e. they spread hatred in the society.

This is the description of the chain of hatred as a part of the 'āsurī sampat'. Subsequently, verses XVIII.53-54 describe how a seeker of spiritual perfection gets rid of this chain and becomes 'samah sarveṣu bhūteṣu', i.e. has equal vision towards all, free from hatred.

11.12. Although the Gītā has presented another chain of vices in verses II.62-63, we have included only the chain of hatred as an anti-social element, because the other chain starts from attachment and ends in self-destruction, i.e. its adverse effect is more at the individual level, rather than at the social level. We recall, in this connection, the difference that we pointed out in paragraph 10.16, between the first and the second variants of samatva—the first linked with 'śreyas' and the second linked with 'lokasaṃgraha'. Since the chain of hatred is an obstacle in the way to 'lokasaṃgraha', it calls for greater attention in this book, in comparison to the other chain of vices which is an obstacle in the way to 'śreyas'.

(d) ***Tāmasika Varieties of Buddhi, Tapas, etc.***

11.13. Although unrighteousness and hatred cause particular alarm when their adverse effect engulfs large sections of the society, the root of the whole trouble really exists in the minds of men and is called 'tāmasika buddhi' in the Gītā. This is what prompted Mahatma Gandhi to take the view that the real struggle between the good and the bad goes on in the heart of each individual. How 'tāmasika buddhi' creates trouble is explained by the Gītā in verse XVIII.32—

adharmaṃ dharmamiti yā manyate tamasā'vritā
sarvārthān viparītāṃśca buddhiḥ sā pārtha tāmasī

Simple Meaning—That way of thinking is harmful which is perverted, i.e. which considers good as bad, and bad as good, thus prompting one to act contrary to social norms and values.

11.14. Verse XVIII.28 describes 'tāmasika kartā', i.e. a person who puts into effect the wrong way of thinking—

ayuktaḥ prākritaḥ stabdhaḥ śaṭho naiṣkritiko'lasaḥ
viṣādī dīrghasūtrī ca kartā tāmasa ucyate

Simple Meaning—A tāmasika doer lacks discipline, he or she cheats others and ruins their work, and does everything inefficiently.

11.15. Verse XVII.19 says that even those practices, which are normally considered good, are put to wrong use, because of the influence of tamas. For example, 'tapas' generally has the meaning of self-discipline, but in the hands of a tāmasika person, it becomes 'tāmasika' too—

mūḍhagrāheṇā'tmano yat pīdayā kriyate tapaḥ
parasyo'tsādanārthaṃ vā tattāmasamudāhritaṃ

Simple Meaning—That tapas is tāmasika which is performed with a foolish obstinacy by means of self-torture or for causing injury to others.

11.16. Gītā's condemnation applies not only to 'tāmasika tapas' but also to 'ghora tapas'. Relevant verses (XVII.5-6) occur in the same chapter in which the above warning against 'tāmasika tapas' is given, and these are quoted below—

aśāstravihitaṃghoraṃ tapyante ye tapo janāḥ
dambhāhaṃkārasaṃyuktāḥ kāmarāgabalānvitāḥ
karṣayantaḥ śarīrasthaṃ bhūtagrāmamacetasaḥ
māṃ caivā'ntaḥśarīrasthaṃ tān viddhyāsuraniścayān

Simple Meaning—Lord Krishna says, those men, vain and conceited and impelled by the force of lust and passion, who perform violent austerities, which are not ordained by the scriptures, being foolish, oppress the group of elements in their body and Me also dwelling in the body. Know them to be demoniac in their resolves.

Parallel Elements in the Mānas

11.17. From the Gītā-based presentation of anti-social elements, we now turn to the Mānas. In the light of paragraph 11.3, the remaining part of this chapter will consist of the following five sections, all based on the Mānas.

(e) ***Binding Forces of Māyā***

11.18. These can be viewed as corresponding to the 'āsurī sampat' or demoniac forces of the Gītā. Although the word 'māyā' occurs in the Gītā too, the Mānas-description thereof is not only more detailed, but it also has a stronger social dimension. For example, the following verse from Uttarakāṇḍa gives a list of the commanders of the dangerous army of 'māyā'—

vyāpi raheu sansār mahn
māyā kaṭak prachanḍ
senāpati kāmādi bhaṭ
dambh kapaṭ pākhanḍ

Simple Meaning—The aggressive army of 'māyā' has taken hold of the whole world. It has three commanders—lust, greed, and anger—and three associates—arrogance, hypocrisy and dishonesty.

11.19. In another context, i.e. in Araṇyakāṇḍa, Tulasī says that forces of 'māyā' have been able to conquer all beings by making them narrow-minded—

main aru mor tor tain māyā
jehi bas kīnhe jīv nikāyā

Simple Meaning—Māyā obtains control over people's minds in a subtle way. Whoever adopts a divisive approach which favours 'I' and 'mine'—and opposes 'you' and 'yours'—know that person to be under the binding force of 'māyā'.

(f) ***Asant or Unrighteous People***

11.20. Tulasī's descriptions of unrighteous people are almost as detailed as those of the righteous ones. In fact, Tulasī asks for the blessings of both 'sant' and 'asant', i.e. the righteous and the unrighteous, because, as a true bhakta, he sees Lord Rāma in every being. The motive behind

Tulasī's strong criticism of the 'asant' is to warn common people in three ways, viz. (i) not to become an asant, (ii) not to have the company of 'asant', and (iii) not to be fooled by the outwardly sweet but inherently dangerous behaviour of asant. Without going into much detail, we shall confine ourselves to these three points only.

11.21. To start with, Tulasī says in Bālakāṇḍa that virtues and vices co-exist in the world, and it is for each individual to make the right choice (i.e. not to become an 'asant')—

jad chetan guṇ dosh maya
vishwa kīnha kartār
sant hans gun gahahin paya
pariharī vāni vikār

Simple Meaning—The creator has put together both virtues and vices. It is our function to act like a swan (who takes in milk and leaves out water), i.e. to become a 'sant' and not an 'asant'.

11.22. Secondly, the Mānas is full of repeated warnings, "Avoid the company of 'asant' ". For example, Bālakāṇḍa itself says—

hāni kusang susangati lāhū
lokahu ved vidit sab kāhū

Simple Meaning—Remember that the company of 'asant' means 'loss' and the company of 'sant' means gain. This is the message of the Vedas and is known to all the people.

And a similar message is given in Kishkindhākāṇḍa—

vinsai upjai gyān jimi
pāi kusang susang

Simple Meaning—Company of 'asant' means 'disappearance of jñāna, i.e. knowledge', and company of 'sant' means 'acquisition of knowledge'.

11.23. Finally, the advice not to become a victim of a wicked person's hypocrisy is also given again and again in the Mānas. For our present purposes, the following quotation from Araṇyakāṇḍa should suffice—

navani nīch kai ati dukhdāyī
jimi ankush dhanu urag bilāī
bhaydāyak khal kai priya vāṇī

Simple Meaning—If an 'asant' bows down to you, be careful because his real intention is to harm you. A snake bows down before biting you. Even sweet words of an 'asant' are just a cover for inflicting injury on you.

(g) *Slippery Path of Vices Starting from Egotism*

11.24. The condemnation of egotism in the Mānas is parallel to that in the Gītā. Tulasī has demonstrated, by means of Rāvaṇa's action, that starting from egotism, a chain of vices took control and pushed him down the path of destruction. For example, Sundarakāṇḍa describes how Rāvaṇa, because of egotism, completely ignored Hanumān's advice—

jadapi kahī kapi ati hit vānī....
bolā vihasi mahā abhimānī

Simple Meaning—Although Hanumān's suggestions were aimed at doing good to Rāvaṇa, the latter only scoffed at them because he was extremely arrogant.

11.25. A little later, a clearer sign of Rāvaṇa's downfall was visible when he hit his younger brother, Vibhīshaṇ. Rāvaṇa's wife, Mandodarī tried to help too, but Tulasī says, in the same canto (i.e. Sunarakāṇḍa)—

mandodarī adhik akulānī....
vihasā jagat vidit abhimānī

Simple Meaning—Mandodarī was able to foresee the crisis and she tried to avert it, but again, Rāvaṇa, whose arrogance was known the world over, merely laughed and paid no heed to her advice.

11.26. The upshot of what Tulasīi says about Rāvaṇa in Laṅkākāṇḍa is that his egotism pushed him along a slippery path of vices—

ati abhimān....kāl vivash....
nij agh gayau kumāragagāmī

Simple Meaning—Rāvaṇa was too arrogant to listen to any advice, as if death was calling him. He kept on going on the wrong path and ultimately perished by his own sins.

(h) *Tāmasika Buddhi Leading to Conflicts*

11.27. Here too the Mānas follows the Gītā in describing tāmasika buddhi as the pushing force that causes conflicts in the society, but the expression preferred by Tulasī to denote 'tāṁasika buddhi' is 'kumati' which means 'wrong way of thinking'. Sundarakāṇḍa has the most famous saying of the Mānas on this point—

jahān sumati tahan sampati nānā
jahān kumati tahan vipati nidānā

Simple Meaning—Right way of thinking (sumati) leads to happiness and prosperity, but 'kumati' is bound to result in disaster.

11.28. In the same context, the definition of 'kumati' is also given—and this is similar to that of the Gītā—

tav ur kumati basī viprītā
hit anhit mānau ripu prītā

Simple Meaning—Under the influence of kumati (i.e. a perverted way of thinking), one considers good as bad, and enemy as friend.

11.29. Vibhīshaṇa attributes Rāvaṇa's downfall to 'kumati'. To a lesser degree, Kaikeyī's role in creating conflicts in Ayodhyā is also linked by Bharat to 'kumati', as described in Ayodhyākāṇḍa—

jab tain kumati kumat jiyan thayaū

Simple Meaning—Bharat says to Kaikeyī—Although you are my mother, I must say that you have fallen a prey to 'kumati', and therefore I have to oppose you.

11.30. Tulasī says in Uttarakāṇḍa that the most dangerous outcome of 'kumati' or 'tāmasika buddhi' is visible in kaliyuga—

tāmas bahut rajogun thorā
kali prabhāv virodh chahun orā

Simple Meaning—Kaliyuga's problems arise because of the preponderance of tāmasika buddhi (combined with a little bit of rājasī buddhi, but none at all of sāttvika buddhi) and the net result is 'conflicts all around'.

This is an appropriate point to move on to 'kaliyuga' in the next section.

(j) *Kaliyuga—A Synonym for Anti-Social Situation*

11.31. This is a special feature of the Mānas because Tulasīdāsa had first-hand experience of the degeneration caused by kaliyuga, and he wrote strongly about it in order to persuade people to start the process of social reform and spiritual regeneration. Tulasī's ideas on this subject appear in a concentrated form in Uttarakāṇḍa. What makes kaliyuga particularly dangerous is that, even administrators, pandits, and sannyasins, who can be expected to do good to people, themselves contribute to anti-social activities. For example, Tulasī calls kaliyugi kings as "citizen-eaters"—

bhūp prajāsan....
nrip pāp parāyan dharma nahīn
kari danḍ viḍamb prajā nithī

Simple Meaning—Kings become sinners. They punish innocent people and constantly harass them, as if they are eating them up.

11.32. What about pandits and jñānins? Tulasī says, they boast a lot but their conduct is deplorable—

pandit soi jo gāl bajāvā...
nirāchār je shruti path tyāgī
kaliyug soi gyānī so virāgī

Simple Meaning—Pandits in kaliyuga neither know the Vedas nor do they act according to them, but they are experts in boasting. The same is true of jñānins.

11.33. Tulasī's harshest criticism is against sannyāsins and the so-called gurus because they cheat innocent people by pretending to be yogins—

nāri muī griha sampatī nāsī
mūnḍ munḍāi hohin sannyāsī
jāken nakh aru jatā viśālā
soi tāpas prasiddha kalikālā
guru sis badhir andḥ kā lekhā
ek na sunai ek nahin dekhā

Simple Meaning—Tulasī warns—Do not be misled by those who have shaved off their head or who have long hair and long nails. Find out who they really are and what they know. Most of them took sannyasa because their wife died and they lost their property. They are nothing but beggars. Similarly, gurus have no vision of knowledge and so can be called 'blind', and their disciples can be called 'deaf' because they are not interested in listening to guru's advice.

11.34. Keeping in mind the anti-social situation of kaliyuga, Tulasī repeatedly declared the aim of the Mānas as—

mangal-karani kali-mal-harani

i.e. to remove the evils of kaliyuga and to bring about the good of all. In this way, the kaliyuga-section of the Mānas has been written only to strengthen the call for the good of all.

CHAPTER TWELVE

Call to Promote Virtues—Daivī Sampat or Rāma-rājya

12.1. In the preceding chapter, we considered problems created by anti-social elements which constitute a serious challenge to those who strive for the good of all. Both the Gītā and the Mānas believe that, deriving support from the knowledge of such problems, appropriate action can be taken by social workers to ensure the victory of the good over the evil forces. The achievement of the victory can obviously be facilitated if the good forces join hands together. Under such circumstances, we have the assurance of the Vedic scriptures that God's Avatāra will also appear and provide decisive support to the good forces. In the present chapter, we bring together in one place the various elements that strengthen the hands of those who work for improvements in the society. As in the previous chapter, similarities between the Gītā and the Mānas will again be obvious. However, a special part of this presentation will be devoted to the description, given in the Mānas, of what an ideal society based on the principle of the good of all may look like—this feature being unique to the Mānas. In terms of the ten key words or phrases that we listed in chapter two, the topic that we are now covering occupies the tenth, i.e. the last place. This also means that answers to questions two and three listed in paragraph 1.54—parts of which have occupied the last ten chapters—will be completed at the end of this chapter. That will leave two more questions to be answered in the next (and the final) chapter.

Terminology to Denote Elements that Support the Good of All

12.2. Socially beneficial ideas relating to virtues and values are presented in the Gītā in five different contexts, viz.

(a) Daivī sampat, i.e. divine virtues;
(b) Virtues listed as part of jñāna;
(c) Sāttvika varieties of jñāna, sukha, etc.
(d) Dharma with emphasis on its social and universal aspects; and
(e) Characteristics of those who have attained spiritual perfection.

12.3. Besides containing parallels to these, the Mānas has a special feature called "Rāma-rājya" (meaning Rāma's rule), which provides a picture of an ideal society based on the principle of universal welfare. We shall present in Appendix Four the full text of the relevant Mānas-section which occurs in Uttarakāṇḍa, accompanied with simple English language meaning thereof. A gist of the same will be given in this chapter too.

12.4. Out of the five contexts listed above in paragraph 12.2, the fourth one has already been explained in this book in chapter three, and the fifth one similarly in chapter five. So there is no need to repeat that material here. Accordingly, the rest of this chapter will be devoted to items (a) to (c) of paragraph 12.2, and parallel descriptions thereof in the Mānas, and finally, the Rāma-rājya picture of the Mānas.

(a) ***Daivī Sampat or Divine Virtues***

12.5. Verses XVI.1-3 of the Gītā have listed as many as twenty-six virtues (constituting daivī sampat). However, before presenting them, we want to draw attention to Hiriyanna's suggestion regarding a two-way classification of virtues. This suggestion was made by Hiriyanna in a different context. He utilized a list of nine virtues (dharmasādhanaṃ) given in Yājñavalkya Smṛti to illustrate the practical difference between "self-regarding" and "other-regarding" virtues. We feel it is a useful classification and we shall apply it to the virtues that are included in daivī sampat. We also want to mention that "other-regarding" virtues are popularly known as social values.

12.6. Hiriyanna based his suggestion on the following verse of Yājñavalkya Smṛti—

ahimsā satyamasteyaṃ
saucamindriyanigrahaḥ
dānam damo dayā kṣāntiḥ
sarveṣāṃ dharmasādhanaṃ

Hiriyanna explained this verse and gave his suggestion in the following words—

"Yājñavalkya, in the Smṛti which goes by his name, has listed nine virtues to be cultivated by all, viz. non-injury, sincerity, honesty, cleanliness, control of the senses, charity, self-restraint, love, and forbearance. It will be seen that some of these, like non-injury and charity, have a reference to the good of others or are altruistic, while others, like sincerity and self-restraint, serve to develop one's own character and will. It should not, however, be thought that this division into self-regarding and other-regarding virtues is a hard and fast one; for, as an individual has no life of his own independently of society, the former has a bearing on the latter, as surely as the latter has on the former."[1]

12.7. Having looked at Hiriyanna's suggestion, we take up verses XVI.1-3 of the Gītā, one by one—

abhayaṃ sattvasaṃśuddhirjñānayogavyavasthitiḥ
dānaṃ damaśca yajñaśca svādhyāyastapa ārjavaṃ

Simple Meaning—Nine virtues are listed in the first verse—fearlessness, purity of mind, wise apportionment of knowledge and concentration, sharing, self-control, yajña, study of the scriptures, tapas, and uprightness.

ahimsā satyamakrodhas tyāgaḥ śāntriapaiśunaṃ
dayā bhūteṣvaloluptvaṃ mārdavaṃ hrīracāpalaṃ

Simple Meaning—Eleven virtues are listed in the second verse—non-violence, truth, freedom from anger, non-possessiveness, tranquillity, aversion to fault-finding, compassion to living beings, freedom from covetousness, gentleness, modesty, and absence of fickleness.

tejaḥ kṣamā dhritiḥ śaucaṃ adroho nā'timānitā
bhavanti sampadaṃ daiviṃ abhijātasya bhārata

Simple Meaning—Six virtues are listed in the third verse—vigour, forgiveness, fortitude, purity, freedom from malice and absence of excessive pride—all these (twenty-six) virtues constitute divine nature.

12.8. Rather than going into the subtle distinction between the various virtues, Gītā-commentators have suggested a selective approach. Also, since our focus is on the good of all, we are specially interested in the 'other-regarding' virtues like non-violence, sharing, compassion to living beings, freedom from malice, and absence of excessive pride. In fact, Mahatma Gandhi felt that by putting into practice just three virtues, viz. fearlessness, truth, and non-violence, a significant contribution to the good of the society can be made.

12.9. Adopting an approach similar to Gandhi's, Vinoba has stressed the significance of fearlessness and absence of excessive pride. Here is a part of his long commentary—

> "Fearlessness has been given the first place. This is not mere accident, but deliberate. Without truth, good qualities have no value; but then, for truth, fearlessness is essential. In an atmosphere charged with fear, good qualities cannot grow, in fact, they themselves become bad qualities, and good efforts and tendencies get weakened. Fearlessness is the commander of all good qualities; but the army has to be watched on both the front and the rear. The direct attack will, of course, be in front, but one may also be stealthily set upon from behind. While, in front, fearlessness stands alert, humility guards the rear.... In the absence of humility there is no knowing when victory will turn into defeat."[2]

(b) ***Virtues Listed as Part of Jñāna***

12.10. The above-mentioned list can be called 'the first list of (twenty-six) virtues'. The second list of (twenty) virtues has been given in the Gītā (verses XIII.7-11) as part of jñāna, i.e. knowledge. Before presenting this second list in full, we want to make two observations. First, that virtues like non-violence occur as such in both the lists. Secondly, virtues like absence of excessive pride, occurring in the first list, have their synonyms like humility in the second list.

12.11. Now we take up verses XIII.7-11, one by one—

amānitvamadambhitvamahiṃsā kṣāntirārjavam
ācāryopasanaṃ śaucaṃ sthairyamātmavinigrahaḥ

Simple Meaning—Nine virtues are listed in the first verse—humility, integrity, non-violence, patience, uprightness, service of the teacher, purity, steadfastness, and self-control.

indriyārtheṣu vairāgyamanahaṃkāra eva ca
janmamṛtyujarāvyādhiduḥkhadoṣānudarśanam

Simple Meaning—Three virtues are listed in the second verse—indifference to the objects of sense, non-egotism and the perception of the evil of birth, death, old age, sickness and pain.

asaktiranabhiṣvaṅgaḥ putradāragṛhādiṣu
nityaṃ ca samacittatvaṃ iṣṭāniṣṭopapattiṣu

Simple Meaning—Three virtues are listed in the third verse—non-attachment, absence of clinging to son, wife, home and the like, and a constant equal-mindedness to all desirable and undesirable happenings.

mayi cānanyayogena bhaktiravyabhicāriṇī
viviktadeśasevitvamaratirjanasaṃsadi

Simple Meaning—Three virtues are listed in the fourth verse—Unswerving devotion (bhakti) to God with wholehearted discipline resort to solitary places, dislike for a crowd of people.

adhyātmajñānanityatvaṃ tattvajñānārthadarśanam
etajjñānamiti proktamajñānaṃ yadato'nyathā

Simple Meaning—Two virtues are listed in the fifth verse—constancy in the knowledge of the Spirit, insight into the end of the knowledge of Truth—all these (twenty) virtues are declared to be knowledge, and the absence of these is ignorance.

12.12. We have already drawn attention to some of the twenty virtues which are either identical with or parallel to the virtues of daivī sampat. Another notable virtue in this (i.e. the second) list is 'anahaṃkāra' which is similar to 'nirahaṃkāra'. Without going into further detail, we reproduce a part of Dr. Radhakrishnan's commentary on these verses which highlights Gītā's intention to combine both theory and practice in jñāna—

"It is clear from this list of (twenty) qualities that jñāna or knowledge includes the practice of the moral virtues. Mere theoretical blearning will not do."[3]

(c) ***Sāttvika Varieties of Jñāna, Sukha, etc.***

12.13. For purposes of promoting the good of all, the right type of social values need to be imparted to all the people. Such values are closely associated in the Gītā with 'sāttvika jñāna', the basic content of which is summarized in verse XVIII.20—

sarvabhūteṣu yenaikaṃ bhāvamavyayamīkṣate
avibhaktaṃ vibhakteṣu tajjñānaṃ viddhi sāttvikam

Simple Meaning—That knowledge is sāttvika (good) by which the one Imperishable Being is seen in all existences. Since this Being is "undivided in the apparently divided", sāttvika jñāna fosters the spirit of "unity in the midst of diversity".

We recall that we utilized this verse in chapters two and three to emphasize that the phrase 'avibhaktaṃ vibhakteṣu' provides the basis of 'dharma that unites'. We feel that pluralistic societies all over the world can obtain valuable support from sāttvika jñāna to prevent the spread of divisive tendencies.

12.14. Another important concept, which the materialistic society of modern times urgently needs, relates to clarifying the real meaning of happiness. The Gītā warns that excessive consumerism only gives an illusion of happiness. Verses XVIII.37-38 contain such a warning—and we present them in the reverse order—

viṣayendriyasaṃyogādyattadagre'mṛtopamam
pariṇāme viṣamiva tatsukhaṃ rājasaṃ smṛtam

Simple Meaning—That happiness is merely 'rājasi', i.e. temporary and illusory, which arises from the contact of the senses and their objects—because this looks like nectar at first but turns out to be like poison at the end.

yattadagre viṣamiva pariṇāme'mṛtopamam
tatsukhaṃ sāttvikaṃ proktaṃātmabuddhiprasādajam

Simple Meaning—That happiness is sāttvika, i.e. real, which springs from a clear understanding of the self (i.e. from a knowledge of who we are and what is our real purpose of life in the world)—This may look like poison at first but proves to be like nectar at the end.

12.15. For the conflict-ridden world of today, the Gītā gives the message that 'ahiṃsā', i.e. non-violence is essential for achieving the good of all. Verse XVII.14 glorifies 'ahiṃsā' as an element of sāttvika tapas—

.....ahiṃsā ca śārīraṃ tapa ucyate

Simple Meaning—Tapas, i.e. self-discipline includes 'ahiṃsā'.

12.16. Before closing this section, we want to draw attention to 'sāttvika shraddhā', i.e. faith in a high ideal, not only because it can give the right direction to common people but also because it will help understand the reference thereto in the Mānas (that will be made in paragraph 12.24). For this purpose, parts of two verses (XVII.4 and VII.23) need to be put together—

yajante sāttvika devān...
devān devayajo yānti

Simple Meaning—Sāttvika shraddhā prompts one to worship gods (not demons) ....and worshippers of gods go to gods.

Two points need to be clarified here. First, that all forms of gods are forms of the One Supreme and so their worship is the worship of the Supreme. Secondly, the Gītā wants us to grasp the principle that we can become what we want to become. Dr. Radhakrishnan's explanation of 'sāttvika shraddhā' is summarized below—

> "Shraddhā is not acceptance of a belief. It is striving after self-realization by concentrating the powers of the mind on a given ideal... It is the pressure of the spirit on humanity, the force that urges humanity towards what is better, not only in the order of knowledge but in the whole order of spiritual life."[4]

Parallel Lists of Virtues in the Mānas

12.17. We presented in paragraphs 12.5-12 two long lists of virtues given in the Gītā. The Mānas also has two similar lists, one in Laṅkākāṇḍa and the second in Uttarakāṇḍa. The next two sections are devoted to these lists—and these will be followed by two more sections (on 'par-hit' and Rāma-rājya).

(d) ***Virtues Symbolizing 'Chariot of Victory' in Mānas***

12.18. This list of virtues is given in Laṅkākāṇḍ. The occasion is the decisive battle between Rāma and Rāvaṇa. Vibhīshaṇ notices that, while Rāvaṇa has a big chariot, Rāma has none. A doubt arises in the mind of Vibhīshaṇ as to how a chariot-less Rāma can win such a crucial battle—

nāth na rath....
kehi vidhi jitab vīr balwānā

Simple Meaning—Vibhīshaṇ asks Lord Rāma, how, without a chariot, do you hope to achieve victory over a great warrior like Rāvaṇa who has such a big chariot?

12.19. In His reply, Lord Rāma tells Vibhīshaṇ that a physical chariot, made of commodities, is not so important for victory as a mental chariot whose components are 'virtues'—

sunahu sakhā kah kripānidhānā
jehin jaya hoi so syandan ānā

Simple Meaning—Rāma tells Vibhīshaṇ, my dear friend, I want you to know that a big-looking chariot may have an impressive, outer appearance, but it cannot ensure victory in the battle of life. What is needed for victory is a 'chariot of virtues', i.e. inner qualities.

Before commenting on the list of twenty-two virtues listed by Lord Rāma, we want to say that Vibhīshaṇ's doubt was set at rest because he understood that Rāma-Rāvaṇa battle is more spiritual than physical.

12.20. Now we look at that part of the text which contains the word 'par-hit'—

sauraj dhīraj tehi rath chākā....
bal vivek dam par-hit ghore....
īsh bhajan sārathī sujānā

Simple Meaning—Courage and patience are the wheels of this chariot....self-confidence, self-discipline, right knowledge, and desire to do good to others—these are the four horses.... bhakti is the charioteer.

12.21. Instead of presenting the entire list, it may be more interesting to compare it with 'daivī sampat' of the Gītā. We find that truth, self-discipline, forgiveness and sharing occur as such in both the lists, while non-violence, patience, compassion and purity are referred to through their synonyms. We conclude this section by pointing out that Pandit Ram Kinkar Upadhyay has attached special importance to the victory-chariot for purposes of comparing the Gītā and the Mānas. One of the main conclusions that he has drawn is that the virtues of the victory-chariot represent a harmonious combination of karmayoga, bhaktiyoga and jñānayoga.

(e) ***Virtues that Light the Lamp of Jñāna in the Mānas***

12.22. This is the second long list of virtues in the Mānas. The occasion is the dialogue between Kākbhushuṇḍi and Garuḍa, which constitutes an important section of Uttarakāṇḍa. Between this list of the Mānas and the second list of the Gītā given in paragraphs 12.10-12, there is contextual similarity in the sense that both of them are related to jñāna or knowledge.

12.23. The imagery that Tulasī has employed for explaining the need for jñāna is very interesting. He says that, although the jīva, i.e. the individual self, is, according to Vedānta, a part of the Cosmic Self, it gets entangled with 'māyā' or ignorance. For liberation, this knot between 'jīva' and 'māyā' needs to be untied, and one way of doing this is to light the 'lamp of jñāna'. This is how the Mānas puts it—

īshvar ansh jīva avināshī....
so māyābas bhayau....
granthi chhūt kimi parai na dekhī

Simple Meaning—Jīva is essentially immortal and free like Īshwara, but the knot between jīva and māyā creates bondage. Light is needed so that the knot can be seen and then untied.

12.24. Just as the lighting of a lamp requires wick and ghee (clarified butter), similarly many virtues are needed for the acquisition of jñāna. Tulasī has listed as many as twenty-seven virtues. For example, the first six of these virtues are—

sāttvika shraddhā....
jap tap vrat yam niyam apārā
je shruti kah shubh dharm achārā

Simple Meaning—The starting point (i.e. the first virtue) is 'sāttvika shraddhā'—as explained in the Gītā, reference para 12.16 above. Next comes 'good dharma' (conduct) (as laid down by Shruti, i.e. Vedas and Upaniṣads), five elements of which are—jap (recitation of God's name), tapas (self-discipline), vrat (strong determination), yam (which includes non-violence), and niyam (which includes purity).

12.25. Instead of going over the entire list of twenty-seven virtues (i.e. twenty-one more, following the six listed above), we rather make two observations of a comparative nature. First, we want to say that implicit reference to the Gītā (as done above for sāttvika shraddhā) is quite common in the Mānas (e.g. in Rāma-Lakshmaṇ dialogue in Araṇyakāṇḍa). Secondly, there is a lot of similarity between this Mānas-list of virtues and the corresponding ones of the Gītā (reference paragraph 12.11 above). In particular, we want to draw attention to an important similarity, viz. that, just as bhakti (devotion) is included in the jñāna-promoting virtues of the Gītā, Tulasī has not only done that, but has also gone a step further. Tulasī has warned that the 'lamp of jñāna' runs the risk of being extinguished by the strong wind of 'attachment to sense-objects'. It is safer, says Tulasī, to depend on the light of the 'shining jewel of bhakti' which cannot be extinguished.

(f) ***Mānas Proclaims 'Par-Hit' as the Essence of All Scriptures***

12.26. Although the lists of virtues glorified by the Mānas are quite long, the essence of the message is crystallized in one word, viz. 'par-hit' or doing good to others. Tulasī asks people not to interpret it as his message, but rather as the message of the Vedas and the Upaniṣads He declares in Bālakāṇḍa—

shruti kah param dharam upkārā

i.e. the essence of Shruti (i.e. Vedas and Upaniṣads) is that 'upkāra' (doing good to others) is the highest dharma.

And Tulasī goes one step further in Uttarakāṇḍa—

par-hit saris dharam nahin bhāī....
nirṇaya sakal purān ved kar

Simple Meaning—The conclusion of all the scriptures (including Vedas, Purāṇas, etc.) is that there is no dharma as great as 'par-hit'.

12.27. Whether it is called 'upkār' or 'par-hit', the Mānas does not want to narrow down the scope of one's actions done for the good of others. In fact, Tulasī's vision is so wide that he thinks of 'vishva-upkār' (good of the universe). This is how he presents Bharat's character in Ayodhyākāṇḍa—

bhayavu vishva upkārū

i.e. the entire 'vishva' (universe) benefited from Bharat's high ideals.

Tulasī uses the same expression in relation to Rāma in Vinay-Patrikā—

rāj rājendra.....vishva upkārī

i.e. Lord Rāma assumed kingship only for 'vishva-upkār'.

More light on this last statement will be thrown in the next section (which will conclude this chapter).

(g) ***Rāma-rājya—the Ideal Society of the Mānas***

12.28. This is one of the most famous sections of the Mānas which occurs in Uttarakāṇḍa. Here is a picture of what an ideal society based on the principle of jagmangal (good of the world) may look like. That this is not a theocracy, follows from Tulasī's low opinion about priests, expressed in the same canto—

uprohitya karma ati mandā

i.e. the priests usually play an anti-social role.

12.29. Rather than depend on narrow-minded priests who promote superstitions and consequent exploitation of common people, Tulasī's Rāma-rājya is based on the principle of social harmony and equality—

rāmrāj baiṭhen trailokā
harshit bhaye gaye sab sokā
bayaru na kar kāhū san koī
rām pratāp vishamtā khoī....
sab nar karahin paraspar prītī
chalahin svadharma nirat shruti nītī

Simple Meaning—In Rāma-rājya, all the people were happy. There was no trace of enmity or inequality. People loved one another. Everyone followed sva-dharma i.e. the path of fulfilment of all obligations, towards oneself as well as towards others.

12.30. Tulasī makes it clear that the 'dharma' of the people in Rāma-rājya was broad-based, the four pillars of which were—truth, purity, compassion, and sharing. Helping one another was the characteristic feature of this dharma—

chāriu charan dharma jag māhīn
pūri raha sapnehun agh nāhīn.....
rām bhagati rat nar aru nārī
sakal param gati ke adhikārī......
sab udār sab par upkārī

Simple Meaning—People in Rāma-rājya did not commit any sin because they were guided by truth and purity. Their bhakti was not self-centred, rather they were motivated by compassion and sharing. Since they helped one another, there was no doubt about their attaining the highest state of liberation.

12.31. Tulasī had the farsightedness to paint the picture of Rāma-rājya as a prosperous society in which no one suffered from poverty, ignorance and disease—

rām rāj kar sukh sampadā
barani na sakai phanīs sāradā
alpmrityu nahin kavniu pīrā
sab sundar sab viruj sarīrā
nahin daridra kou dukhī na dīnā
nahin kou abudh na lachchhanhīnā
sab nīrdambh dharmarat punī

nar aru nāri chatur sab gunī
sab gunagya pandit sab gyānī
sab kritagya nahin kapaṭ sayānī

Simple Meaning—Even Saraswatī and the thousand-headed Sheshnāg cannot describe the happiness and prosperity of the people in Rāma- rājya. No one died before getting old. No one suffered from pain. All enjoyed good health. No one was poor, nor unhappy, nor helpless. No one was ignorant. All were pandits, full of knowledge and other qualities. All were righteous, polite and grateful.

12.32. Even modern experts in socio-economic development would be satisfied with such a description of Rāma-rājya. Similarly, environmental specialists too would feel happy to read about the plentiful supply of clean air, water, etc.—

sītal surabhi pavan bah mandā....
saritā sakal bahahin bar bārī....
sasi sampann sadā rah dharnī....
mānge vārid dehin jal rāmchandra ke rāj

Simple Meaning—The air was pleasant and fragrant. Flowing rivers provided clean water. Greenery was in abundance. Rainfall was perfect too, i.e. neither drought nor floods caused any problem.

12.33. We have already mentioned that Mahatma Gandhi was highly impressed with Tulasī's description of Rāma-rājya. What pleased him most was the non-violent basis of the society, a picture of which was provided in a poetic style—

danḍa jatinh kar bhed jahn
nartak nritya samāj
jitahu manahi sunia as
rāmchandra ke rāj

Simple Meaning—No one committed any crime, so there was no need of 'danḍa', i.e. punishment—but the word 'danḍa' also means a 'walking stick', so only sannyasins carried a 'danḍa'. Similarly, there was no need to use the policy of 'bhed', i.e. divide and rule—but 'bhed' is also a technical word in music and dancing, and that was its only use. Finally, since there was no enemy, the word 'jito', i.e. 'conquer', was used only to give the message of conquering one's own mind.

12.34. In this way, through the Rāma-rājya description, the Mānas calls on everyone to work for jagmangal or vishava-upkār—both the expressions meaning the good of the world. An essential step in doing that is to choose such representatives (who perform the function of law-making, administration, etc.) who are like 'Rāma', i.e. persons with high ideals. Therefore, Mantharā's words that occur in Ayodhyākāṇḍa, viz.—

kou nrip hou hamahin kā hānī

which means "I don't care who will be king"—should not be interpreted as Tulasī's views, but rather the views of an anti-social maid-servant.

Similarly, the following words of Sundarakāṇḍa (which are obviously deplorable)—

ḍhol ganvār shūdra pashu nārī
sakal tarnā ke adhikārī

which mean that "a drum, rustic, shudra, animal and woman need a beating"—should be interpreted as the views of the "foolish ocean" (as Tulasī' has described the speaker of these words), and not Tulasī's own. How can one ever associate such deplorable words with the poet who described the ideal society of Rāma-rājya?

CHAPTER THIRTEEN

How to Re-invigorate the Call for the Good of All

13.1. This is the last chapter of the book, and in order to specify its content, we need to take into account the objective that we set before us in paragraph 1.54, and also what we have accomplished so far. We listed five questions and envisaged that the answers thereto would mark the fulfilment of the objective. Out of these five questions, the first one was answered in chapter one, and questions two and three have been answered simultaneously in chapters two to twelve. Therefore, the task assigned to the present chapter is to provide answers to questions four and five which were spelt out in paragraph 1.54. We shall take up these two questions, one at a time.

The Fourth Question

13.2. First, we feel it would be helpful to reproduce question four here, viz. "How did the people respond to the message of the Gītā and the Mānas? More specifically, when and to what extent, did the Pandits and others oppose or accept the message, and how did the society lose or gain thereby?"

Obviously, an appropriate answer to this question has to analyse the socio-religious history of India, and of people of Indian origin who were taken to countries like Trinidad, Surinam, Guyana, Mauritius, Fiji, and South Africa. The time-span of the people's response to the message of the Gītā runs into thousands of years but we will have to select the main elements thereof, taking care, however, to include the initial period of half-hearted acceptance as well as the subsequent period of whole-hearted acceptance. The time-span for a similar analysis relating to the

Mānas is four hundred and twenty five years because Tulasī began writing the Mānas in 1573 and completed it in 1575.

13.3. In the light of the above, a systematic answer to question four will now be presented in the following six sections—

(a) Why there was delay in accepting Gītā's message fully;
(b) Why there was initial opposition to the Mānas;
(c) Period of neglect brought to an end by karmayogins and bhaktas;
(d) Important events associated with Gītā's acceptance;
(e) How the Mānas joined Gītā-based movements; and
(f) How Mānas came to the cultural rescue of Indian emigrants

We shall do the section-wise presentation, one by one.

(a) ***Why There Was Delay in Accepting Gītā's Message Fully***

(i) *Historical Analysis*

13.4. The attitude of ancient Indian pandits i.e. scholars, towards the Gītā was obviously ambivalent, i.e. a mixture of respect and neglect. From the philosophical viewpoint, the Gītā was given as much respect as the Upaniṣads. However, for social and practical purposes, the message that the Gītā contained was almost neglected. This neglect proved to be a disaster for the society when it came face to face with serious problems. A few examples will help clarify this.

13.5. Perhaps the most alarming issue was the fragmentation of the society and the attitude of neglect of the poorer sections in the minds of pandits. The Gītā gave a warning and suggested a solution in verse V.18—

vidyāvinayasampanne brāhmaṇe gavi hastini
śuni caiva śvapāke ca paṇḍitāḥ samadarśinaḥ

Simple Meaning—Pandits are those who have equal vision towards all, for example, towards a learned and humble brahmin, a cow, an elephant, a dog or a dog-eater.

13.6. This was a challenge for the pandits, but rather than accept the Gītā's suggestion, they started justifying the sad plight of the neglected people by giving a perverted interpretation of the law of karma. Priests said that the suffering of the poor people was due to their past karma and so it was unnecessary to show any sympathy towards them. The

Gītā pleaded for an attitude of compassion, for example, in verse XII.13—

adveṣṭā sarvabhūtānām maitraḥ karuṇa eva ca

Simple Meaning—A bhakta has no ill-will towards any being (not even towards those who have ill-will towards him or her). A bhakta is also compassionate and friendly.

13.7. Neither the rich nor the poor appreciated the sound advice of the Gītā, because they were both under the tāmasika influence of the priests. The rich were too arrogant to show compassion. The poor were victims of superstition and fatalism, which brought about laziness, faintheartedness and loss of self-respect. The Gītā gave a call to lift them up, for example, in verse II.3—

kṣudraṃ hṛdayadaurbalyaṃ tyaktvottiṣṭha parantapa

Simple Meaning—Cast off this petty faintheartedness and arise.

13.8. But many people thought, why arise and work hard, why not take to begging instead? To them too, the Gītā said, begging is anti-social. Furthermore, the Gītā told those who supported beggary that even charity given to an unworthy recipient was tāmasika, i.e. bad.

13.9. But rather than follow Gītā's advice about sāttvika and tāmasika acts, the common people put their faith in priests who misguided them by giving an allurement as to how to book their seat in heaven. Evil customs like child-sacrifice, child marriage, and burning of widows gripped the society, which meant torturing people in the name of religion.

13.10. Either through fear of hell or through false hopes for heaven, the priests exploited ignorant people. Here too, the Gītā warned, for example, in verses II.42-43—

kāmātmānaḥ ..... svargaparāḥ...
.... avipaścitaḥ

Simple Meaning—Those people are unwise and devoid of true knowledge, who believe that going to heaven is the highest goal and who act with such desire.

13.11. It was in 1818 that Raja Rammohan Roy started a reform movement based on the advice of the Gītā (and supported by Upaniṣads too), to save widows from the heaven-related clutches of the priests (who had joined hands with others in a conspiracy). Because of the importance of this movement, we shall give details thereof in a later section. At this point, we need to appreciate that for a very long time, the Gītā's social message remained neglected.

13.12. The neglect of the sannyāsa-related message of the Gītā lasted even longer. Since most of the sannyāsins were escapists, who lived on beggary, and who took no interest in social problems, the Gītā declared in verse VI.1 that their conduct was inappropriate to the needs of the day—

> *anāśritaḥ karmaphalaṃ kāryaṃ karma karoti yaḥ*
> *sa saṃnyāsī ca yogī ca na niragnirna cākriyaḥ*

> ***Simple Meaning***—A real sannyāsī or a yogī is one who performs his or her duty (including service to society) without expecting any return for oneself—and it is improper to escape from agni (i.e. household duties) for this purpose.

13.13. The so-called sannyāsa-school of scholars played an obstructive role and prevented the spread of the Gītā's message of social service. Now that we look back on the situation that existed for many centuries, we can say that India lost her independence because large sections of the society were neglected. In a poetic language we can say that, although we had a diamond-like message in the Gītā, we ignored it, and so we became a helpless prey to poverty and degeneration.

13.14. It was in 1897 that Swami Vivekananda acted on the Gītā's message and gave a new orientation to the sannyāsins. We shall write about this in a later section. But the point to note is that valuable time was lost in putting the Gītā's message to full use. Furthermore, before concluding the present section, we shall refer to three more reasons which contributed to the neglect of the Gītā's message.

(ii) *Analysis of the Role of Old Commentaries*

13.15. The first of these (three) reasons is related to the type of commentaries that were written on the Gītā in the distant past. These commentaries were written from a philosophical angle and they considered questions as to whether the Gītā supports the Advaita philosophy or Vishishtādvaita philosophy. If the commentaries had been written from a social or practical angle, they would have examined whether the Gītā gives priority to social goals or to individual goals. The first such new type of commentary, viz. that by Lokamanya Tilak, appeared in the beginning of the twentieth century.

13.16. Among old commentators, two names are most prominent, viz. Shankaracharya and Ramanujacharya. Shankaracharya had picked up jñānayoga (leading to renunciation of karma) as the central message of the Gītā. Ramanujacharya (unhappy with the Māyā-doctrine of Shankara) emphasized Bhakti-yoga as the main teaching. In both the cases, karmayoga was pushed to the background. The neglect of the social message of the Gītā continued till the arrival of Tilak's commentary. Brown gives Tilak credit for using his deep knowledge and an activist approach to life, to write a commentary, strong enough to challenge the hold of Shankara and Ramanuja—

> "Tilak accuses other commentators, including Shankara and Ramanuja...of distorting the text so as to force an interpretation consistent with the views of each cult. But Tilak himself, being free of any cult, believes he is able to give a scientific analysis of the true import of the Gītā."[1]

13.17. Along with Tilak, credit should be given to Vivekananda for having prepared the ground for the acceptance of new ideas. He had started emphasizing, in his talks, the activist message of the Gītā. Without entering into deep interpretational controversies of the type that Tilak considered necessary for his mission of shaking up old notions, Vivekananda had picked up the social service component of karmayoga to revolutionize the concept and practice of sannyasa. The complementary roles of Vivekananda and Tilak in making karmayoga the center-piece of socio-religious thinking in the country, in the beginning of the twentieth century, have been highlighted by Subramaniam—

> "This (the turn of the century) was the time when Tilak's new interpretation of the Gītā, equating it with karmayoga was firing the imagination of the Indian intelligentsia and of the nationalists in particular....And just recently, Vivekananda had increased that stress with his lectures on karmayoga, his highly activist conduct and his activist approach to all things religious and social."[2]

(iii) *Analysis of Prasthānatraya*

13.18. The expression 'Prasthānatraya' denotes three authoritative scriptures, viz. the Upaniṣads, the Brahmasūtras, the Gītā, taken collectively. Attempts were made in the past to prove that their philosophical views are the same. This traditional view of Prasthāna-traya tended to ignore such of the ideas and terms of the Gītā as were not found in the other two. A fear was expressed by D.S. Sarma that since the term "lokasaṃgraha" does not occur in the Upaniṣads, it might not receive due attention.

13.19. Writing in a similar vein, Vinoba and his brother Balkoba, identified 'sthitaprajña' and 'lokasaṃgraha' as two of the most important terms of the Gītā, neither of which occur in the Upaniṣads. It might be mentioned in this connection (reference paragraph 8.30 of this book) that Vinoba subsequently identified 'lokānām asambhedāya...setuḥ' as the Upaniṣadic expression that could be compared to 'lokasaṃgraha'.

13.20. In writing a new commentary on the Gītā, Tilak had to give a new interpretation of Prasthānatraya also, according to which the three scriptures need not support the same yoga—

> "Some people think that, as the Upaniṣads are generally in support of sannyāsa, there will arise a mutual opposition between the three parts of the Prasthānatraya, if the Gītā is explained as being in support of action, and the authoritativeness of the three parts will be endangered....
>
> "As the Upaniṣads support the path of sannyāsa, and the Gītā supports the path of karmayoga, these two parts of the Prasthānatraya can be seen to be mutually cooperative like two hands, instead of being mutually antagonistic....
>
> "If the Gītā did not contain anything more than the Upaniṣads and the Brahmasūtras, there would be no point in including the Gītā in the Prasthānatraya."[3]

(iv) *Analysis Based on Literary Style and Terminology*

13.21. It is well-known that the Gītā has used a conversational style, and also that several of its words are not to be found in the Upaniṣads. D.S. Sarma is of opinion that these two things together probably led to a delay in understanding the social message of the Gītā. For example, Lord Krishna spoke about lokasaṃgraha on His own initiative, and not in reply to a specific question by Arjuna. Also, the teaching on lokasaṃgraha was given at 'the second stage' (so to speak)—the 'first stage' having been devoted to Arjuna's question on 'śreyas'. About Sarma's view relating to terminology, we have already made a reference in paragraph 13.18. (For more details, please see the author's own book *"The Social Role of the Gītā : How and Why"*, Chapter 8).[4]

(b) ***Why There was Initial Opposition to the Mānas***

13.22. The initial attitude of the pandits towards the Mānas was worse than what it had been towards the Gītā. For example, in the case of the Gītā, as we saw in the previous section, the overall attitude was respectful, but its social message was ignored. The Mānas received no such respect from the pandits of Banaras, for quite some time. In fact, they showed open hostility. According to their own explanation, their opposition was based on language, i.e. they did not like Tulasī's writing the scripture in a language other than Sanskrit. But at the back of what they said, there was opposition to Tulasī's reformist ideas. However, before we give examples thereof, we want to reproduce below a portion of Tulasī's biography published by Gītā Press, Gorakhpur, that describes what the pandits of Banaras did—

> "The news of the honour received by the Mānas at the Vishwanath temple aroused jealousy in the minds of the pandits. They joined hands, not only to oppose the Mānas, but also to destroy the book itself, if they could steel it from Tulasī's cottage. They employed two thieves for this purpose. However, when the thieves arrived at the cottage, they saw two guards who looked like Rāma and Lakshmaṇa. God's 'darshan' brought about an immediate purification of the thieves, and they told the pandits accordingly.
>
> "When Tulasī heard about this episode, he felt as if his keeping the manuscript with himself was proving to be a source of anxiety to Lord Rāma. So he gave the book to his friend Todarmal for safe custody. He also arranged for additional copies of the book to be prepared to meet the growing demand therefor.
>
> "Having failed to destroy the Mānas, the pandits approached Madhusudan Saraswati to evaluate the book and provide them with an assessment. Madhusudan was thrilled to go through the Mānas and he expressed his opinion in the following Sanskrit verse—
>
> *ānandakānane hyasmin*
> *jangamastulasītaruḥ*
> *kavitāmanjarī bhāti*
> *rāmabhramarabhūshitā*
>
> ***Simple Meaning***—I feel as if Banaras is a garden which is lucky to have a 'Tulasī-plant', because Tulasī's noble poetry has attracted Lord Rāma (just as the tulasī-plant attracts bees).
>
> "Even Madhusudan's words of praise were not able to put an end to the pandits' opposition to the Mānas."[5]

13.23. The latter part of the above-mentioned biography of Tulasī shows that, with the passage of time, the attitude of the pandits changed, and the Mānas too, like the Gītā, was recognized as great. However, the same type of ambivalence persisted, i.e. showing symbolical respect to the Mānas as such, but ignoring the reformist message thereof.

Some examples (that follow) will make this clear.

13.24. Tulasī wanted that pandits and sannyāsins should reverse their behavioural trends, i.e. give up deception and boasting, and start performing acts of social service instead. But these people were in no mood to listen to Tulasī, as shown by the following words of Uttarakāṇḍa—

mārag soi ja kahn jo bhāvā
pandit soi jo gāl bajāvā.....
jāken nakh aru jatā visālā
soi tāpas prasiddh kalikālā

Simple Meaning—No one wants to listen to any advice. There is also no desire to do good deeds as taught by the scriptures. Pandits feel that they can earn respect, simply by talking big. Similarly, sannyāsins feel that their long hair and long nails are enough to win fame.

13.25. Because of lack of education, common people put faith in priests, who in turn viewed money-making as their function rather than fulfiling the religious needs of the society. Tulasī's deploration of the priests, because of their commercial mentality, is evident from the following words from Uttarakāṇḍa and Ayodhyākāṇḍa, respectively—

uprohitya karma ati mandā.....
bechahin ved dharam duhi lehīn

Simple Meaning—Tulasī says, priests are doing a bad job because their focus is on money—they are behaving as if they are selling the Vedas and milking the dharma.

13.26. It was Tulasī's hope that by attracting people towards bhaktiyoga and karmayoga, a way out of fatalism, lethargy and faintheartedness could be found. He wanted people to be inspired by Hanumān and the vānaras, and therefore he filled Kishkindhākāṇḍa and Sundarakāṇḍa with calls for action (based on bhakti) and for giving up cowardice—

tāsu dūt tum taji kadarāī
rām hridaya dhari karahu upāī....
daiva daiva ālasī pukārā

Simple Meaning—Rāma's servants do not behave like cowards, their bhakti enables them to find a way out of difficulties, and they know that only lazy people are fatalists.

13.27. Although pandits, priests and sannyāsins tried to keep people away from the Mānas, the message of Tulasī, like that of the Gītā, was unstoppable. After a long period of neglect, the tide was turned. Karmayogins took the lead by using the Gītā for social reform. Gradually, the scope of their work was widened, and bhaktas too joined hands, to bring about 'sakal mangal', i.e. the good of all. This is the topic of the next and the following sections.

(c) *Period of Neglect Brought to an End by Karmayogins and Bhaktas*

13.28. Since the Gītā as well as the Mānas give assurance about the victory of good over evil, a day was bound to come when neglect would give way to action. The Gītā had declared in verse IX.31—

na me bhaktaḥ praṇaśyati

i.e. God's bhakta cannot be destroyed.

And Uttarakāṇḍa (of the Mānas) too gave the same message—

tāte nās na hoi dās kar

i.e. a bhakta may suffer but he or she cannot perish.

13.29. Tulasī's optimism is reflected in Vinay Patrikā—and since his aim was sakal mangal, the hope expressed in the following lines can be interpreted as being both personal and social—

ab lon nasāni
ab na nasaihoṇ
rām kripā bhavnishā sirānī
jāge phir na dasaihoṇ

Simple Meaning—Tulasī says—By God's grace, the period of decay will not last any longer. Māyā had put me into slumber, but I am now awake, and on the basis of strength that I get from Lord Rāma, I can declare that Māyā cannot do any more damage to me—and to the society to which I belong.

13.30. But the question was—will an Avatāra come and save the situation or will God's work (mat-karma or Rāma kāj) be done by some one else? The answer was contained in verse III.25 of the Gītā—

kuryādvidvāṃstathā'saktaṣ cikīrṣurlokasaṃgraham

Simple Meaning—A learned karmayogin, desirous to help others and looking for no selfish gain, is fit to do God's work.

And such a karmayogin was Rammohan Roy. He took the lead, on a modest scale, and then came other karmayogins and bhaktas, paving the way for more to come and to take up more comprehensive tasks for the good of all. For a brief account of some of them, we move on to the next section.

(d) ***Important Events Associated With Gītā's Acceptance***

13.31. The first application of the Gītā for a great social cause, about which records are available, was set in motion by Rammohan Roy in 1818. The social problem which Roy tried to tackle was the burning of widows, popularly known as 'suttee'. But the message of the Gītā which Roy utilized in a debate with suttee-advocates has a potential for wider applicability. In order to present a clear picture of the problem of 'suttee' as well as Roy's solution thereof, the following details are necessary.

Opposing an Evil That was Committed in the Name of Religion

13.32. The Mahābhārata says that Pandu's second wife, Mādrī, became a 'suttee' by burning herself with the dead body of her husband. But with the lapse of time, i.e. by the seventeenth century, a perverted form of 'suttee' took shape in Bengal. Three factors—legal, financial, religious—were responsible for making 'suttee' a uniquely cruel and difficult problem.

13.33. The legal aspect was connected with the type of inheritance law that was made applicable to joint Hindu families in Bengal. While the rest of India followed the 'Mitākshar' law, Bengal followed 'Dāyabhāga' law. We need not explain this in detail, but the main provision of Dāyabhāga law was this—after the death of one of the brothers in a joint Hindu family, his widow had practically the same right in the family property as her late husband had. This looks like a device intended to benefit the widow, but it gave rise to a dangerous 'trick' in the minds of the surviving brothers. They thought that if the widow was somehow eliminated, they would obtain a larger share of the family property.

13.34. But what was the source of the substantial wealth that came in the hands of the joint Hindu families? The new source of such wealth was the profitable trading opportunities that were made available in Calcutta by the British East India Company. Many families suddenly became rich, and they did not want that the widow should transfer her late husband's share to the family of her parents.

13.35. But how did religion enter into this legal and financial set-up? The religious element was brought in by the priests whose attitude had degenerated along with the decline in values. The result was that priests joined hands with the rich families, and devised 'tricks' to eliminate the widow. This was done in two ways.

13.36. First, the priests in Bengal wilfully manipulated a mantra of the Rig-Veda. In this mantra, the word 'agre' (meaning, in the front) was used to convey the idea that married women would sit with their husbands "in the front", while performing religious ceremonies. By a simple 'trick', the priests changed "agre" to "agne" (meaning—fire). Then they told the widows that even Rig-Veda wanted them to sit with their husbands "in the fire". This manipulation done by the priests in Bengal was brought to light by Max Mueller in the latter part of the nineteenth century—because he found that all other versions of the Rig-Veda (except the ones in Bengal) had the word 'agre'— and not 'agne'— in the mantra under consideration.

13.37. The second 'trick' devised by the priests was even more appalling. They concocted a stupefying drink by means of which the widow would be made to lose her normal intellectual capability. The priests would then pretend that the widow had said 'yes' when asked whether she wanted to become a 'suttee'. Along with the drink, the priests would give an allurement that a 'suttee' goes to heaven. As part of the conspiracy, the rich families rewarded the priests by authorizing them to collect from the ashes the ornaments which were worn by the widow at the time of being burnt with the dead body of her husband.

13.38. We must give credit to Rammohan Roy that, through study and observation, he was able to see and tell what was going on in the name of religion. But he also knew that the best way to get rid of this evil custom was to bring about a change in public opinion, by means of education and open discussion.

13.39. Christian missionaries suggested to Roy that the easiest way to end the 'suttee' custom was to give up Hinduism and to get converted to christianity. However, Roy did not agree, because he was confident that by depending on scriptures like the Gītā, social reform was possible, and that would be most beneficial to the society.

13.40. The debate that took place in 1818 between Roy, on the one hand, and suttee-advocates, on the other, was an important event in the socio-religious history of the world. The main argument of Roy was that, to obtain a 'yes' reply from the widow after giving an allurement about heaven, violated the 'nishkama-karma' doctrine of the Gītā. His explanation was so convincing that even the suttee-advocates replied, "what you have said we shall carefully consider." In any case, the British Government was able to assert thereafter that the suttee-custom was not in accordance with authoritative Hindu scriptures. Although the decision to impose a legal ban on suttee was taken by the Governor-General in 1829, Rammohan Roy has been rightly given due credit for making serious efforts for this cause from 1818 onwards.

13.41. By interpreting the Gītā appropriately, so as to oppose an evil that was being committed in the name of religion, Rammohan Roy not only tackled the 'suttee' problem, but he also gave to social reformers a useful tool. Terrorists using suicide-bomb techniques (even today) give allurements about heaven to ignorant followers. Those trying to bring an end to such terrorism can possibly make use of Roy's approach, with such modification as may be considered necessary.

Establishing an Organization to Serve the Poor

13.42. The second major social application of the Gītā is attributed to Swami Vivekananda. He combined the karmayoga of the Gītā and the Vedanta of the Upaniṣads, to arrive at a new philosophy of sevā (service), called "practical Vedanta". The organization that was started to carry on "sevā" on a big scale was named by Vivekananda after his Master, Paramhansa Ramakrishna.

13.43. The Ramakrishna Mission, established in 1897, although non-political, was still revolutionary in certain respects. Monks were to be the pillars of the new organization, but their motto marked a clear departure from the tradition inasmuch as it stressed 'social service' as the best way to Moksha (liberation). Vivekananda coined a new Sanskrit phrase for this, namely, "ātmano mokṣārthaṃ jagaddhitāya ca" meaning, 'for one's mokṣa as well as for the good of the world.'

13.44. Vivekananda's ideas were so revolutionary, that some of his own colleagues (i.e. brother-disciples of Śrī Ramakrishna) initially expressed what could be called 'fraternal resistance'. However, when the depth of Vivekananda's feelings and commitment to the new ideal became clear then a united front emerged. In this way, Vivekananda succeeded in ensuring that the Ramakrishna Mission adopted the karmayoga-based socio-spiritual approach to India's problems.

13.45. Vivekananda's emphasis on 'social service' as an important element in socio-spiritual re-awakening in the country, strengthened further by dedicated work done by the Ramakrishna Mission over the years, gradually moulded the approach of many "political or social reform groups" also, as noted recently by Madeleine Biardeau. She made a special study of social service groups in India during the nineteen eighties, with a view to identifying their sources of inspiration. Her findings confirm Vivekananda's great contribution in bringing into prominence the social role of the Gītā—

> "The term 'seva', 'service' is one that recurs quite frequently in the names of many political or social reform groups.... Undoubtedly, the influence of Vivekananda who had been so impressed in his travels to the West by charitable institutions, and of his Ramakrishna Mission as well, lent great credence to the idea of selfless service. It is nevertheless more than likely that all of this took place within pre-existing ideological frames of reference, and that the Bhagavad-Gītā was its greatest source of inspiration."[6]

Using the Gītā to Obtain Political Independence of India

13.46. The most well-known application of the Gītā was organized by Tilak, Aurobindo and Gandhi, for obtaining the political independence of India. It was in 1897—the same year in which Vivekananda established the Ramakrishna Mission—that Tilak suggested a political application of the Gītā. He was imprisoned and deprived of adequate food for nearly one year. He would have died, but Max Mueller and other scholars intervened to get him out of prison. But once started on a revolutionary path, Tilak kept up pressure for Swarāj (self-rule), and the British viewed him as the biggest enemy of the empire. Tilak's slogan was "Swaraj is my birth right and I shall have it". In 1908, he was again imprisoned for six years and sent to Mandlay (Burma). There, in a remote prison, he wrote his famous commentary on the Gītā, in Marathi, entitled *"Gītā Rahasya"* which was published in 1915. Translations in Hindi, English and many other languages followed.

13.47. In 1908, Aurobindo too was imprisoned—because of the same incident for which Tilak was detained. In the Alipore Jail of Calcutta, Aurobindo studied the Gītā and decided to follow the path of karmayoga. In 1909, after coming out of the prison, he edited the journal *"Karmayogin"* through which he suggested that freedom fighters should keep before their eyes "Lord Krishna of Kurukṣetra", rather than "Lord Krishna of Vrindāvan". In the same year, he published an "open letter to countrymen" which contained a prophecy. He wrote that, following Lord Krishna's call, he will retire from politics in 1910. But, he added, there is no cause for disappointment, because a new leader will arrive who will be like the 'sthitaprajña' of the Gītā, and who will fight without arms, and still win India's independence.

13.48. As already announced, Aurobindo reached Pondicherry in 1910, and he stayed there till 1950. One of the great books that he wrote there is *"Essays on the Gītā."* His own spiritual discipline led him to the status of a 'Pūrṇayogin', i.e. one who rises up to perfection, but then descends to the level of ordinary people to help all mankind. Aurobindo worked for the good of all, and after his passing away, his followers have tried to maintain those activities.

13.49. Looking back on all the events, we can say that Aurobindo's prophecy was fulfilled in 1919. Gandhi succeeded Tilak as the leader of Congress. He declared that we shall achieve India's independence by non-violent satyagraha—a new technique based on the Gītā. In the plenary session of the Congress, nearly two-thirds of the delegates supported Gandhi's declaration. When asked to define a Satyagrahī, Gandhi referred to the sthitaprajña of the Gītā whose qualifications are—truth, non-violence, selfless service, willingness to suffer, and dedicating all this to God. In Gandhi's opinion, the same virtues make a person spiritually perfect.

13.50. Pandits who tend to interpret the Gītā literally, raised an objection against Gandhi's derivation of the ahiṃsā doctrine therefrom. Gandhi clarified that his commentary on the Gītā depends not so much on words, but more so on actual experimentation, i.e. the ideas that came to him when he tried to act according to the principles of the Gītā. Vinoba supported Gandhi's approach—he said that Maitrāyaṇī Upaniṣad also suggests that we go from 'shabda' (word) to 'ashabda' (spirit underlying the word).

13.51. A favourite statement of Gandhi was—there is no such thing as defeat in non-violence. But this does not mean that success is achieved immediately or without hard work. For example, India's struggle for independence (on the basis of the Gītā), which can be assumed to have started from Tilak's imprisonment in 1897, (not taking into account earlier efforts), took fifty years. That is why, Gandhi attached great importance to the Constructive Programme which gave immense scope for everyone to participate. All of this was 'lokasaṃgraha' in the language of the Gītā. In order to spread this message to all the sections of the society, Gandhi took the help of the Mānas too. But more on that in the next section.

(e) ***How the Mānas Joined Gītā-Based Movements***

13.52. Just as the use of the Gītā for the freedom movement depended on new commentaries rather than the old ones, similarly the Mānas too was utilized by means of 'jagmangal-oriented' interpretations. For example, the famous words of Bālakāṇḍa—

parādhīn sapnehu sukh nāhīn

which mean that "one who is dependent can never be happy" were interpreted by freedom fighters so as to be applicable to the country and all its citizens—irrespective of the fact that this implied a widening of the scope that these words had in the Mānas.

13.53. When people asked Gandhi whether he can tell them how a non-violence-based society would look like, he referred to the description of Rāma-rājya in the Mānas. As we already mentioned in paragraphs 12.28-33, Rāma-rājya is not a theocracy—rather it is a society based on truth, non-violence, justice, or jag-mangal, for short. Now, having drawn attention to the support that the Mānas gave, we can complete the account relating to India's freedom struggle by saying that success was finally achieved in 1947.

13.54. Once the similarity between the Gītā and the Mānas was recognized during the freedom struggle, more and more movements drew support jointly from both of them. A large number of social service organizations were set up. Among movements that had greater visibility—because of extensive field work and close association with economic and political issues—the pride of place has to be given to the Bhoodan movement of Acharya Vinoba. Initially, he had appealed to land-holders to voluntarily share land with the landless, by explaining to them the Gītā's concept of 'dānaṃ'—

> 'Dānaṃ' (sharing) was recommended by the Gītā in order that we can discharge our debt to society. This, and not doing good to others, is its real meaning. For example, I have received from the society boundless service. When I came into this world, I was weak and helpless. The society brought me up so that I, then so little, have grown so big. Therefore, I, in my turn, should serve the society. 'Doing good' is serving someone from whom we have received no service. But in this case, we have already received everything from society. The service that we render to free ourselves from this debt to society is 'dānaṃ'. To help human society to progress is 'dānaṃ'.[7]

13.55. Subsequently, Vinoba told the people that the Mānas too supports his Bhoo-dan (land-gift) movement. To explain this, he used the following quotations from Ayodhyākāṇḍa and Bālakāṇḍa, respectively—

sampati sab raghupati kai āhī....
kīrati bhaniti bhūti bhali soī
sursari sam sab kahn hit hoī

Simple Meaning—All property belongs to God.... Only that glory, poetry and prosperity can be called good which, like the holy river Ganga, does good to all.

Without going into further detail, we want to say that, with the joint support of the Gītā and the Mānas, Vinoba did achieve a fair degree of success.

(f) *How Mānas Came to the Cultural Rescue of Indian Emigrants*

13.56. For the social causes mentioned so far, the ideological support came either from the Gītā and Upaniṣads, or from the Gītā and the Mānas. But Indian labourers, who were taken to countries like Trinidad in the nineteenth century and in the early part of the twentieth century, depended solely on the Mānas for their cultural survival. These countries provide a very important example where the jag-mangal message of the Mānas was not only understood but also put into action, successfully, in the face of heavy odds. We can even say that these emigrants devoted themselves whole-heartedly to the Mānas—avoiding the type of criticism often reflected in the attitude of the intellectual class back home in India.

13.57. The writer of this book (accompanied with his wife) has personally visited Trinidad and shared with the people there the glorification of the Mānas, which enabled them, not only to retain their identity, but also to raise their status, as equals of others in all respects. Experiences of Indian emigrants to other countries (e.g. Surinam, Guyana, Fiji, Mauritius, South Africa, etc.) are believed to be similar.

13.58. It is a highly fruitful topic of research to identify some of the specific elements of the Mānas which provided inspiration, courage and patience to the Indian emigrants. First, the fact that Lord Rāma, Sītā and Lakshmaṇa spent fourteen years in exile, gave immense strength to the emigrants who were initially taken there on a five-year contract. Secondly, Ayodhyākāṇḍa told them that—

sibi dadhīchi harichand naresā
sahe dharam hit koṭi kalesā

i.e. Shibi, Dadhīchi, Harishchandra, and others became famous because they made sacrifices to maintain their dharma. Message like this contributed to the ability of the emigrants to suffer hardships for the sake of their dharma.

13.59. Thirdly, the emigrants were encouraged by the Mānas to move forward, i.e. to concentrate attention on what to do next, because Kishkindhākāṇḍa told them that—

āge chale bahuri raghurāyā

i.e. Lord Rāma kept on moving forward—undeterred by difficulties.

13.60. Fourthly, Hanumān presented to them the highest ideal—how he went to Laṅkā, gave Rāma's message to Sītā, faced the demons fearlessly, and served Lord Rāma wholeheartedly. Fifthly, the fact that Rāma and Hanumān, although belonging to two different races, joined hands for a great cause, gave to the people of Trinidad a very strong message of social harmony and unity, without any discrimination based on race, colour, creed, etc.

13.61. Obviously, the success of the Indian emigrants owes much to their ability to identify the right leaders, who explained the Mānas to them and organized programmes in the fields of education, health, job opportunities, etc. Research is being conducted to find out who these leaders were and what they did, in the face of many difficulties. People of Trinidad recall with great pride one such leader, viz. the late Bhadase Sagan Maharaj. Although we end here the answer to question four (reference paragraph 13.2) we feel it would be a valuable addition to Mānas-related literature if biographies of important leaders of Indian emigrants in all the countries were published for wide circulation.

The Fifth and the Last Question

13.62. This brings us to the fifth and the last question that we listed in paragraph 1.54, and the answer to which will mark the fulfilment of the objective that we had set for this book. For the fifth question too, as we did for the fourth one in paragraph 13.2, we begin by reproducing the question itself, viz. "What preliminary suggestion can we give to further promote the message of the Gītā and the Mānas so that individuals as well as the society and the country—and ultimately the whole world—may benefit, socially, culturally, morally, economically, and politically?"

13.63. We purposely used the expression 'preliminary suggestion' in the wording of question five, because no single person can do more than that. What we shall do to answer the fifth question is only to present the outline of a ten-point action plan, with the hope that co-operative efforts will gradually be made to spell out in detail, these as well as other suggestions. The main point that we want to stress is that lessons should be learnt from the long history connected with the message of the good of all. In our opinion, the task of re-invigorating the call for the good of all could begin by taking action, in a co-ordinated manner, on the following ten points—

(i) To conduct an in-depth study of the factors which harmed the society in the past, and to publish the results thereof in simple language so that common people can also understand them.

(ii) Once the reasons for social decline are identified, then a cooperative effort will need to be made to find remedial measures. To publish the measures too in simple language.

(iii) To create public awareness about the harm to individuals and to the society that is being caused in the name of religion. Quite often, such harm is caused by giving an allurement about heaven. The fact that such allurement is not supported by the Gītā and the Mānas will need to be made known to people through social education.

(iv) Parallel to item (i) above, studies should also be made as to when and how the society made all-round progress—the intention being to promote similar steps now, particularly those based on non-violence.

(v) Research to be conducted to identify programmes of various types which have benefited the society on different occasions, and in different fields—including programmes currently in operation—and to make the results known to common people.

(vi) To popularise those commentaries and books on the Gītā and the Mānas which give prominence to their message for the good of all.

(vii) To organize national and international conferences on the Gītā and the Mānas aimed at pupularising their social message.

(viii) To make co-ordinated plans to support the efforts that Indian emigrants are making to preserve their dharma, culture, language, etc. in countries like Trinidad.

(ix) To ensure full co-operation between scholars, social workers and common people in the planning and execution of programmes related to the social message of the Gītā and the Mānas. Similar cooperation to be extended to other books too, if the message is the same, i.e. the good of all.

(x) To organize special programmes to attract the younger generation to the social values of the Gītā and the Mānas, keeping in mind that many of them are falling prey to the glamour of self-centred materialistic values.

Appendix One

Six Descriptions of the Spiritually Perfect in the Gītā

The purpose and the content of this Appendix were indicated in paragraph 5.20 of this book. Here we present all the fifty-seven verses of the Gītā (from chapters II, V, VI, XII, XIV and XVIII) through which spiritually perfect persons have been described. Depending on the context, short titles of these descriptions also vary. The six titles together with the corresponding verses are listed below—

(i) Sthitaprajña—verses II.54-72 (i.e. 19 verses)
(ii) Jīvanmukta—verses V.19-29 (i.e. 11 verses)
(iii) Sāmya-yogī—verses VI.27-32 (i.e. 6 verses)
(iv) Bhakta —verses XII.13-20 (i.e. 8 verses)
(v) Triguṇātīta—verses XIV.21-27 (i.e. 7 verses)
(vi) Brahmabhūta—verses XVIII.51-56 (i.e. 6 verses).

The descriptions are now presented one by one.

Sthitaprajña (II.54-72)

Arjuna uvāca
sthitaprajñasya kā bhāṣā samādhisthasya keśava
sthitadhīḥ kiṃ prabhāṣeta kimāsīta vrajeta kim

Simple Meaning—Arjuna wants to know the characteristics of a person of speadfast wisdom.

Śrībhagavānuvāca
prajahāti yadā kāmān sarvān pārtha manogatān
ātmanyevātmanā tuṣṭaḥ sthitaprajñas tadocyate

Simple Meaning—Lord Krishna says, a sthitaprajña is one who puts away all selfish desires, and who does not need any external object for one's happiness and contentment.

duḥkheṣvanudvignamanāḥ sukheṣu vigataspṛhaḥ
vītarāgabhayakrodhaḥ sthitadhīrmunirucyate

Simple Meaning—Two points are highlighted here—remaining 'same' in joys and sorrows, and freedom from passion, fear and rage.

yaḥ sarvatrā'nabhisnehas tattat prāpya śubhāśubham
nā'bhinandati na dveṣṭi tasya prajñā pratiṣṭhitā

Simple Meaning—A sthitaprajña is even-minded, i.e. he remains the same whether he gets what others call good or bad.

yadā saṃharate cā'yam kūrmo'ngānīva sarvaśaḥ
indriyānī'ndriyārthebhyas tasya prajñā pratiṣṭhitā

Simple Meaning—The importance of self-discipline is highlighted here, i.e. keeping the senses under control. Lord Krishna says, even a tortoise can do that.

viṣayā vinivartante nirāhārasya dehinaḥ
rasavarjaṃ rasopyasya paraṃ dṛṣṭvā nivartate

Simple Meaning—Through abstinence, we can achieve external avoidance from sense-objects, but inner taste for them persists. Through bhakti, the inner taste can also go away.

yatato hyapi kaunteya puruṣasya vipaścitaḥ
indriyāṇi pramāthīni haranti prasabhaṃ manaḥ
tāni sarvāṇi saṃyamya yukta āsīta matparaḥ
vaśe hi yasyendriyāṇi tasya prajñā pratiṣṭhitā

Simple Meaning—The message of these two verses can be summarized like this—to become a sthitaprajña, one needs to be 'yatatah... vipascitah... matparah' i.e. to make a combined use of karmayoga, jñānayoga, bhaktiyoga.

dhyāyato viṣayān puṃsaḥ saṅgasteṣū'pajāyate
saṅgātsaṃjāyate kāmaḥ kāmāt krodho bhijāyate
krodhādbhavati sammohaḥ sammohāt smrtivibhramaḥ
smṛtibhraṃśād buddhināśo buddhināśāt praṇaśyati

Simple Meaning—In these two verses, Lord Krishna gives a warning about 'a chain of destruction' which has eight components—thinking of sense-objects, attachment, desire, anger, bewilderment, loss of memory, destruction of intelligence, complete destruction.

rāgadveṣaviyuktaistu viṣayānindriyaiścaran
ātmavaśyairvidheyātmā prasādamadhigacchati
prasāde sarvaduḥkhānāṃ hānirasyo'pajāyate
prasannacetaso hyāsu buddhiḥ paryavatiṣṭhate

Simple Meaning—These two verses glorify 'inner purification', the chief symptom of which is 'freedom from attachment and aversion'. If we have inner purification, and also control over the mind and senses, then outwardly we can make use of sense-objects and still achieve peace, i.e. the end of all sorrow.

nāsti buddhirayuktasya na cāyuktasya bhāvanā
na cābhāvayataḥ śāntir aśāntasya kutaḥ sukham.

Simple Meaning—One who does not practice 'nishkama karmayoga' is called 'ayukta'—his situation is pitiable, because his intellect is unstable, he does not have the right feelings, and he has neither peace nor happiness.

indriyāṇāṃ hi caratāṃ yanmano'nuvidhīyate
tadasya harati prajñāṃ vāyurnāvamivā'mbhasi

Simple Meaning—The importance of self-discipline and control over senses is stressed here by saying that if discipline is imperfect, then intellect is carried away (as a boat is carried away by wind).

tasmādyasya mahābāho nigṛhītāni sarvaśaḥ
indriyāṇī ndriyārthebhyas tasya prajñā pratiṣṭhitā

Simple Meaning—'Control over senses' has been stressed again, and since this is the last verse conveying this message in the context of sthitaprajña, it begins with the word 'tasmat' which means 'therefore'.

ya niśā sarvabhūtānāṃ tasyāṃ jāgarti saṃyamī
yasyāṃ jāgrati bhūtāni sā niśā paśyato muneḥ

Simple Meaning—A selfish person engrossed in sense-objects and caring for none else is diametrically opposite to a sthitaprajña, in regard to life's goal and approach, as night is the opposite of day.

āpūryamāṇamacalapratiṣṭhaṃ samudramāpaḥ praviśanti yadvat
tadvatkāmā yaṃ praviśanti sarve sa śāntimapnoti na kāmakāmī

Simple Meaning—A sthitaprajña is all-absorbing and yet peaceful, like an ocean. He is the opposite of 'kamakami' who is running after desires and has no peace.

vihāya kāmānyaḥ sarvān pumāṃścarati niḥspṛihaḥ
nirmamo nirahaṃkāraḥ sa śāntimadhigacchati

Simple Meaning—A sthitaprajña is 'niramamo nirahaṃkarah', i.e. he has gone beyond the sense of mineness and egotism. In other words, all his actions are for the good of the world.

eṣā brāhmī sthitiḥ pārtha nai'nāṃ prāpya vimuhyati
sthitvā'syāmantakāle-pi brahmanirvāṇamṛcchati

Simple Meaning—A sthitaprajña attains 'brahmi sthiti', i.e. he has attained Brahman while still alive. Bewilderment cannot touch him.

Jīvanmukta (V.19-29)

ihai'va tairjitaḥ sargo yeṣāṃ sāmye sthitaṃ manaḥ
nirdoṣaṃ hi samaṃ brahma tasmād brahmaṇi te sthitāḥ

Simple Meaning—Those who have equal vision towards all are jīvanmuktas, i.e. they are liberated (spiritually) while still alive. They are established in God, because God is flawless and the same in all.

na prahṛṣyet priyaṃ prāpya no'dvijet prāpya cā'priyaṃ
sthirbuddhirasaṃmūḍho brahmavid brahmaṇi sthitaḥ

Simple Meaning—A jīvanmukta is established in Brahman and four of his characteristics are mentioned in this verse—even-mindedness towards the pleasant and the unpleasant, steadfast wisdom, freedom from bewilderment, and a true knowledge of Brahman.

bāhyasparśeṣvasaktātmā vindatyātmani yat sukham
sa brahmayogayuktātmā sukhamakṣayamaśnute

Simple Meaning—A jīvanmukta has no attachment to external objects, he is self-controlled in yoga on God, and therefore he enjoys internal happiness and undying bliss.

ye hi saṃsparśajā bhogā duḥkhayonaya eva te
ādyantavantaḥ kaunteya na teṣu ramate budhaḥ

Simple Meaning—A jīvanmukta is wise, he knows that pleasures derived from sense-objects are temporary and they only lead to sorrow, and so he does not get entangled with them.

śaknoti'hai'va yaḥ soḍhuṃ prākśarīravimokṣaṇāt
kāmakrodhodbhavaṃ vegaṃ sa yuktaḥ sa sukhī naraḥ

Simple Meaning—A jīvanmukta is one who, even before giving up his body, is able to resist the rush of desire and anger. He is a yogin, he is the happy man.

yo'ntaḥsukho'ntarārāmas tathā'ntarjyotireva yaḥ
sa yogī brahmanirvāṇaṃ brahmabhūto 'dhigacchati

Simple Meaning—A jīvanmukta finds his happiness within, his joy within and likewise his light only within. He is a yogin, he becomes divine and he attains to 'brahmanirvāna' (beatitude of God).

labhante brahmanirvāṇaṃ ṛṣayaḥ kṣīṇakalmaṣāḥ
chinnadvaidhā yatātmānaḥ sarvabhūtahite ratāḥ

Simple Meaning—Rishis whose sins are destroyed, whose doubts or dualities are cut asunder, whose minds are disciplined and who rejoice in doing good to others—they attain to 'brahmanirvāna'.

kāmakrodhaviyuktānāṃ yatīnāṃ yatacetasām
abhito brahmanirvāṇaṃ vartate viditātmanām

Simple Meaning—jīvanmuktas are free from desire and anger, they have subdued their minds, they have knowledge of the self—so they experience 'brahmanirvana' from all sides.

sparśānkṛtvā bahirbāhyāṃś cakṣuścai'vā'ntare bhruvoḥ
prāṇāpānau samau kṛitvā nāsābhyantara cāriṇau
yatendriyamanobuddhir munirmokṣaparāyaṇaḥ
vigatecchābhayakrodho yaḥ sadā mukta eva ṣaḥ

Simple Meaning—A muni practising dhyanayoga, who has controlled the senses, mind and understanding, who is intent on liberation, who has cast away desire, fear and anger—he is ever freed.

bhoktāraṃyajñatapasāṃ sarvalokamaheśvaram
suhṛdaṃ sarvabhūtānāṃ jñātvā māṃ śāntimṛicchati

Simple Meaning—An aspirant practising karmayoga, jñānayoga and bhaktiyoga in a coordinated manner, knows that God is the Enjoyer of yajñas and tapas, He is the Great Lord of all the worlds, and He is the Friend of all beings (who does good to them without expecting any return). The aspirant learns how to become a friend of all beings and therefore attains peace.

Sāmyayogi (VI.27-32)

praśāntamanasaṃ hyenaṃ yoginaṃ sukhamuttamam
upaiti śāntarajasaṃ brahmabhūtamakalmaṣam

Simple Meaning—A yogin who has become one with God, whose mind is peaceful, whose passions are at rest, and who is stainless—he enjoys supreme happiness.

yuñjannevaṃ sadā'tmānaṃ yogī vigatakalmaṣaḥ
sukhena brahmasaṃsparśam atyantaṃ sukhamaśnute

Simple Meaning—A yogin following the path of harmonization, puts away all sins, and experiences easily the infinite bliss of contact with the Eternal.

sarvabhūtasthamātmānaṃ sarvabhūtāni cā'tmani
īkṣate yogayuktātmā sarvatra samadarśanaḥ

Simple Meaning—A person whose self is harmonized by yoga, sees the Self abiding in all beings and all beings in the Self—he has equal vision everywhere.

yo māṃ paśyati sarvatra sarvaṃ ca mayi paśyati
tasyā'haṃ na praṇaśyāmi sa ca me na praṇaśyati

Simple Meaning—Lord Krishna says, he who sees Me (i.e. God) everywhere and who sees all in Me (i.e. in God), I am never away from him and similarly he is never away from Me.

sarvabhūtasthitaṃ yo māṃ bhajatyekatvamāsthitaḥ
sarvathā vartamāno'pi sa yogī mayi vartate

Simple Meaning—The yogin who, established in oneness, worships Me abiding in all beings, lives in Me, howsoever he may be active.

ātmaupamyena sarvatra samaṃ paśyati yo'rjuna
sukhaṃ vā yadi vā duḥkhaṃ sa yogī paramo mataḥ

Simple Meaning—A sāmyayogi is guided by the philosophy of 'atmaupamya' which sees the same Ātman in all the beings. Furthermore, his sympathetic behaviour towards all reflects this philosophy fully, in the sense that he is happy when others are happy and he is unhappy when others are unhappy.

Bhakta (XII.13-20)

adveṣṭā sarvabhūtānāṃ maitraḥ karuṇa eva ca
nirmamo nirahaṅkāraḥ samaduḥkhasukhaḥ kṣamī

Simple Meaning—A bhakta has no ill-will towards any being, he is also compassionate and friendly, he is beyond the sense of I and mine, he is even-minded towards sorrows and pleasures, and he has the quality of forgiveness.

saṃtuṣṭaḥ satataṃ yogī yatātmā dṛḍhaniścayaḥ
mayyarpitamanobuddhir yo madbhaktaḥ sa me priyaḥ

Simple Meaning—Lord Krishna says, the yogi, who is ever-content, self-controlled, unshakable in determination, with mind and understanding given up to Me—he, My devotee, is dear to Me.

yasmāno'dvijate loko lokanno'dvijate ca yaḥ
harṣāmarṣabhayodvegair mukto yaḥ sa ca me priyaḥ

Simple Meaning—A bhakta is not a source of annoyance to any, and, in turn, he is not annoyed by anyone, he is free from joy and anger, fear and agitation, and he is dear to Me.

anapekṣaḥ śucirdakṣa udāsīno gatavyathaḥ
sarvārambhaparityāgī yo madbhaktaḥ sa me priyaḥ

Simple Meaning—A bhakta renounces the fruits of all his actions, his acts are skilled, pure and passionless, he avoids arguments that cause trouble, he has no egotistic feeling of being a doer, and he is dear to Me.

yo na hṛṣyati na dveṣṭi na śochati na kāṅkṣati
śubhāśubhaparityāgī bhaktimān yaḥ sa me priyaḥ

Simple Meaning—A bhakta neither rejoices nor hates, neither grieves nor desires, he dedicates all his actions to God and does not consider himself the doer, thus devoted he is dear to Me.

samaḥ śatrau ca mitre ca tathā mānāpamānayoḥ
śītoṣṇasukhaduḥkheṣu samaḥ saṅgavivarjitaḥ

Simple Meaning—A bhakta behaves alike to foe and friend, also to good and evil repute, he is alike in cold and heat, pleasure and pain, and he is free from attachment.

tulyanindāstutirmaunī saṃtuṣṭo yena kenacit
aniketaḥ sthiramatir bhaktimānme priyo naraḥ

Simple Meaning—A bhakta holds equal blame and praise, he is restrained in speech, he does not believe in insatiable desires, he has no attachment to his abode, he is a sthitaprajña and is dear to Me.

ye tu dharmyāmṛtamidaṃ yathoktaṃ paryupāsate
śraddadhānā matparamā bhaktāste 'tīva me priyāḥ

Simple Meaning—Lord Krishna concludes the description of a bhakta by saying—those who with faith, holding Me as their supreme goal, follow this immortal wisdom, those devotees are exceedingly dear to Me.

Triguṇātita (XIV.21-27)

arjuna uvāca

kairliṅgaistrīn guṇānetān atīto bhavati prabho
kimācāraḥ kathaṃ cai'tāṃ strīn guṇānativartate

Simple Meaning—Arjuna wants to know the characteristics of one who has gone beyond the three guṇas. What is his way of life? How is this state of spiritual perfection reached?

śrībhagavānuvāca

prakāśaṃ ca pravṛittiṃ ca mohameva ca pāṇḍava
na dveṣṭi sampravṛittāni na nivṛittāni kāṅkṣati
udāsīnavadāsīno guṇair yo na vicālyate
guṇā vartanta ityeva yo'vatiṣṭhati ne'ṅgate
samaduḥkhasukhaḥ svasthaḥ samaloṣṭaśmakāñcanaḥ
tulyapriyāpriyo dhīras tulyanindātmasaṃstutiḥ
mānāpamānayostulyas tulyo mitrāripakṣayoḥ
sarvārambhaparityāgī guṇātītaḥ sa ucyate

Simple Meaning—Lord Krishna describes the characteristics of a triguṇātita in these four verses. He does not abhor illumination (sattva), activity (rajas), and delusion (tamas) when they arise nor longs for them when they cease. He is unperturbed by the guṇas and is not entangled in them. Knowing that it is the guṇas that act, he concentrates attention on God and does not waver. Above all, he is even-minded. He regards pain and pleasure alike, looks upon a clod, a stone, and a piece of gold as of equal worth, and remains the same amidst the pleasant and the unpleasant things. He has equal vision, regards blame and praise as one, remains the same in honour and dishonour, and treats alike both friends and foes. He has no egotistic feeling of being a doer.

māṃ ca yo'vyabhicāreṇa bhaktiyogena sevate
sa guṇān samatītyai'tān brahmabhūyāya kalpate

Simple Meaning—About the way for reaching the state of liberation,

Lord Krishna says, the way is to serve Me (and My creation) with unfailing devotion of love.

brahmaṇo hi pratiṣṭhā'ham amṛtasyā 'vyayasya ca
śāśvatasya ca dharmasya sukhasyai 'kāntikasya ca

Simple Meaning—Lord Krishna concludes this section by saying—I am the abode of Brahman, the Immortal and the Imperishable, of eternal dharma and of absolute bliss.

Brahmabhūta (XVIII.51-56)

buddhyā viśuddhayā yukto dhṛityā'tmānaṃ niyamya ca
śabdādīn viṣayāṃstyaktvā rāgadveṣau vyudasya ca
viviktasevī laghvāśī yatavākkāyamānasaḥ
dyānayogaparo nityaṃ vairāgyaṃ samupāśritaḥ
ahaṅkāraṃ balaṃ darpaṃ kāmaṃ krodhaṃ parigraham
vimucya nirmamaḥ śānto brahma bhūyāya kalpate

Simple Meaning—These three verses go together. Before writing their simple meaning, we want to draw attention to the words "ahaṃkāraṃ... vimucya nirmamaḥ" which, like "nirmamo nirahaṃkaraḥ", convey the idea of serving the world.

Now, the meaning of the three verses. Lord Krishna describes how a person becomes worthy of becoming one with Brahman. Equipped with a pure understanding, firmly restraining oneself, turning away from sense-objects, he casts aside dualities like attraction and aversion. He remains unattached to people, regulates his food, controls his speech, body and mind, practises dhyana-yoga and cultivates the spirit of mental renunciation. He casts aside 'ahaṃkāra', i.e. egotism, also force, arrogance, desire, anger, possessiveness, goes beyond the sense of 'mine', and attains tranquillity of mind.

bharmabhūtaḥ prasannātmā na śocati na kāṅkṣati
samaḥ sarveṣu bhūteṣu madbhaktiṃ labhate parām
bhaktyā māmabhijānāti yāvān yaścā'smi tattvataḥ
tato māṃ tattvato jñātva viśate tadanantaraṃ

Simple Meaning—Lord Krishna continues—having become one with Brahman, and being tranquil in spirit, he neither grieves nor desires. Regarding all beings as alike, he attains supreme devotion to Me. Through devotion, he comes to know Me, what My measure is and who I am in truth; then, having known Me in truth, he enters into Me.

sarvakarmāṇyapi sadā kurvāṇo madvyapāśrayaḥ
matprasādādavāpnoti śāśvataṃ padamavyayam

Simple Meaning—This is the final verse of this section. Lord Krishna makes it clear that, in the state of perfection, all the yogas (karma, bhakti, jñāna) merge into one. Having mentioned bhakti and jñāna, the Lord now says—such a purna-yogin, taking refuge in Me, performs all the actions, i.e. he devotes himself to selfless service, and dedicating that to the Lord, he reaches, by My grace, the eternal, undying abode.

APPENDIX TWO

Initial Declaration of the Mānas About Jag-Mangal and Sarva-Hit

The purpose and the content of this Appendix were indicated in paragraph 8.46 of this book. Although declarations about jag-mangal and sarva-hit are made throughout the Mānas, we attach special significance to the one made in the beginning itself, i.e. in Bālakāṇḍa. We present here a part of the relevant Hindi text with simple meaning thereof in English.

jaḍa chetan jag jīva jat
sakal rāmmaya jāni
bandaun sab ke pad-kamal
sadā jori jug pāni

Simple Meaning—Tulasī says—I know that Lord Rāma pervades all the beings of the world, and so I pray to all of them with folded hands.

dev danuj nar nāg khag
pret pitar gandharva
bandaun kinnar rajnichar
kripā karahu ab sarva

Simple Meaning—Devas, daityas, human beings, snakes, birds, gandharvas, kinnaras and rakshasas—I pray to all of them and ask for their blessings.

ākar chāri lākh chaurasī
jāti jīva jal thal nabhvāsī

siyārām-maya sab jag jānī
karaun praṇām jori jug pānī

Simple Meaning—There are eighty-four lakhs of species who live either on earth or in the sea or in air. I know that Sītā and Rāma pervade all of them, and so I pray to all of them with folded hands.

jāni kripākar kinkar mohū
sab mili karahu chhāri chhal chhohū
nij budhi bal bharos mohi nāhīn
tāten vinay karaun sab pāhīn

Simple Meaning—All of you are full of compassion. Please consider me as your servant and be kind to me. I have no confidence in my own capabilities, therefore I seek your blessings.

karan chahaun raghupati gun gāhā
laghu mati mori charit avagāhā
sūjh na ekau ang upāū
man mati rank manorath rāū

Simple Meaning—I want to narrate the virtues of Lord Rāma, but my intellect is small while Rāma-kathā is unfathomable. I have limited capability but my desire is limitless, therefore I do not see any feasible way to fulfil my desire.

mati ati nīch ūnchi ruchi āchhī
chāhiya amiya jag jurai na chhāchhī
chhamihahin sajjan mori ḍhiṭhāī
sunihuhin bāl-vacan man lāī

Simple Meaning—My intellect is low, but the desire is very high—it is as if I want nectar, while even buttermilk is beyond my means. Saints will pardon me for my insistence to write Rāma-kathā, and will listen to my childlike words.

jaun bālak kah totari bātā
sunahin mudit man pitu aru mātā
hansihahin kūr kutil kuvichārī
je pardūshan bhūshan-dhārī

Simple Meaning—When a child utters a few unintelligible words, the parents not only listen to them but also feel delighted. But cruel people with perverted ideas make fun of the child because they take delight in the shortcomings of others.

nij kavitta kehi lāg na nīkā
saras hou athavā ati phīkā
je parbhaniti sunat harshāhīn
te bar purush bahut jag nāhīn

Simple Meaning—Who does not like his own poetry? Everyone does—and it does not matter whether the poetry is good or bad. But good people are those who listen to others' poetry with delight—and such good people are rare in this world.

jag bahu nar sar sari sam bhāī
je nij bādhi badhahin jal pāī
sajjan sakrit sindhu sam koī
dekhi pūr vidhu bādhai joī

Simple Meaning—Most of the people in this world are small-minded like ponds and rivulets, who feel elated by their own growth. Good people are rare like the ocean—which has high tide when the moon is full (i.e. good people feel elated when others prosper).

bhāg chhot abhilāsh baḍ
karaun ek visvās
paihahin sukh suni sujan sab
khal karihahin upahās

Simple Meaning—My luck (i.e. capability) is small but my desire to write Rāma-kathā is big. I am confident that good people will feel happy with my poetry (in spite of its poor quality), and wicked people will make fun of me.

khal parihās hoi hit morā
kāk kahahin kalkanth kathorā
hansahin bak dādur chātakhī
hansahin malin khal vimal batakhī

Simple Meaning—Wicked people's making fun of me will only do good to me. Crows say that the nightingale's voice is harsh. Just as a bagula-bird makes fun of the swan, and a frog makes fun of chatak, similarly wicked people make fun of good poetry.

kavitrasik na rām-pad nehū
tinh kahn sukhad hās-ras ehū
bhāshābhaniti bhori mati morī
hansibe jog hanse nahin khorī

Simple Meaning—Those who cannot appreciate poetry and who have no devotion to Lord Rāma, will laugh at my poetry and feel happy. I do not blame them because my poetry is fit to be laughed at—for two reasons. First, I am writing in common people's language (and not in Sanskrit). Secondly, my intellectual capability is low.

prabhupad prīti na sāmujhi nīkī
tinhahi kathā suni lāgihi phīkī
hari har pad rati mati na kutarkī
tinh kahn madhur kathā raghuvar kī

Simple Meaning—Those who are not devoted to Lord Rāma and who lack in good understanding, will find no sweetness in Rāma-kathā. On the other hand, those who worship Lord Vishnu and Lord Shiva with love and whose understanding is not spoilt by bad argumentation, will find Rāma-kathā extremely sweet.

rām bhagati bhūshit jiyan jānī
sunihạhin sujan sarāhi subānī
kavi na houn nahin vacan pravīnū
sakal kalā sab vidyā hīnū

Simple Meaning—Knowing that my poetry is adorned with the jewel of Rām-bhakti, good people will listen to it and admire it too. However, such admiration is not due to poetic qualities because I am neither a poet not expert in the use of words. In fact, I am devoid of all poetic and related qualities.

ākhar arath alankriti nānā
chhand prabandh anek vidhānā
bhāvbhed rasbhed apārā
kavit dosh gun vividh prakārā
kavit vivek ek nahin moren
satya kahaun likhi kāgad koren

Simple Meaning—Experts in the theory of poetry-writing have made a long list of requirements relating to the proper use of words, metre, ideas and symbols, but I have no knowledge of any of them—and please accept this as a true statement.

bhaniti mori sab gun rahit
vishvavidit gun ek
so vichāri sunihahin sumati
jinh ken vimal vivek

Simple Meaning—Although my poetry has no literary quality, yet it has a different type of merit which is valued all over the world (and which is specified in the verse that will follow). Because of that merit, people of good understanding and pure knowledge will listen to my poetry.

ehi mahn raghupati nām udārā
ati pāwan purān shruti sārā
mangal bhavan amangal hārī
umā sahit jehi japat purārī

Simple Meaning—The merit of my poetry is that it glorifies the purifying name of Lord Rāma—and this is the essence of all scriptures. The name of Lord Rāma is the abode of mangal (i.e. good), and it takes away all amangal (i.e. bad). This name is dear to Lord Shiva and Pārvatī.

bhaniti vichitra sukavikrit joū
rām nām binu soh na soū
vidhubadanī sab bhānti sanvārī
soh na vasan binā var nārī

Simple Meaning—The greatness of poetry is due to Rāma-nām and nothing else. Even if a famous poet writes technically perfect poetry, it cannot be called great unless Rāma-nām is in it. For example, a lady receives respect due to socially admired clothes and not because of physical features and ornaments.

sab gun rahit kukavikrit vānī
rām nām jas ankit jānī
sādar kahahin sunahin budh tāhī
madhukar saris sant gungrāhī

Simple Meaning—Just as bees go in for honey, similarly saints are attracted by merit, and therefore they admire the poetry which has the stamp of Rāma-nām, even if it has no literary quality and it is composed by an ordinary poet (who is not famous).

jadapi kavit ras ekau nāhīn
rām pratāp pragaṭ ehi māhīn
soi bharos moren man āvā
kehin na susang badappan pāvā

Simple Meaning—Although my poetry, has no literary quality, it has the merit that comes from singing the glory of Lord Rāma. This gives me confidence, because anyone can become great by good company.

dhūmau tajai sahaj karuvāī
agaru prasang sugandh basāī
bhaniti bhades vastu bhali barnī
rām kathā jag-mangal karnī

Simple Meaning—Even smoke (which is naturally bitter) becomes pleasant when accompanied with the nice smell of 'agar'. Similarly, although my poetry is technically not beautiful, it will become meritorious because of its association with the best thing in the world, i.e. Rāma-kathā, which will bring about jag-mangal (i.e. good of the world).

This is the first declaration of the Mānas about jag-mangal. Declaration of 'sarva-hit' occurs a little later.

mangal karani kali mal harni
tulsī kathā raghunāth kī
gati kūr kavitā sarit kī
jyon sarit pāvan pāth kī
prabhu sujas sangati bhaniti bhali
hoihi sujan man bhāvnī
bhav ang bhūti masān kī
sumirat suhāvni pāvnī

Simple Meaning—Rāma-kathā will bring about 'mangal', and will remove the evils of kaliyuga. The flow of my poetry is zigzag, but so is the flow of the holy river Gangā. The merit of my poetry lies in the narration of the purifying deeds of Lord Rāma, and so it will appeal to the hearts of saints. Even the ashes of the cremation ground become pure due to association with Lord Shiva.

priya lāgihi ati sabahi mam
bhaniti rām jas sang
dāru vichāru ki karai koi
bandiya malaya prasang

Simple Meaning—Just as ordinary wood becomes sandalwood (which is liked and used in religious ceremonies) due to association with 'malay-mountain', similarly my poetry (which has no poetic quality) will be liked by all because of the narration of the glories of Lord Rāma.

syām surabhi paya visad ati
gunad karahin sab pān
girā grāmya siya rām jas
gāvahin sunahin sujān

Simple Meaning—Although 'shyama-cow' is black, but its milk is fine and healthy and is liked by all. Similarly, in spite of my use of 'villagers' language', my narration of the glories of Rāma and Sītā will not only be listened to by good people, but they will also sing my poetry.

mani mānik mukutā chhabi jaisī
ahi giri gaj sir soh na taisī
nrip kirīt taruni tanu pāī
lahahin sakal sobhā adhikāī
taisehi sukavi kavit budh kahahīn
upjahin anat anat chhavi lahahīn

Simple Meaning—Wise people say that good poetry is honoured not where it is born (i.e. written) but somewhere else (where the ideas contained therein are valued). There is nothing strange in this—even 'mani-jewel' and pearl are valued not in places where they are found in nature, but more so by the users (who put them in crowns and ornaments).

bhagati hetu vidhi bhavan vihāī
sumirat sārad āvati ḍhāī
rām charit sar binu anhavāyen
so shram jāi na koti upāyen

Simple Meaning—When a poet prays to Goddess Saraswati, she responds to the poet's devotion and comes running to the poet, from Brahmalok. Saraswati naturally gets tired, and in order to enable Saraswati to refresh, the poet should arrange that she takes a dip in the holy lake of the glories of Lord Rāma.

kavi kovid as hridayn vichārī
gāvahin hari jas kalimal-hārī
kīnhen prākrit jan gun gānā
sir dhuni girā lagat pachhitānā

Simple Meaning—The practical meaning of the symbolic statement made in the preceding verse is this—wise poets sing only the glories of God, and not of worldly people. If Saraswati's help is taken to sing glories of worldly people, she would feel unhappy. However, when a poet sings glories of God with Saraswati's help, the resultant poetry is so good that it can remove the evils of kaliyuga.

hridaya sindhu mati sīp samānā
svāti sārdā kahahin sujānā
jon barsai var vāri vichārū
hohi kavit mukutāmani chārū

Simple Meaning—Just as an ordinary shell becomes a pearl after receiving water from 'swāti', similarly, the inspiration and good ideas received from Saraswati enable the poet to write beautiful and meritorious poetry.

juguti vedhi puni pohiahin
rāmcharit var tāg
pahirahin sajjan vimal ur
sobhā ati anurāg

Simple Meaning—Just as pearls need a thread to become a beautiful garland, similarly the poetry needs glories of Lord Rāma to achieve a purifying effect (i.e. it helps develop bhakti in the hearts of listeners).

je janme kalikāl karālā
kartab vāyas vesh marālā
chalat kupanth ved mag chhānde
kapat kalevar kalimal bhānde
vanchak bhagat kahāi rām ke
kinkar kanchan koh kām ke
tinh mahn pratham rekh jag morī
dhīng dharamdhvaj dhandhak dhorī

Simple Meaning—Tulasī says, please ignore my shortcomings. I admit that I am sinner number one, from many angles, e.g. among those who look like swans but act like crows, or among those who give up Vedas and adopt the evil ways of kaliyuga, or among those who pretend to be bhaktas but are experts in cheating, or among those who have fallen prey to lust, anger and greed, or among those who only carry the banner of perverted dharma.

jon apne avgun sab kahaūn
bādhai kathā pār nahin lahaūn
tāte main ati alap bakhāne
thore mahn jānihahin sayāne

Simple Meaning—Tulasī continues—if I narrate all my shortcomings, I will have to keep going and still see no end to my narration. Therefore, I have indicated my shortcomings only briefly, hoping that wise people will be able to make out fully what I want to say.

samujhi vividh vidhi vintī morī
kou na kathā suni deihi khorī
etehu par karihahin je asankā
mohi te adhik te jadmati rankā

Simple Meaning—I have pleaded for mercy in many ways, and I do hope that no body will blame me for having written such imperfect poetry. In spite of my plea, if anyone criticizes me, I can only call that person a bigger fool than me.

kavi na houn nahin chatur kahāvahun
mati anurūp rām gun gāvaun
kahn raghupati ke charit apārā
kahn mati mori nirat sansārā

Simple Meaning—I am not a poet; I am not an expert in the use of words. I am only singing and narrating the virtues of Lord Rāma, in accordance with what little intellect I have. Please, just imagine, while glories of Lord Rāma are infinite, my intellect is not only small, but is also ineffective because of attachment to the world.

jehin mārut giri meru udāhīn
kahahu tūl kehi lekhe māhīn
samujhat amit rām prabhutāī
karat kathā man ati kadarāī

Simple Meaning—How can cotton escape from being swept away by the strong wind which can shake even mountains? Due to my limited capability, I hesitate to write about the infinite glories of Lord Rāma.

sārad ses mahes vidhi
āgam nigam purān
neti neti kahi jāsu gun
karahin nirantar gān

Simple Meaning—Saraswati, Sheshnāg, Shiva, Brahmā, and all the scriptures narrated God's qualities but could see no end thereto, and therefore said, in the end, 'neti', i.e. this is not the end, because God's qualities are infinite.

sab jānat prabhu prabhutā soī
tadapi kahen binu rahā na koī

tahān ved as kāran rākhā
bhajan prabhāu bhānti bahu bhākhā

Simple Meaning—Although all know that God's qualities are infinite, still they have tried to narrate them in accordance with their own limited understanding. Vedas have supported all such efforts.

ek anīh arūp anāmā
aj sachchidānand par dhāmā
vyāpak vishvarūp bhagwānā
tehin dhari deh charit krit nānā

Simple Meaning—Brahman is unmanifested, it has no name and form, it is never born, it is 'sat-chit-ānand', it is the ultimate abode, it pervades all and appears as the world. The same God took Avatāra and did everything as 'lila', i.e. sport.

so keval bhagatan hit lāgī
param kripāl pranat anurāgī
jehi jan par mamtā ati chhohū
jehi karunā kari kīnh na kohū

Simple Meaning—God's 'līlā' is for the good of the bhaktas because God is the most compassionate and He loves those who approach Him. In fact, God is attached to His bhaktas, and He is always kind to them—and never angry.

gayī bahor garīb nevajū
saral sabal sāhib raghurājū
budh barnahin harijas as jānī
karahin punīt suphal nij vānī

Simple Meaning—If we lose something valuable (like peace of mind), God can restore it for us. He is like Brother to the poor. He likes simple people. He is omnipotent. He is the Lord of all. He took Avatāra as Lord Rāma. Knowing all this, the wise people narrate God's virtues—and this narration gives purity and effectiveness to their words.

tehin bal main raghupati guṇ gāthā
kahihaun nāi rāmpad māthā
muninh pratham hari kīrati gāī
tehin mag chalat sugam mohi bhāī

Simple Meaning—I am encouraged by the example set by the wise people, and so I surrender myself to the feet of Lord Rāma and get ready to start my own narration of Rāma's 'līlā' and virtues. And how do I start? I feel it will be easier for me to go along the path which was followed by Vālmīki, Vyas, etc. when they sang the glories of God.

ati apār je sarit var
jon nrip setu karāhin
chadhi pipīlikau param laghu
binu shram pārahi jāhin

Simple Meaning—Even small ants can easily cross big rivers by going along the bridge which kings build over such rivers. Similarly, I feel I should be able to write Rāma-kathā by drawing support from the writings of earlier Munis.

ehi prakār bal manahi dekhāī
karihaun raghupati kathā suhāī
vyās ādi kavi pungava nānā
jinh sādar hari sujas bakhānā
charan kamal bandaun tinh kere
puravahun sakal manorath mere

Simple Meaning—By acquring confidence in this way, I shall start writing the glorious Rāma-kathā. Before starting, I shall read again and again the writings of Vyās and other great poets who have narrated God's virtues with utmost respect. I bow to the feet of all those poets, and I pray that they may kindly bless me and give to me the knowledge, writing skill, etc. through which I may be able to fulfil all my wishes.

kali ke kavinh karaun parnāmā
jinh barne raghupati gun-grāmā
je prākrit kavi param sayāne
bhāshān jinh haricharit bakhāne
bhaye je ahahin je hohihahin āge
pranavaun sabahin kapaṭ sab tyāgen

Simple Meaning—I also pray to the poets of kaliyuga who have narrated the virtues of Lord Rāma. Then I pray to poets who wrote in 'Prākrit-bhāshā', who narrated the virtues of Lord Rāma in the language of the common people—among them I salute those who existed in the past, also those who are living now and those who will come in the future—I pray to all of them in full sincerity, with no trace of hypocrisy.

hohu prasann dehu vardānū
sādhu samāj bhaniti sanmānū

jo prabandh budh nahin ādarhīn
so śhram bādi bāl kavi karhīn

Simple Meaning—I pray to all of you—please be kind to me and grant me a boon that my poetry may be honoured by good people. I ask for this boon, because if the poetry of a writer is not honoured by good people, then that writer is obviously a fool who is putting all his efforts in this task in vain.

kīrati bhaniti bhūti bhali soī
sursari sam sab kahn hit hoī

Simple Meaning—This is the famous statement of Tulasīdāsa that glorifies 'sarva-hit'. He says—only that glory, poetry and prosperity can be called good which, like the holy river Gangā, contributes to the good of all. Tulasī's declaration about 'jag-mangal' was made a little earlier in this Appendix.

rām sukīrati bhaniti bhadesā
asmanjas as mohi andesā
tumhari kripā sulabh sou more
siyani suhāvani ṭāṭ paṭore

Simple Meaning—Tulasī says, in accordance with the preceding statement, Lord Rāma's glory is obviously good because it contributes to the good of all. But what about my poetry through which I will narrate Rāma's glory? Obviously, my poetry is not beautiful. I am worried about this lack of correspondence (i.e. good glory expressed through bad poetry). O poets, if you are kind to me, this problem can be sloved. Just as silk-embroidery can beautify even a coarse gunny-bag made of jute, similarly, Rāma's glory will beautify my ugly poetry.

saral kavit kīrati vimal
soi ādarahin sujān
sahaj bayar visrāi ripu
jo suni karahin bakhān

Simple Meaning—Tulasī concludes this section by telling what he wants his poetry to achieve—the language of the poetry to be simple and easy, the content of the poetry to be great (because of narration of Rāma's glory), and the effectiveness of the poetry to be so great that even an enemy (after listening to the poetry) may give up enmity and utter sweet words of praise. Only this type of poetry, says Tulasī, will be honoured by wise people.

APPENDIX THREE

Kaliyuga—Tulasī's Description of a Society Under the Grip of Unrighteousness

This Appendix was referred to in paragraph 11.3. Under the title 'kaliyuga', Tulasī describes a society which is under the grip of unrighteousness. This description occurs in Uttarakāṇḍa (i.e. canto VII of the Mānas). The narrator is Kākbhushuṇḍi and the listener is Garuḍa. Underlying the narration is a clear message "Do not succumb to kaliyuga."

kalimal grase dharma sab
lupt bhaye sad-granth
dambhinh nij mati kalpi kari
pragat kiye bahu panth

Simple Meaning—Kākbhushuṇḍi says, the evils of kaliyuga overpowered all elements of dharma. Good books (like the scriptures) disappeared. In their place, came sin-promoting books of self-appointed preachers who directed people along unrighteous paths.

bhaye log sab moh-bas
lobh grase shubh karma
sunu harijān gyān-nidhi
kahaun kachhuk kali-dharma

Simple Meaning—O wise Garuḍa, please listen to the alarming situation that prevailed in kaliyuga. People were confused and bewildered. Good deeds were abandoned because of excessive greed.

baran dharma nahin āshram chārī
shruti virodh rat sab nar nārī
dvij shruti bechak bhup prajāsan
kou nahin mān nigam anusāsan

Simple Meaning—The traditional 'varṇāshrama-dharma' disappeared. Opposition to Vedas was predominant. No one attached any importance to the values and discipline that the Vedas taught. Even Brahmins became victims of commercialization—it looked as if they were selling the Vedas. Kings and administrators (who were supposed to protect the people) behaved as if they were 'eating people up'.

mārag soi jā kahn jo bhāvā
pandit soi jo gāl bajāwā
mithyārambh dambh rat joī
tā kahn sant kahai sab koī

Simple Meaning—Everyone said, "I will do what I want", i.e. no one observed any social norms. Boasting became the main characteristic of pandits. Similarly, hypocrisy and arrogance earned people the title of 'saints'.

soi sayān jo pardhan hārī
jo kar dambh so baḍ āchārī
jo kah jhūth maskhari jānā
kaliyug soi gunvant bakhānā

Simple Meaning—One who could grab other people's money was considered wise. Outward pretensions took the place of good conduct. Telling lies and cutting jokes were considered great qualities.

nirāchār jo shruti path tyāgī
kaliyug soi gyānī so virāgī
jāke nakh aru jatā visālā
soi tāpas prasiddha kalikālā

Simple Meaning—If some one's conduct is contrary to the Vedas, people think that he has knowledge and a spirit of renunciation. Long hair and long nails were supposed to be the only characteristics of a 'tapasvin' (i.e. one who is expert in tapas or self-discipline).

asubh vesh bhūshan dharen
bhachchhābhachchh je khāhin

tei jogī tei siddha nar
pūjya te kaliyug māhin

Simple Meaning—Yogins and siddha's (perfect persons) were those people whose appearance and attire were anti-social and who observed no discipline in eating. Such people were the object of worship.

je apkārī chār
tinh kar gaurav mānya tei
man kram vachan labār
tei vaktā kalikāl mahn

Simple Meaning—Those who could harm others, earned respect. Those who could tell lies and glorify bad conduct became known as orators.

nāri vivas nar sakal gosāin
nāchahin nat markat kī nāīn
sab nar kām lobh rat krodhī
dev vipra shruti sant virodhī

Simple Meaning—Day-to-day conduct of men was contrary to the teachings of Vedas and saints. They were victims of desire, anger and greed. They lost confidence in their own decision-making, so they depended entirely on their wives and practically danced to their tunes (like juggler's monkey).

gun mandir sundar pati tyāgī
bhajahin nāri par purush abhāgī
saubhāginī vibhūshan hīnā
vidhavanh ke singār navīnā

Simple Meaning—Unhealthy relationships were common in families. Even wives of worthy husbands wanted to have an affair with other men. Due to extra-marital affairs, widows received more ornaments than married women.

gur shish badhir andh kā lekhā
ek na sunai ek nahin dekhā
harai shishya dhan shok na haraī
so gur ghor narak mahn paraī

Simple Meaning—Performers of sva-dharma were hard to find—even 'gurus' and 'shishyas' (teachers and pupils) were no exception. The shishya did not listen to Guru's instructions, and so could be called 'deaf'. The guru had no knowledge, i.e. vision of the Supreme, and so could be called 'blind'. Of course, for such a pitiable condition, the guru was more to blame, because he only wanted money from the shishya and did nothing to remove his sorrows.

mātu pitā bālakanhin bolāvahin
udar bharai soi dharma sikhāvahin

Simple Meaning—The problem of survival was so acute that parents wanted to teach only such dharma to children as may enable them to earn enough to survive.

brahma gyān binu nāri nar
kahahin na dūsari bāt
kauḍi lāgī lobh bas
karahin vipra gur ghāt

Simple Meaning—There was no correspondence between saying and doing. Everyone talked about 'knowledge of Brahman', but in practice they even committed murders for a small amount of money.

par triya lampat kapat sayāne
moh droh mamtā laptāne
tei abhedvādi gyānī nar
dekhā main charitra kaliyug kar

Simple Meaning—It was fashionable to talk of Vedānta and to show off their theoretical knowledge about the identity of Brahman and jīva, but their conduct was horrible, e.g. womanizing, cheating, harming others, and falling prey to bewilderment and arrogance.

āpu gaye aru tinhahū ghālahin
je kahn sat mārag pratipālahin
kalpa kalpa bhari ek ek narkā
parahin je dūshahin shruti kari tarkā

Simple Meaning—Those who, in the name of argumentation, opposed the social values of the Vedas, not only destroyed themselves, but they also created confusion among those who wanted to maintain dharma.

nāri muyī griha sampati nāsī
mūnḍ munḍāi bhaye sannyāsī
sab nar kalpit karahin achārā
jāi na barni anīti apārā

Simple Meaning—Sannyasins of kaliyuga were not inspired by knowledge or desire to serve the society, rather they were opportunists and escapists—when their wife died and they lost property, they just shaved off their head and took on the appearance of a sannyasin. They, as well as others, committed immoral acts, leading to a sharp decline in social values.

bhaye varan sankar kalī
bhinnasetu sab log
karahin pāp pāvahin dukh
bhav ruj shok viyog

Simple Meaning—Cross-breeding was common, social norms and ideals were discarded, and all sorts of crimes were committed. No wonder that people suffered from various types of diseases and were subjected to sorrows.

shruti sammat hari bhakti path
sanjut virati vivek
tehi na chalahin nar moh bas
kalpahin panth anek

Simple Meaning—Under the influence of kaliyuga, people gave up bhakti-yoga (which was approved by scriptures and accompanied with right knowledge), and in its place, they took to tāmasika (bad) practices, guided by wrong ways of thinking.

bahu dām sanvārahin dhām jatī
vishayā hari līnh na rahi viratī
tapsī dhanvant daridra grihī
kali kautuk tāt no jāt kahī

Simple Meaning—Perverted thinking destroyed the value-system and everything went upside-down. Householders became poor while sannyasins and tapasvins became rich. Sannyasins spent money for decorating their place of stay, which made it clear that they were deeply attached to sense-objects.

kulvanti nikārahin nāri satī
grih ānahin cheri niberi gatī

Simple Meaning—Ill-treatment of women was quite common. Many of them, in spite of possessing admirable qualities, were turned out of homes, to make room for a mistress.

sut mānahin mātu pitā tab lon
abalānan dīkh nahīn jab lon
sasurāri piāri lagī jab ten
ripurūp kutumb bhaye tab ten

Simple Meaning—Family relationships suffered another kind of deterioration. As soon as a son got married, he became so attached to his wife and in-laws, that he broke his ties with his own parents and treated them almost like enemies.

nrip pāp-parāyan dharma nahīn
kari daṇḍ viḍamb prajā nitahīn
dhanavant kulīn malīn apī
dvij chinha janeu ughār tapī

Simple Meaning—Kaliyuga made everything topsy-turvy (i.e. upside down). The king, instead of protecting people, harassed them and punished innocent citizens. Social values got perverted. High status did not depend on virtues but only on money. Brahmins' identification was not linked with learning but only with the wearing of a sacred thread. Similarly, tapasvin's identification was not linked with knowledge or social service but only with the smearing of ashes on their body.

nahin mān purān na vedahi jo
hari sevak sant sahī kali so
kavi vrinda udār dunī na sunī
gun dūshak vrāt na kopi gunī

Simple Meaning—Those whom people called saints or bhaktas earned these titles by unrighteous means (which included condemnation of scriptures). Poets tried to earn recognition by finding fault with others. Virtues like broad-mindedness were difficult to find.

kali bārahin bār dukāl parai
binu ann dukhī sab log marai

Simple Meaning—Famines occurred frequently in kaliyuga and many people died because of lack of food.

sunu khages kali kapaṭ hath
dambh dvesh pākhanḍ
mān moh māradi mad
vyāpi rahe brahmanḍ

Simple Meaning—O Garuḍa, 'tamas' prevailed in kaliyuga, resulting in the spread of vices like cheating, arrogance, hatred, hypocrisy, lust, anger, greed and so on.

tāmas dharma karahin nar
jap tap vrat makh dān
dev na barsahin dharnī
baye na jāmahin ḍhān

Simple Meaning—Whatever religious practices (japa, tapas, yajña, danam, etc.) people performed, they carried them out with a tāmasika (bad) spirit. Because of this, the gods did not care for the people. Indra did not give them adequate rain and mother earth did not help in the germination of grain seeds.

ablā kach bhūshan bhūri chhudhā
dhanhīn dukhī mamtā bahudhā
sukh chāhahin mūdh na dharma-ratā
mati thori kathori na komaltā

Simple Meaning—Women's condition was particularly bad. They were considered 'ablā' (powerless). They could not afford to buy any ornament, so their hair was the only ornament. They did not get adequate food. Whatever difficulties they had to face due to poverty, were aggravated because of their attachment to children. They had no proper education. Out of desperation, they thought that by giving up 'dharma', they might get happiness. Due to improper way of thinking, they gave up softness and became harsh.

nar pīdit rog na bhog kahīn
abhimān virodh akāranhīn
laghu jīvan samvat panch-dasā
kalpānt na nās gumān asā

Simple Meaning—Although people suffered from diseases and could not enjoy life, still they did not give up their arrogant attitude. They did not learn any lesson from the realities of life. Although it should be clear to them that they would not remain alive for more than a few years, still they talked big and behaved arrogantly as if they would never die. Their arrogant behaviour was an obstacle to social harmony. There were so many conflicts in the society, and in many cases it was even difficult to identify the cause of conflict.

kalikāl bihāl kiye manujā
nahin mānat kau anujā tanujā

nahin tosh vichār na shitaltā
sab jāti kujāti bhaye mangatā

Simple Meaning—Under the evil influence of kaliyuga, men did not observe even the minimum rules of family life. Even their own daughters and sisters did not feel secure. In fact, lust was not the only problem, because there was complete moral and social degeneration. Contentment, discrimination, calmness—all virtues disappeared. People gave up 'purushārtha', i.e. useful work to earn their living, and took to begging instead.

irishā parushāchchhar loluptā
bhari pūri rahī samata vigatā
sab log viyog visok haye
varnāshram dharma achār gaye

Simple Meaning—'Samatā' (feeling of equality) disappeared, giving way to jealousy, harsh language, and greed-based desire of people to acquire everything for their own selves. Because of the disappearance of the co-operative spirit, people felt lonely and left out, with no one to sympathize even when they were in the grip of sorrow. All this happened because people gave up the dharma and good conduct that went with 'varṇāshrama' system.

dam dān dayā nahin jānpanī
jadtā parvanchantāti ghanī
tanu poshak nāri narā sagre
par-nindak je jag mo bagre

Simple Meaning—'Sāttvika' virtues like self-discipline, sharing, compassion, and right knowledge, disappeared, and their place was taken by 'tāmasika' vices like ignorance, desire to cheat, too much of selfishness, and finding fault with others.

sunu vyālāri kāl kali
mal avgun āgār
gunau bahut kaliyug kar
binu prayās nistar

Simple Meaning—O Garuḍa, although kaliyuga had all the evils and vices, it also had one good point, viz. that the way to obtain release from 'sansāra' was easier in kaliyuga than in the other three yugas.

kritajug tretā dvāpar
pujā makh aru jog

jo gati hoi so kali hari
nām ten pāvahin log

Simple Meaning—Whereas in satya-yuga, tretā-yuga and dvāpara-yuga, the release from 'sansāra' could be obtained by pujā, yajña and yoga, the same goal could be obtained in kaliyuga by the Lord's name.

kritajug sab jogī vigyānī
kari hari dhyān tarahin bhav prānī
tretā vividh yajna nar karahīn
prabhuhi samarpi karma bhav tarahīn
dvāpar kari raghupati pad pūjā
nar bhav tarahin upāya na dūjā
kalijug keval hari gun gāhā
gāvat nar pāvahin bhav thāhā

Simple Meaning—All the people in satya-yuga were yogins and vijñānins (i.e. they had knowledge) and the way to obtain release from sansāra was 'dhyān' (meditation). In tretā-yuga, people performed 'yajña' and they could obtain release by dedicating all their actions to God. In dvāpar-yuga, the way to obtain release was 'pujā' (worshipping the feet of the Lord). In kaliyuga, the way to obtain release was 'to sing the virtues of the Lord'.

kalijug jog na jagya na gyānā
ek adhār rām gun gānā
sab bharos taji jo bhaj rāmahi
prem samet gāv gun-grāmahi
soi bhav tar kachhu sansay nāhīn
nām pratāp pragat kali māhīn
kali kar ek punīt pratāpā
mānas punya hohin nahin pāpā

Simple Meaning—Kākbhushuṇḍi explains further the way to obtain release from 'sansāra' in kaliyuga. He says, yoga, yajña, and jñāna are not so effective in kaliyuga (as they are in the other yugas). "Singing the virtues of Lord Rāma" is the most effective way in kaliyuga. But this needs to be done whole-heartedly and with complete devotion. 'Rāma-nām' is supreme in kaliyuga, and it can remove all the vices, and put virtues in their place.

kalijug sam jug ān nahin
jon nar kar visvās

gāi rām gun gan vimal
bhav tar binahin prayās

Simple Meaning—Kākbhushuṇḍi concludes his explanation about the relative merit of kaliyuga. He says, it should be considered a great thing that, in kaliyuga, release from 'sansāra' can be obtained easily by singing the virtues of Lord Rāma.

pragat chāri pad dharma ke
kali mahn ek pradhān
jen ken vidhi dinhen
dān karai kalyān

Simple Meaning—Tulasī says, dharma has four important elements, viz. satya (truth), dayā (compassion), tapas (self-discipline), and dānam (sharing). In kaliyuga, 'dānam' is most effective.

nit jug dharma hohin sab kere
hridayan rām māyā ke prere
suddha satva samatā vigyānā
krit prabhāv prasann man jānā
sattva bahut raj kachhu rati karmā
sab vidhi sukh tretā kar dharmā
bahu raj svalp satva kachhu tāmas
dvāpar dharma harash bhay mānas
tāmas bahut rajo gun thorā
kali prabhāv virodh chahun orā

Simple Meaning—These are the closing verses of the kaliyuga section of Uttarakāṇḍa in the Mānas. Tulasī says, under the influence of Lord Rāma's 'māyā', the proportions of the three guṇas (sattva-rajas-tamas) vary from yuga to yuga—and that explains the difference between the yugas. Satyā-yuga has pūrṇa sattva-guna, and so we have in that yuga—equality, knowledge and happiness. Tretā-yuga has sattva-guna too but it is mingled with a little bit of rajas, therefore we have in that yuga 'happiness' and 'desire to be active in karma'. In dvāpar-yuga, rajas is predominant (with small proportions of sattva and tamas), therefore we have, in that yuga, a mixture of joy and fear. Finally, in kaliyuga, tamas is predominant (with a small proportion of rajas), and so we have in kaliyuga 'conflicts all around'.

Appendix Four

Rāma-rājya—Tulasī's Description of an Ideal Society Based on Jag-Mangal

This Appendix was referred to in paragraph 12.3. Having described kaliyuga (as in Appendix Three), Tulasī wants people to know that Lord Rāma put an end to unrighteousness and freed the society from the disharmony caused by 'tamas'. The description of the ideal society based on jag-mangal occurs in Uttarakāṇḍa—and Tulasī's message is, "strive for Rāma-rājya".

rām rāj baithen trailokā
harshit bhaye gaye sab sokā
bayaru na kar kāhū san koī
rām pratāp vishamtā khoī

Simple Meaning—When Rāma-rājya was established, all the three worlds and all the people became happy because their sorrows came to an end. Enmity disappeared—giving way to mutual friendliness. The feeling of inequality also disappeared—because all are equal in the eyes of Lord Rāma.

varanāshram nij nij dharam
nirat ved path log
chalahin sadā pāvahin sukhahi
nahin bhaya sok na rog

Simple Meaning—People followed 'varṇāshram dharma', i.e. the path of righteousness established by the Vedas. All were happy, free from fear, sorrows and diseases.

daihik daivik bhautik tāpā
rām rāj nahin kāhuhi vyāpā
sab nar karahin paraspar prītī
chalahin svadharma nirat shruti nītī

Simple Meaning—All types of difficulties and sorrows came to an end. People loved one another. They followed 'svadharma' in accordance with the ethical principles of the Vedas.

chāriu charan dharma jag māhīn
pūri rahā sapnehu agh nāhīn
rām bhagati rat nar aru nārī
sakal param gati ke adhikārī

Simple Meaning—All the four elements of 'dharma'—truth, purity, compassion, sharing—were wide-spread, i.e. there was no 'adharma' at all. All men as well as women followed the path of 'Rāma-bhakti', and so all were entitled to the highest state of liberation.

alpa-mrityu nahin kavniu pīrā
sab sundar sab viruj sarīrā
nahin daridra kou dukhī na dīnā
nahin kou abudh na lachchhan-hīnā

Simple Meaning—No one died before getting old. No one suffered pain. All had healthy and beautiful bodies. No one was poor, nor unhappy, nor helpless. No one was ignorant. Everyone looked to the future with a bright outlook.

sab nirdambh dharmarat punī
nar aru nāri chatur sab gunī
sab gunagya pandit sab gyānī
sab kritagya nahin kapat sayānī

Simple Meaning—All were polite, pious and devoted to dharma. Men as well as women were endowed with good qualities. All were pandits and full of knowledge, and they valued the qualities of others. People were nice and helpful to one another, and they were grateful to those who helped them.

rām rāj nabhges sunu
sachrāchar jag māhin
kāl karma subhāv gun
krit dukh kāhuhi nāhin

Simple Meaning—Kākbhushuṇḍi tells Garuḍa, no one in Rāma-rājya was unhappy—all types of sorrows came to an end.

bhūmi sapta sāgar mekhlā
ek bhūp raghupati koslā
bhuvan anek rom prati jāsū
yah prabhutā kachhu bahut na tāsū

Simple Meaning—Lord Rāma ruled over the whole world, i.e. all the lands and all the seas. In fact, Lord Rāma is infinite and all the worlds are contained in just a small portion of the infinite, so don't feel surprised at the earlier statement.

so mahimā samujhat prabhu kerī
yah varnat hintā ghanerī
sou mahimā khages jinh jānī
phiri ehin charit tinhahun rati mānī

Simple Meaning—Kākbhushuṇḍi says, O Garuḍa, once you realise that Lord Rāma is infinite, then any description of His rule will look like telling only a part of His greatness. For bhaktas, this knowledge helps in strengthening their devotion to the glories of Lord Rāma.

rām rāj kar sukh sampadā
barni na sakai phanīs sārdā
eknāri vrat rat sab jhārī
te man vach kram pati hitkārī

Simple Meaning—Even Sheshnāg and Saraswatī can not describe how happy and prosperous people were in Rāma-rājya. Family life was wonderful too. Men were monogamous and wives contributed wholeheartedly to the welfare of the family.

daṇḍa jatinh kar bhed jahn
nartak nritya samāj
jītahu manahi suniya as
rām chandra ken rāj

Simple Meaning—No one committed any crime, so there was no need of 'daṇḍa' i.e. punishment—but the word 'daṇḍa' also means a 'walking stick', so only sannyāsins carried a 'daṇḍa'. Similarly, there was no need to use the policy of 'bhed', i.e. divide and rule—but 'bhed' is also a technical word in music and dancing, and that was its only use. Finally, since there was no enemy, the word 'jīto', i.e. 'conquer', was used only to give the message of conquering one's own mind.

phūlahin pharahin sadā taru kānan
rahahin ek sang gaj panchānan
khag mrig sahaj bayaru visrāī
sabanhi paraspar prīti badhāī

Simple Meaning—The condition of the forests was wonderful too. Leaves and flowers were so nice to look at. Elephants and lions lived together. Birds and animals gave up their natural spirit of enmity, and, in its place, cultivated love for one another.

kūjahin khag mrig nānā vrindā
abhay charahin van karahin anandā
sītal surabhi pavan bah mandā
gunjat ali lai chali makrandā

Simple Meaning—Birds sang sweet songs. Animals roamed about fearlessly. The air was pleasant and fragrant. Bees were hovering around flowers to make honey. Their humming sound was so sweet.

latā vitap māngen madhu chawahīn
manbhāvato dhenu paya sravahīn
sasi sampann sadā rah dharnī
tretān bhai kritjug kai karnī

Simple Meaning—Trees, plants and creepers responded and made as much honey available as people wanted. Cows gave milk in plenty. The greenery of farms made the land beautiful, and food supply was abundant. Although Rāma-rājya was in tretā-yuga, people's happiness and prosperity were as in satya-yuga.

pragatīn girinh vividh mani khānī
jagadātamā bhūp jag jānī
saritā sakal bahahin var bārī
sital amal svād sukhkārī

Simple Meaning—Mines containing jewels appeared in the hills—to make jewels easily available to the citizens of Rāma-rājya. The water of the rivers was clean, unpolluted, sweet and purifying.

sāgar nij marjādā rahahīn
ḍārahin ratna taṭanhin nar lahahīn
sarsij sankul sakal taḍāgā
ati prasanna das disā vibhāgā

Simple Meaning—The seas did not encroach upon land—but they did manage to make pearls easily available to people living on the coast. The ponds were full of lotus flowers. People in all parts of the world were very happy.

vidhu mahi pūr mayūkhanhi
ravi tap jetnehi kāj
māngen vārid dehi jal
rāmchandra ken rāj

Simple Meaning—The moon-light was soft and pleasant like nectar. The sun adjusted its heat to the needs of the people. The clouds gave as much of rain-water as people wanted.

pati anukūl sadā rah sitā
sobhā khāni susīl vinītā
kausalyādi sāsu grih māhīn
sevai sabanhi mān mad nāhīn

Simple Meaning—Sītā co-operated wholeheartedly with Rāma. She contributed fully to the glory of Rāma-rājya. She too performed her sva-dharma (to show respect and to care for Kauśalyā, Kaikeyī and Sumitrā) with great dignity. In spite of being Rāma's wife, Sītā did not let the high status adversely affect her behaviour towards common people, i.e. she was polite and free from arrogance.

sevahin sānukūl sab bhāī
rām charan rati ati adhikāī
rām karahin bhrātanh par prītī
nānā bhānti sikhāvahin nītī

Simple Meaning—Bharat, Lakshman and Shatrughna helped and served Rāma in all ways, with love and respect. Similarly Rāma loved His brothers and imparted training to them so that they can share the task of administration.

harshit rahahin nagar ke logā
karahin sakal sur durlabh bhogā
ah-nishi vidhihi manāvat rahahīn
shrī raguvīr charan rati chahahīn

Simple Meaning—All the citizens were happy. Their condition was even better than that of the gods. They were Rāma-bhaktas, and they prayed that their devotion to Rāma should remain firm for ever, because that was the secret of their happiness.

dui sut sundar sitā jāye
lav kush ved purānanh gāye
dou vijayī vinayī gun mandir
hari pratibimb manahum ati sundar
dui dui sut sab bhrātanh kere
bhaye rūp gun shīl ghanere

Simple Meaning—Sita gave birth to two beautiful sons—Lav and Kush—whose glory has been narrated in the Vedas and Purāṇas. Like Rāma, they were experts in the use of arms and at the same time, they were polite and had all the virtues. Rāma's brothers also had two sons each—and all of them were equally meritorious.

gyān girā gotīt aj
māyā man gun pār
soi satchidānand ghan
kar nar charit udār

Simple Meaning—Brahman who is beyond the reach of sense, mind and intellect, who is the Lord of Māyā (of the three guṇas, i.e. sattva-rajas-tamas), who is sat-chit-ānand—appeared as Rāma and carried out 'līlā' (i.e. sport) in human form.

avadhpurī vāsinh kar
sukh sampadā samāj
sahas sesh nahin kahi sakahin
jahn nrip rām virāj

Simple Meaning—With Lord Rāma as the king, the citizens of Ayodhyā were naturally happy and prosperous, so much so that even a thousand Sheshnāg cannot give a complete description thereof.

nāradādi sanakādi munīsā
darshan lāgi kosalādhīsā
din prati sakal ayodhyā āvahin
dekhi nagaru virāg visrāvahin

Simple Meaning—Rishis like Nārada, and Munis like Sanakādi were always anxious to have 'darshan' of Lord Rāma. So all of them came to Ayodhyā everyday. The prosperity of the city was so enchanting that even Rishis and Munis were moved.

ramānāth jahn rājā
so pur barni ki jāi

animādik sukh sampadā
rahīn avadh sab chhāi

Simple Meaning—After describing the grandeur of Ayodhyā (parts of which we have not included here), Tulasī summarizes his narration by saying, "How can any one give a complete picture of the city's happiness and prosperity where Lord Rāma Himself was the king?"

In the closing verses of this section (which are presented below), Tulasī explains the symbolic significance of Rāma-rājya. His main message is this—when virtues fill our heart and vices disappear, we can say that Rāma-rājya is being established.

jab ten rām pratāp khagesā
udit bhayau ati prabal dinesā
pūri prakāsh raheu tihun lokā
bahuntenh sukh bahutanh man sokā

Simple Meaning—Symbolically, the establishment of Rāma-rājya is like 'sun-rise' which illumines the three worlds. Its effects on virtues and vices are different, e.g. virtues are happy while vices are unhappy.

jinhahi sok te kahaun bakhānī
pratham avidyā nisā nasānī
agh ulūk jahn tahān lukāne
kām krodh kairav sakuchāne

Simple Meaning—First we look at vices which are unhappy. The night of ignorance comes to an end, sins like owl hide, kumud-flowers like lust and anger lose their bloom.

vividh karma gun kāl subhāu
e chakor sukh lahahin na kāu
matsar mān moh mad chorā
inh kar hunar na kavnihun orā

Simple Meaning—Bondage-causing thoughts and actions (inspired by rajas and tamas guṇas) are like chakor-bird (who does not like sun-light). Jealousy, arrogance, hatred and confusion are like thieves (who cannot steal during day-time).

dharam taḍāg gyān vigyānā
e pankaj vikse vidhi nānā

sukh santosh virāg vivekā
vigat sok e kok anekā

Simple Meaning—Now we look at virtues which are happy. Spiritual knowledge and scientific knowledge supported by dharma—these are like lotus-flowers (that bloom with sun-rise). Happiness, contentment, internal renunciation and power of discernment—these are like chakvā-bird (who likes sunlight).

yah pratāp ravi jāken
ur jab karai prakāsh
pachhile bāḍhahin pratham je
kahe te pāvahin nās

Simple Meaning—Tulasī concludes this section by summarizing the content of the preceding verses. As soon as you illumine your heart with the light of the glories of Lord Rāma, virtues (listed in the preceding verses) will grow, while vices (also listed above) will disappear.

Notes

Chapter One

1. Shivananda, *Gītā-Rasāmrita.* Sarva Seva Sangh Prakashan, Varanasi, 1986 (second edition), p.525.
2. K.M. Panikkar, *The Foundations of New India.* Allen and Unwin, London, 1963, pp. 39-40.
3. Swami Ranganathananda, *The Message of the Upaniṣads.* Bharatiya Vidya Bhavan, Bombay, 1971, p.122.
4. Vinoba Bhave, *Talks on the Gītā.* Sarva Seva Sangh Prakashan, Varanasi, 1978 (sixth edition), p. 93.
5. C. Rajagopalachari, *Ramayana.* Bharatiya Vidya Bhawan, Bombay, 1968, pp. 15-16.
6. S. Radhakrishnan, *The Bhagavad-Gītā.* Harper and Row, New York, 1973, p.11.
7. Shivananda, *Gītā-Rasāmrita*, op.cit., p. 361.
8. Shripal Singh Kshem, *"Goswāmiji Kā Samanvaya-yoga".* In Mānas-Chandan, vol.III, No.11, 1998, pp. 14-18.
9. Vinoba Bhave, *Sthitaprajña-Darshan.* Sarva Seva Sangh Prakashan, Varanasi, 1946.
10. T.L. Vaswani, *Śrī Rāma : The Beloved of Aryavarta.* Gītā Publishing House, Poona, 1962, p. 26.
11. Balkoba Bhave, *Gītā-Tattva-Bodh.* Sarva Seva Sangh Prakashan, Varanasi, 1981 (second edition).
12. Shivananda, *Gītā-Rasāmrita, op.cit.*
13. Ram Kinkar Upadhyay, *A Comparative Study of Mānas and Gītā.* Tulasī Tattvanusandhan Kendra, Kanpur, 1987.

Chapter Three

1. S. Radhakrishnan, *The Bhagavad-Gītā,* op.cit., pp. 13-14.

2. Ibid, pp. 155-160.
3. Swami Chidbhavananda, *The Bhagavad-Gītā.* Tapovanam, Tirupparaitturai, 1975, pp. 105-106.
4. B.G. Tilak, *Writings and Speeches.* Ganesan, Madras, 1922, p. 263.
5. S. Radhakrishnan, *The Bhagavad-Gītā,* op.cit. p. 326.
6. P.M. Thomas, *Twentieth Century Indian Interpretations of Bhagavad-Gītā.* Indian Society for Promoting Christion Knowledge, Delhi, 1987, p. 164.
7. V. Nargolkar, *The Creed of Saint Vinoba.* Bharatiya Vidya Bhawan, Bombay, 1963, p. 62.
8. S.P. Agarwal, *The Social Message of the Gītā Symbolized as Lokasaṃgraha.* Motilal Banarsidass, Delhi, 1995.
9. P. Sankaranarayanan, *"Human Person, Society and State : The Classical Hindu Approach". In Human Person, Society and State,* ed. by P.D. Devanandan and M.M. Thomas, Committee for Literature on Social Concerns, Bangalore, 1957, p. 75.
10. S. Radhakrishnan, *The Bhagavad-Gītā,* op.cit., p. 268.
11. Ibid, p. 383.
12. Ibid, p. 274.
13. Arvind Sharma, author of *'Hinduism for our Times',* spoke about 'mahajana' to the author of this book during personal discussion in July 1991.
14. Vinoba Bhave, *Talks on the Gītā,* op.cit., pp. 154-157.
15. Karan Singh, *Prophet of Indian Nationalism.* George Allen and Unwin, London, 1963, pp. 143-144.

Chapter Four

1. R.S. Betai, *Gītā and Gandhiji,* Gujarat Vidyapith, Ahmedabad, 1970, p. 235.
2. Swami Vivekananda, *Complete Works.* Advaita Ashrama, Calcutta, 1972 (fourteenth edition), vol. III, p. 142.
3. S.P. Agarwal, *Lokasaṃgraha-Sandesah.* Motilal Banarsidass, Delhi, 1999.
4. Śrī Aurobindo, *Essays on the Gītā.* Śrī Aurobindo Ashram, Pondicherry, 1970 (eighth edition), p. 372.

5. M. Hiriyanna, *The Essentials of Indian Philosophy,* Mac millan, New York, 1949, pp. 54-56.
6. Shriman Narayan (ed.), *Selected Works of Mahatma Gandhi,* Navajivan, Ahmedabad, 1968, vol. IV, p. 302.
7. Vinoba Bhave, *Talks on the Gītā,* op.cit., pp. 94-104.
8. Ibid, pp. 214-215.

Chapter Five

1. S. Radhakrishnan, *The Bhagavad-Gītā,* op.cit., p. 75.
2. K. Mishra, *"Indian Value System and Social Development".* Paper presented at the Annual Conference of the Association of Asian Studies at Laval University, Quebec, 1989, pp. 2-3.
3. S. Radhakrishnan, *The Bhagavad-Gītā,* op.cit., p. 188.
4. Ibid, pp. 75-76.
5. Mahadev Desai, *The Gospel of Selfless Action or the Gītā according to Gandhi,* Navajivan, Ahmedabad, 1946, p. 127.
6. S. Radhakrishnan, *The Bhagavad-Gītā,* op.cit., p. 123.
7. Ibid, p. 182.
8. Ibid, p. 299.
9. Ibid, p. 299.
10. Swami Chinmayananda, *The Holy Geeta.* Central Chinmaya Mission Trust, Bombay, 1990, p. 876.
11. Ibid, p. 1083.

Chapter Six

1. B.G. Tilak, *Gītā-Rahasya,* Tilak Brothers, Poona, 1971 (third edition), p. 460.
2. K.M. Panikkar, *The Foundations of New India,* op.cit., pp. 39-40.
3. S. Radhakrishnan, *The Bhagavad-Gītā,* op.cit., p. 135.
4. K.N. Upadhyaya, *Early Buddhism and the Bhagavad-Gītā,* Motilal Banarsidass, Delhi, 1971, p. 488.
5. Sri Aurobindo, *The Doctrine of Passive Resistance,* Pondicherry, 1952, pp. 77-78.
6. M.K. Gandhi, *The Bhagavad-Gītā,* Orient Paperbacks, New Delhi, pp. 79-80.

7. Ibid, p. 86.
8. D.S. Sarma, *"The Path of Yoga in the Gītā"*, In the Cultural Heritage of India, vol.III, H. Bhattacharya, ed., The Ramakrishna Mission Institute of Culture, Calcutta, 1953, p. 403.
9. Mahadev Desai, *The Gospel of Selfless Action*, op. cit., p. 133.
10. Swami Chidbhavananda, *The Bhagvad-Gītā,* op.cit., p. 829.
11. K. Klostermaier, *A Survey of Hinduism,* State University of New York Press, Albany, New York, 1989, p. 105.
12. S. Radhakrishnan, *The Bhagavad-Gītā,* op.cit., p. 151.

Chapter Seven

1. Donald Bishop (ed.), *Indian Thought : An Introduction,* John Wiley and Sons, New York, 1975, pp. 62-79.
2. K.N. Upadhyaya, *Early Buddism and the Bhagavad-Gītā,* op.cit., p. 462.
3. Ibid, pp. 464-466.
4. B.G. Tilak, *Gītā-Rahasya,* op.cit., p. 534.
5. Ibid, pp. 464-465.
6. Shriman Narayan (ed.), *Selected Works of Mahatma Gandhi,* op.cit., vol. VI, pp. 189-190.

Chapter Eight

1. Śrī Aurobindo, *Essays on the Gītā,* op.cit., p. 128.
2. B.G. Tilak, *Gītā-Rahasya,* op.cit., pp. 456-457.
3. Ibid, p. 451.
4. Mahadev Desai, *The Gospel of Selfless Action,* op. cit., p. 183.
5. Vinoba Bhave, *Talks on the Gītā,* op.cit., pp. 28-32.
6. D.S. Sarma, *"The Path of Yoga in the Gītā",* op.cit., pp. 422-423.
7. R.N. Dandekar, *"The Bhagavad-Gītā",* In Wim. Theodore de Bary (ed.), *Sources of Indian Tradition,* Motilal Banarsidass, Delhi, p. 281.
8. Śrī Aurobindo, *Essays on the Gītā,* op.cit., p. 201.
9. S. Radhakrishnan, *The Bhagavad-Gītā,* op.cit., p. 142.
10. S.P. Agarwal, *Tulasī-Rāmayaṇa : Jagmangal-Parāyaṇa,* Motilal Banarsidass, Delhi, 1997.

11. S.P. Agarwal, *Mānas evam Gītā : Lokmangal-Gunjitā,* Motilal Banarsidass, Delhi, 1998.

Chapter Nine

1. Swami Chinmayananda, *The Holy Geeta,* op.cit., pp. 170-174.
2. Vinoba Bhave, *The Steadfast Wisdom,* Sarva Seva Sangh Prakashan, Varanasi, 1985 (third edition), p. 114.

Chapter Ten

1. S. Radhakrishnan, *The Bhagavad-Gītā,* op.cit., p. 204.
2. Swami Ranganathananda, *The Message of the Upaniṣads,* op.cit., pp. 109-110.
3. B.G. Tilak, *Gītā-Rahasya,* op.cit., pp. 603-604.
4. Swami Vivekananda, *Complete Works,* op.cit., vol. III, pp. 430-433.
5. S. Radhakrishnan, *The Bhagavad-Gītā,* op.cit., p. 205.
6. Ibid, p. 192.
7. Ibid, p. 182.
8. Romain Rolland, *The Life of Vivekananda and the Universal Gospel,* Advaita Ashrama, Calcutta, 1970 (seventh impression), p. 166.
9. R.S. Betai, *Gītā and Gandhiji,* op.cit., p. 196.
10. V. Nargolkar, *The Creed of Saint Vinoba,* op.cit., pp. 58-59.
11. B.G. Tilak, *Gītā-Rahasya,* op.cit., p. 1164.

Chapter Eleven

1. Mahadev Desai, *The Gospal of Selfless Action,* op.cit., p. 94.
2. Swami Vivekananda, *Complete Works,* op.cit., vol. I., p. 478.
3. Ram Kinkar Upadhyay, *A comparative study of Mānas and Gītā,* op.cit., pp. 82-83.
4. Ibid, pp. 143-152.
5. Swami Vivekananda, *Our Women, Advaita Ashrama,* Calcutta, 1990, p. 43.
6. Swami Ranganathananda, *The Message of Kanyakumari,* Vivekananda Kendra, Madras, 1981, p. 9.

Chapter Twelve

1. M. Hiriyanna, *"Philosophy of Values"*, In the Cultural Heritage of India, op.cit., vol. III, pp. 647-648.
2. Vinoba Bhave, *Talks on the Gītā,* op.cit., pp. 190-191.
3. S. Radhakrishnan, *The Bhagavad-Gītā,* op.cit., p. 305.
4. Ibid, p. 343.

Chapter Thirteen

1. D.M. Brown, *"The Philosophy of Bal Gangadhar Tilak : Karma vs Jñāna in the Gītā-Rahasya", In the Journal of Asian Studies,* vol. XVII, No. 2 (Feb. 1958), p. 200.
2. V. Subramaniam, *"Karamayoga and the Rise of the Indian Middle Class",* In the Journal of Arts and Ideas, Nos. 14-15, pp.137-139.
3. B.G. Tilak, *Gītā-Rahasya,* op.cit., pp. 490-491.
4. S.P. Agarwal, *The Social Role of the Gītā : How & Why,* Motilal Banarsidass, Delhi, 1993.
5. Hanuman Prasad Poddar, *Shri Ramcharitmānas,* Gitapress, Gorakhpur, 1987 (68th edition), pp. 10-11.
6. Madeleine Biardeau, *Hinduism : The Anthology of a Civilization,* Oxford University Press, Delhi, 1989, pp. 164-165.
7. Vinoba Bhave, *Talks on the Gītā,* op.cit., p. 203.

Index

References are to paragraph numbers, not to pages

Adharma 3.16-3.18, 11.7-11.10
Agarwal, S.P. 3.30, 4.8, 8.46, 13.21
Ahiṃsa 1.13, 1.37, 7.4-7.5, 10.23
Angad 4.26, 4.33-4.36
Arapura, J.G. 8.23
Asant 11.20-11.23
Ashoka, Emperor 1.35
Āsuri Sampat 11.1-11.16
Atmaupamya 10.8-10.9
Aurobindo, Śrī 3.53, 4.11, 6.16, 8.10, 8.27
Avatāra Declaration 3.14-3.21
Avibhaktam vibhakteṣu 3.1-3.53

Balkoba Bhave 1.52
Betai, R. 4.3, 10.19
Bhadase Sagan Maharaj 13.61
Bhāgavat-Puraṇa 1.39
Bhakta 3.6, 5.34-5.36, Appendix One
Bhaktiyoga 4.13, 4.19-4.22, 10.4-10.6
Bharat 9.12-9.16, 11.29
Bhartrihari 1.40
Bhave, Vinoba, *see* Vinoba
Biardeau, M. 13.45
Bishop, D.H. 7.10
Brahmabhūta 5.40-5.42, Appendix One
Brihadaranyaka Upaniṣad 8.30, 9.3
Brihaspati 5.67-5.68
Brown, D.M. 13.16
Buddhism 1.34, 1.36

Chhandogya Upaniṣad 1.12, 1.13, 8.30
Chidbhavananda, Swami 3.16, 6.29
Chinmayananda, Swami 5.39, 5.42, 9.19
Cosmic Vision 3.40-3.44

Dadhichi, Rishi 1.22
Daivi Sampat 12.1-12.9
Dānaṃ 6.28-6.31, 13.54-13.55
Dandekar, R.N. 8.23
Daridra-Narayan 10.18
Desai, Mahadev 5.21, 8.18
Desh-Kāla-Patra 6.1-6.39
Dharma of harmonization 3.2-3.13
Dharma of social service 3.22-3.53

Dhritarashtra 9.3, 9.5-9.6
Divisive behaviour 10.27
Duryodhana 9.5-9.15

Equality 10.18-10.22
Equal vision 10.2-10.22, 13.5
Even-mindedness 10.10-10.17

Faint-heartedness 13.7

Gandhi, Mahatma 1.33, 4.3, 4.20, 5.21, 6.17-6.18, 7.20-7.21, 8.18
Garuḍa 5.69
Gayatri-mantra 1.4
Gita–ten key words 2.2-2.14
Gita Press 13.22

Hanumān 4.27-4.29, 4.39-4.42, 5.64, 10.42, 13.60
Harmonization 3.2-3.13
Hiriyanna, M. 4.15, 12.5-12.6

Inner voice 3.45-3.53
Isha Upaniṣad 1.10

Jag-Abhiram 8.38
Jagat-hit 8.43
Jag-mangal 8.34-8.46, Appendix Two
Jainism 1.24
Janaka 1.24, 8.13
Jaṭayu 4.30-4.31
Jīvanmukta 5.29-5.32, Appendix One
Jñāna 12.10-12.12, 12.22-12.25
Jñāna-yoga 10.2-10.3

Kabir 1.44, 5.15
Kakbhuṣuṇḍī 3.43-3.44, 5.9, 5.60-5.61, 9.4
Kālidāsa 1.40
Kaliyuga 11.31-11.34, Appendix Three
Kāmadev 5.70
Karma-samarpaṇam 4.14-4.22, 4.41-4.46
Karma-yoga 2.9, 4.13, 4.19-4.22, 4.27-4.31, 8.5-8.9
Karmayogin 13.27-13.30
Kathopaniṣad 1.9, 1.11
Kaushalyā 7.29, 10.34
Kevaṭ 10.38
Key words 2.2-2.16
Klostermaier, K. 6.32
Krishna, Lord 3.14, 3.18, 4.3, 6.2, 8.6-8.9, 8.18-8.19
Kshem, Shripal Singh 1.48

Laṅkini 5.71
Lokasaṃgarha 8.1-8.33
Lok-vishrām 8.44-8.45

Mahābhārata 1.21-1.24, 1.34, 3.45, 6.3, 7.6-7.8, 8.31
Mahājana 3.45
Mahāyana Buddism 1.36
Mānas—ten key words 2.15-2.16
Mandodari 4.35
Mangal-bhavan 7.76
Manusmṛti 1.38, 3.46, 6.3, 8.32
Maryada-Purushottam 8.39, 10.36
Mat-karma 4.2-4.9
Māyā 11.18-11.19
Mirābāi 1.48
Mishra, K. 5.4

Nachiketa 1.11
Nargolkar, V. 3.29

Narsi Mehta 1.43
Nimittamātram 4.10-4.13, 4.33-4.40
Nirmamo Nirahaṃkaraḥ 9.1-9.31
Nishkam karma 2.9, 5.23
Non-violence, *see* Ahiṃsā

Panikkar, K.M. 1.19, 6.6
Par-hit 4.30-4.32, 10.39, 12.26-12.27
Paravati 8.42-8.43
Patanjali 1.37
Pauruṣam 7.4-7.5
Place, Time and Worthiness of Cause *see* Desh-Kala-Patra
Poddar, Hanuman Prasad 13.22
Practical Vedānta 10.7
Prasthanatraya 13.18-13.20
Pratapbhanu 4.44-4.46
Purushottama 4.5

Racial equality 10.29-10.32
Radhakrishnan, S. 1.36, 3.3, 3.5, 3.25, 3.32-3.33, 3.41, 5.3, 5.13, 5.35-5.36, 6.12, 6.35, 8.28, 10.2, 10.9, 10.17, 12.12, 12.16
Rajagopalachari, C. 1.26
Raju, P.T. 8.25
Rāma, Lord 1.25-1.33, 4.24-4.25, 5.44-5.55
Rāmcharitmānas, *see* Mānas
Ramakrishna Mission 13.42-13.45
Rāma-kaj 4.23-4.32
Rammohan Roy 13.31-13.41
Rāma-Rajya 8.36-8.38, 12.28-12.34, Appendix Four
Ranganathananda, Swami 1.20, 10.3
Rig-veda 1.8, 13.36
Romain Rolland 10.18

Sakal-mangal 7.23-7.40
Sakal-sukh 7.33-7.34, 7.40
Samadṛshti 10.1-10.42
Samatva 10.10-10.17
Sampati 4.37
Sāmya 10.18-10.26
Sāmya-yoga 10.22
Sāmyayogi 5.33, Appendix One
Sankaranarayanan, P. 3.30
Sansār-hit 8.41
Sant 5.43-5.78
Sarma, D.S. 6.22, 8.22
Sarvabhutahitam 7.1-7.22
Sarvahit 7.32, Appendix Two
Sāttvika 4.13, 5.39, 12.13-12.16
Shabri 10.37
Shankaracharya 3.26, 4.9
Sharma, Arvind 3.45
Shiva, Lord 5.56-5.59
Shivanand 1.5, 1.46
Singh, Karan 3.53
Sītā 1.25-1.32, 7.24
Social service 3.22-3.53, 4.28, 13.42-13.45
Śreyas 8.3-8.8
Sthitaprajña 5.21-5.28, Appendix One
Subramaniam, V. 13.17
Surdas 1.48
Swaraj 13.46

Tāmasika 5.39, 7.4-7.5, 11.13-11.16

Tapas 11.15-11.16

Thomas, P.M. 3.28

Tilak, B.G. 3.24, 6.5, 7.16-7.19, 8.12-8.13, 10.6, 10.25, 13.20

Time, Place and Worthiness of Cause, *see* Desh-Kala-Patra

Trigunātita 5.37-5.39, Appendix One

Trinidad 10.30, 13.57-13.61

Tukārām 1.45

Tulasī 5.72-5.78

Upadhyaya, K.N.6.13, 7.11-7.15

Upadhyay, Ram Kinkar 1.53, 11.6-11.7

Upaniṣads 1.9-1.13, 8.30

Valmiki 5.63

Valmiki Rāmāyaṇa 1.25-1.33

Vashishtha 6.39

Vaswani, Sadhu 1.51

Vedas 1.3-1.8

Vibhishaṇ 5.65

Vidur 9.5-9.6, 10.25

Vinay Patrika 5.78, 13.29

Vinoba 1.23-1.24, 1.50, 3.27-3.29, 3.42, 3.50, 4.21-4.22, 6.19, 8.19, 9.28, 10.22, 11.8, 12.9, 13.54

Virtues 3.14-3.21

Vishrām 4.39, 8.44

Vivekananda, Swami 4.7-4.8, 10.7, 10.18, 11.5, 11.9-11.10

World-tree 3.23-3.30

Yajña 1.6, 1.38, 6.8-6.19, 9.17-9.24

Yajñavalkya 5.62

Yogaruḍha 5.1-5.42, Appendix One

Yoga-Vashishtha 8.33

Yuga-dharma 6.2-6.4